Screening the Nonhuman

Critical Animal Studies and Theory

Series Editors: Anthony J. Nocella II and Scott C. Hurley

This book series is a project of the Institute for Critical Animal Studies, www.criticalanimalstudies.org.

This series addresses human relationships with other animals in the context of socio-political relations and economic systems of power. It sees liberation not as a single-issue phenomenon, but rather as inseparably related to human rights, peace and justice, and environmental issues and movements. Rather than emphasizing abstract theory, the series links theory with practice and emphasizes the immense importance of animal advocacy for a humane, democratic, peaceful, and sustainable world. Taking an interdisciplinary approach to questions of social change, moral progress, and ecological sustainability, the Critical Animal Studies and Theory series connects with disciplines such as feminism, globalization, economics, science, history, education, critical race theory, environmental studies, media studies, ecopedagogy, art, literature, disability, gender, political science, sociology, religion, anthropology, philosophy, and cultural studies. The series will serve as a foundational project for one of the fastest growing and most exciting new fields of scholarship, Critical Animal Studies. Rooted in critical theory as well as the animal advocacy movement, the series argues for an interdisciplinary approach to understanding our relationships with nonhuman animals. Rejecting the notion that nonhuman animals do not have a voice, the series stresses that nonhuman animals do have agency, and thus argues for an animal standpoint. In keeping with the principles of Critical Animal Studies, this series encourages progressive and committed scholarship, and views exploitation of nonhuman animals, such as animal research and studies, as interrelated with other oppressions of class, gender, racism, etc. Against apolitical scholarship, for example human-animal studies, this series encourages engaged critical praxis, promotes liberation of all animals, and challenges all systems of domination.

Titles in the Series

Screening the Nonhuman

Representations of Animal Others in the Media

Edited by Amber E. George and J.L. Schatz

LEXINGTON BOOKS
Lanham • Boulder • New York • London

Published by Lexington Books
An imprint of The Rowman & Littlefield Publishing Group, Inc.
4501 Forbes Boulevard, Suite 200, Lanham, Maryland 20706
www.rowman.com

Unit A, Whitacre Mews, 26-34 Stannary Street, London SE11 4AB

British Library Cataloguing in Publication Information Available

Library of Congress Cataloging-in-Publication Data

Names: George, Amber E., editor. | Schatz, J.L., editor.
Title: Screening the nonhuman : representations of animal others in the media / edited by Amber E.
    George and J.L. Schatz.
Description: Lanham, Maryland : Lexington Books, [2016] | Series: Critical animal studies and
    theory | Includes bibliographical references and index.
Identifiers: LCCN 2016007282 (print) | LCCN 2016015227 (ebook)
Subjects: LCSH: Animals in mass media. | Animal welfare in mass media. | Human-animal relation-
    ships in mass media.
Classification: LCC P96.A53 S37 2016 (print) | LCC P96.A53 (ebook) | DDC 179/.3--dc23
LC record available at https://lccn.loc.gov/2016007282

ISBN 9781498513746 (cloth : alk. paper)
ISBN 9781498513760 (pbk. : alk. paper)
ISBN 9781498513753 (Electronic)

∞™ The paper used in this publication meets the minimum requirements of American
National Standard for Information Sciences Permanence of Paper for Printed Library
Materials, ANSI/NISO Z39.48-1992.

Printed in the United States of America

This book is dedicated to all those struggling to be free.

Table of Contents

Acknowledgments

We would like to acknowledge the publisher and editor of Lexington Press's book series on Critical Animal Studies. We would also like to thank the Executive Board of the Institute for Critical Animal Studies (ICAS) whose guidance was paramount in making this project a success. Of course, we would also like to strongly applaud the hard work of our authors who put together a series of profound pieces that will really imbue media studies with a new life oriented to include all non/humans. It is these endeavors that enable critical animal studies to reach beyond its traditional audience by entering into new disciplines and expanding its lens. However, mostly we would like to thank those out there on the ground doing the necessary praxis that brings us closer to total liberation every day. We hope this book can inspire you to find new forms of awareness and spark change. Thank you. In peace and solidarity.

Introduction: Critical Media Studies and Critical Animal Studies at the Crossroads

Amber E. George and J.L. Schatz

Screening the Nonhuman: Representations of Animal Others in the Media highlights the ecological, social, and political implications of using visual narratives in cultural media to reinforce normalcy, supremacy, and oppression. By making visual media the framework for analysis, *Screening the Nonhuman* explores how these constructs are affirmed and upheld through an intricate interplay among issues of representation, identity politics, and human relationships to the non/human world. Contributors to this book draw upon various modes of analysis to dissect the ways popular culture (re)constructs "the animal" in visual narratives that "other" non/human status, and perpetuates problematic ideologies. While many books in academia explore these issues, few utilize an intersectional approach to analyze the trope of dehumanization against the literal presence of non/human representations. This intervention is a necessary step for critical animal studies. Topics in this book expand from critiques of the film and animation industry, professional and amateur sports, social media platforms, and advertising campaigns from cultures not only in the United States but also around the world. The authors utilize a range of scholarship interweaving critical race studies, queer and feminist scholarship, disability studies, policy analysis, environmental justice, and much more. The theme that ties this book together is that it is not only impossible but also unwise to consider any one strand of thought without contextualizing it with others. We hope that each chapter will challenge readers to expand their conscious understanding of non/human life, and contemplate each chapter as contributing to a greater thesis that spans from one chapter to another.

As such, the methodology of this book takes its roots in critical animal studies that was articulated in 2006 from the Institute for Critical Animal Studies (ICAS), which itself was built upon its 2001 foundation as the Center for Critical Animal Studies. In doing so, this book follows in the principles of ICAS that are

> rooted in animal liberation and anarchism[. This approach], is an intersectional transformative holistic theory-to-action activist led based movement and field of study to unapologetically examine, explain, be in solidarity with, and be part of radical and revolutionary actions, theories, groups and movements for total liberation and to dismantle all systems of domination and oppression, in hopes for a just, equitable, inclusive, and peaceful world. (ICAS, 2016)

These values were later defined in 2007 as part of the "Ten Point Principles of Critical Animal Studies" in the *Journal for Critical Animal Studies*, to articulate what critical animal studies was (Best et al. 2007). These principles include the pursuit of "interdisciplinary collaborative writing and re-search . . . [that] rejects pseudo-objective academic analysis by explicitly clarifying its normative values and political commitments" (Best et al. 2007). A such, we make it clear that this project is not one that is value-neutral but rather is explicitly oriented toward a liberationary outcome for all non/humans. In addition this book eschews "narrow academic viewpoints and . . . theory-for-theory's sake . . . [since it] . . . advances a holistic understanding of the commonality of oppressions . . . [by rejecting] apolitical, conservative, and liberal positions . . . [as well as] reformist, single-issue, . . . strictly animal interest politics in favor of alliance politics" (Best et al. 2007). No doubt, this is why while all the authors in this collection talk about non/human animals in many of their work, the main focus goes beyond what many consider the question of "the animal." We hope that this collection helps champion

> A politics of total liberation which grasps the need for, and the inseparability of, human, nonhuman animal, and Earth liberation. . . . [We believe such an approach necessarily] deconstructs and reconstructs the socially constructed binary oppositions between human and nonhuman animals . . . [while at the same time] . . . openly supports and examines controversial radical politics and strategies used in all kinds of social justice movements, such as those that involve economic sabotage from boycotts to direct action toward the goal of peace. (Best et al. 2007)

Ultimately, our book, like ICAS, "seeks to create openings for constructive critical dialogue on issues relevant to Critical Animal Studies across a wide-range of academic groups, citizens and grassroots activists; the staffs of policy and social service organizations; and people in private, public, and nonprofit sectors" (Best et al. 2007). For more on these principles we strongly recommend *Defining Critical Animals: An Intersectional Social Justice Approach for Liberation* (Nocella et al. 2014).

As a result, each chapter in this collection is part of the larger field and movement of critical animal studies that, as it has grown, has contributed scholarship to geography, education, policy, law, anthropology, sociology, economics, women's studies, religion, bioethics, disability studies, ethnicity studies, and philosophy. Moreover, critical animal studies spark action within movements globally to be more intersectional and promote total liberation. The distinguished scholar-activists in this text challenge readers to consider cultural media as anything but neutral. We seek to elevate critical animal studies to the forefront of critical theory and cultural studies to challenge all forms of normalcy, domination, and authoritarianism in visual media. Conceived of as a corrective, this text questions aspects of critical animal studies that have focused more on the literal real world rather than the fictional representations that surround it. Meanwhile, other books concerning "animals" in the media adopt a human-animal studies perspective that ignores the intersectional analysis that critical animal studies foregrounds. As a result, few academics investigate patterns of oppression between *Homo sapiens* alongside non/human domination on a representational level. Hence, while people may recognize certain instances of injustices they witness as abhorrent, these egregious examples of domination obscure the more mundane forms of violence that happen every day and are even more insidious. Fortunately, through "new paradigms of ecopedagogy, bridge-building with other social movements, and a solidarity-based alliance politics, it is possible to build the new forms of consciousness, knowledge, social institutions that are necessary to dissolve the hierarchical society that has enslaved this planet for the last ten thousand years" (Best, Nocella, Kemmerer, and Gigliotti 2007).

As will be shown throughout this book, the continual representation of animality in the media serves as a precursor to the oppression experienced by human and non/human alike. This happens through discourses of dehumanization that render certain lives ungrievable due to their supposed absence of humanity. For instance, Frank Wilderson III's discussion of anti-blackness contends that "social death" ontologically positions black bodies as the "antihuman" (2010). Furthermore, this is what makes civil society fundamentally incapable of valuing black lives. Moreover, through color symbolism, blackness becomes associated with darkness and evil while whiteness becomes associated with purity. Despite these representations being attached to real bodies, ironically, this process ignores how the ontological positioning of blackness discursively produces the possibility of physical death by rendering black bodies as already socially dead. Furthermore, representations form a self-perpetuating cycle that causes real-world events to shape the subsequent representations that merely repeat the mistakes of the past. Therefore, we must stop believing fictions are merely stories and the way we represent the world is irrelevant to what happens in the world.

Sadly, humans learn to accept non/human oppression as normal through their experiences in educational schooling, religious organizations, media outlets, and other institutions. Hierarchies of superiority based on gender, race, socioeconomic status, sexuality, and disability, among others, sediment in these socializing networks. Evidence of this pattern can be found in several dozen books and hundreds of articles that identify human oppression and the systemic injustice that accompanies it. Thus, there is no shortage of books and college classes that explore the binaries of good/evil, white/black, and man/woman in film, advertising, and television. However, these courses do not extend far enough into the largely ignored experience of non/human representations in academia. Incorporating these perspectives is important because processes of dehumanization prioritize and normalize what it means to be human, often to the detriment of those who fall out of this representational scheme. Lennard Davis describes normality as the "alleged physical state of being normal, while 'normalcy' is 'the political-juridical institutional state that relies on the control and normalization of bodies'" (Davis 2002). The concept of an ideal human body is in opposition to the non/human animal, which oftentimes includes *Homo sapiens* others who are female, non-white, queer, disabled, or are associated with other categories of supposed weakness. This dehumanized status then gives those in power the "right" to disregard subaltern interests, often at the latter's expense.

Today's cultural norms perpetuate values that define good and evil, normal and abnormal, human and "animal" in ways that condone oppression and shape speciesist attitudes and behaviors. Studying these normative forms of popular culture tells us about the humans who consume and produce them. Additionally, consuming and producing is an activity that influences one's choices and simultaneously (re)creates culture, both of which are paramount in unraveling the constructions that give rise to non/human oppression. Instead of exploring these categories of oppression in isolation, our book deploys an intersectional approach that explains how these systems mutually construct one another. By presenting our critique in this way, we make systemic social change possible for non/humans. Unfortunately, our critique is a deviation from current academic practices that ignore how dehumanization serves as a precursor to violence. The willingness to ignore non/human animals is evident in media advertisements that gloss over the horrific reality of factory farms, for instance. Such ads absurdly use cows to encourage eating chicken and Miss Piggy to sell bacon. Regardless of the advertisement, this renders an entire species expendable, and makes their physical deaths irrelevant based on their perceived lack of ontological relevance.

Theorists have formulated strategies of resistance to challenge social constructs and norms regarding gender, race, sexuality, and disability representation, but these fall short of explicitly exploring representations the dehumanization of the non/human. Refusing to acknowledge these linkages of oppression makes it impossible to challenge the underlying structures that enable violence in the first place. As Marjorie Spiegel explains,

> The result [of silence] . . . remove[s] the underlying problems of our society farther and farther from daily experiences and daily consciousness . . . to decrease in the mass of the population, the knowledge, skill, and motivation necessary to deal with them. Whether we defend the violation of another's life through our denial of a reality, which makes us uncomfortable, or through outright enthusiasm for oppressive power relations, the results are devastating. Such dynamics allow us to perpetuate and escalate actions, which prevent others from pursuing their own destinies. (1996, 77–78)

Rupturing these omissions is crucial if we wish to avoid the ecological devastation caused by the same speciesism that ranks humans (white, temporarily able-bodied, first-world, heteronormative, males) above all those cast aside as being non/human. This is all the more important since humans are increasingly communicating with pictures and images rather than print and spoken language. Humans now can create a large variety of visual media quickly, cheaply, and with far-reaching impact across the globe. Thus, we urge readers to take a more self-reflective deliberate approach to visual media and question the labels and categories used in cultural production that divide and separate humans from non/humans. Becoming more practiced in critical analysis can (re)form how we relate to social constructs and reimagine them positively.

Current visual media teaches humans to be speciescist; humans learn if they represent others as so fundamentally different to themselves the difference and distance between species are sufficient to deny all moral consideration. Popular media has both reflected and, in many ways, encouraged the "othering" and disavowal of moral concern. Sadly, this practice is nothing new. For instance, when famed feminist Mary Wollstonecraft published *A Vindication of the Rights of Women* in 1792, the idea that women should be granted equal rights was met with ridicule. It seemed absurd to consider the interests of women, just as it may appear foolish to do so for non/humans today. Women, people of color, and LGBTQIA+ individuals have since ascended from the margins to gain more equity and greater access to opportunity. This is not to say any of these groups has achieved liberation since many are still represented as non/human and suffer similar injustices despite significant social gains. However, it is to say that non/humans who are left battling for moral consideration continue to be met with ridicule. Furthermore, scorn and speculation extend to many other liberatory social justice campaigns that are delegitimized through animality tropes in visual representation.

Accordingly, this collection uses the term non/human rather than "animal" to build upon the growing work of anti-humanist studies that argue the notion of humanity is used as a tool to oppress marginalized *Homo sapiens* and deny full access to being human. Michael O'Rourke calls this process a form of "queering the Non/Human[, which he argues] . . . shatters received notions about what it is that constitutes us as human in the first place" (2008, xvii). In this way,

> Thinking begins not just there with the animal . . . but with all non/human others, and with the reframing of traditional forms of humanism to make way for the becoming human of humanity, its hominisation. . . . In Jean-Luc Nancy's terms, we might say that queering the non/human, as a new kind of process ontology, is transimmanent. . . . This demand for a thinking of engaged being-in-the-world should bring into focus the ethical and political intervention . . . [over] discussions of livable life and grievable death, processes of dehumanisation and abjection, and who gets to count as human. (O'Rourke 2008, xvii–xx)

In succession, humans must be willing to acknowledge the interconnection of the "isms" and the harms associated with using, as Audre Lorde says, "the master's tools" to "dismantle the master's house" when framing our orientations toward the world (Lorde 1986). If we are to elicit social change, one marginalized group cannot visit the same indignities against another group using the same tools of oppression that built the system in the first place.

Therefore, when talking about speciesism it is imperative not to pave over anti-blackness, heteronormativity, ableism, or any other hegemonic ontologies that violently frame human perception. For instance, one should not utilize the language of "moral schizophrenia," in Gary Francione's words, when decrying meat eating, nor should the People for the Ethical Treatment of Animals (PETA) objectify women in their anti-fur ads. Likewise, Mercy for Animals should not make unnuanced parallels between animal agriculture and slavery. At the very least, oppressive language alienates those who could otherwise join in solidarity. More importantly, though, it should serve as a red flag to anyone claiming to be an ally while unapologetically using biased, prejudiced, or discriminatory representations. Therefore, as editors of this collection, we believe that the interrogation of the non/human, as opposed to "the animal," is a necessary remedy to the current pitfalls in animal welfare initiatives that oppress others and prevent total liberation. Investigating these concerns using visual representations is a necessary prerequisite to creating an intersectional foundation strong enough to interrogate hegemonic power structures in human ontology.

We argue, in part, that the very category of the non/human operates from the site of this intersection. This makes the non/human the most effective starting point for analysis, even if speciesism is not at the root of all oppressions because it builds praxis for coalition building. Initiating praxis enables one to interrogate how non/humans have been historically used to signify deviance from the norm in order to justify ontological exclusion and violence. In each instance of physical violence, the representation of animality was foundational to the bloody consequences that followed. While using non/humans as an absent referent may have advanced *Homo sapiens* social justice in the past, this approach fails in the long run since it misses the fundamental roots of such injustice overall. Worse still, this misstep actually undermines other liberatory advances since it merely naturalizes the exclusion of those still deemed non/human.

> From all of this we see that the liberation of animals, while a pressing and worthy goal in its own right, is not of importance only to non-human animals. . . . Advances toward releasing animals from our domination and control of their lives will also serve to lessen the oppression of blacks and others who suffer under the weight of someone else's power. By eliminating the oppression of animals from the fabric of our culture, we begin to undermine some of the psychological structures inherent in a society, which seems to create and fosters masters. With a philosophy of universal respect for others' lives, treating anyone—human or nonhuman—in a cruel manner begins to be unthinkable. (Spiegel 1996, 31–32)

This is why any attempt at altering the world must fully consider the non/human otherwise it will only further cement oppression and make mobilizing sustained action against violence nearly impossible.

While many humans genuinely want to combat social injustices witnessed in the media, others may not want to face the harshness of reality. Resistance is a coping strategy humans who aren't quite ready to challenge the status quo may use to ignore and deny injustice. An integral element in anti-oppression work requires confronting how the gaze of the human viewer perpetuates oppression. By this we mean, humans must be willing to accept that their lifestyle choices are not merely personally flawed but directly contribute to non/human suffering. In other words, if one fails to challenge their choices, they are contributing to the suffering of another. For instance, eating meat or consuming entertainment is not merely a personal choice. Minimally, it is relational because it requires the killing or filming of another being, in most cases without their consent. Once the association becomes relational, it simultaneously becomes political because the ensuing power dynamics allow one to justify one's interest over the other that is consumed. Thus, we ask the reader to explore their relationship to visual rhetoric by considering the connection among coercion, persuasion, and resistance. If one consciously recognizes and then dismantles these normalized practices of power and privilege, then the interconnectedness of oppression is made clearer. Those seeking greater clarity could analyze the language, imagery, and attitudes in visual culture alongside more literal elements of consumption to craft new strategies for justice. Only through consciousness raising, education, introspection, and committing to end behaviors that limit non/humans and humans can this ideal be realized. If we can adopt an anti-oppressive worldview that includes the consideration of non/human animals we can be more authentic activists, allies, and advocates in all spheres of our lives.

Of course, performing such an analysis is often fraught with risk. As Cornel West famously said, "It takes courage to ask—how did I become so well-adjusted to injustice" (West 2008)? People who challenge the norm are often stigmatized. In the instance of race, the diagnosis of "moron" was first developed to justify institutionalizing, and sometimes sterilizing, white women who had relations with black men since they "demonstrated a lack of social intelligence" despite their IQ (Stubblefield 2007). Likewise, "several late nineteenth-century physicians concocted a diagnosable form of mental illness to explain an over concern for animal welfare. Sadly, they pronounced, that animal activists were misguided souls that suffered from 'zoophile psychosis' . . . [with women being] particularly susceptible to the malady" (Beers 2006). In both cases, mental disability was used as a trope to delegitimize individuals who empathize with anyone considered beyond the scope of deserving empathy. More recently, legislation such as the Animal Enterprise Terrorism Act in the United States criminalizes any attempt to expose the cruelties of animal agriculture. The resounding argument states that exposing non/human abuse is an attack on the free market and the success of capitalism. Similarly, activists who continue to organize are considered "mad" due to their actions to protect those who are not deemed worthy of protection.

Even when it is not legislation or mental designations belittling advocates for non/human interests, nonconformists are portrayed in the media as overly zealous, spacey, misguided, neurotic, narcissistic, or even as terrorists. These representations are the basis for institutional repression, and reinforce the very discourses that initially created their justification. Regarding foreign policy, Roxanne Doty explains,

> Discourses create various kinds of subjects and simultaneously position these subjects vis-a-vis one another. For example, a traditional discourse on the family would contain spaces for a subject with traits conventionally defined as "male" and another kind of subject with traits conventionally defined as "female." These subjects would be positioned vis-à-vis one another in a particular way, e.g., female subservient to male. Within the traditional discourse on the family it is impossible to think outside of these categories except in terms of deviance or abnormality. . . . Subjects, then, can be thought of as positions within particular discourses, intelligible only with reference to a specific set of categories, concepts, and practices. . . . An approach that focuses on discursive

practices as a unit of analysis can get at how this "reality" is produced and maintained and how it makes various practices possible. (1993)

Therefore, rather than focus on individual policies, this book begins its departure from the discourses that encapsulate the non/human and make the various practices of oppression possible. Only by interrogating those representations and how humans relate to the construction of non/human animals can it be possible to unravel the violence that happens in the material world once the images leave the screen.

While the arts and humanities are often upheld as a pinnacle of civilization that fans the embers of democracy and western cultural development, art has become a tool for social control and normalization. Filmmakers like Leni Riefenstahl, while championed for her artistic vision, helped inspire Germany to depict the perfected Aryan race (Bach 2008). Simultaneously, cartoonists like Dr. Seuss drew racialized characters resembling Japanese-Americans to persuade the United States to endorse policies of internment (Edwards 2012). As critical animal studies scholar Anthony J. Nocella II notes, beyond these examples and despite great works of philosophy, music, art, and architecture, these advances have enabled colonial and postcolonial violence to expand throughout the world for "civilization" and "humanity." Indeed, the very concept of "civilization" is problematic because it presents as the antithesis to the wild, non-domestic, animalistic, primal, emotional, instinctual, abnormal, disabled, heterosexual, colonized, and feminine (Nocella and Best 2006). Aesthetics serve as the foundation for policies that contain, expel, and exterminate undesirables. It is also an antecedent to labeling constituents as "savages" due to a perceived lack of artistic and cultural development. Rethinking these binaries emphasizes the historical limits placed upon nature, humanity, and non/human animals. As part of our transformative project, focusing on the culturally mediated forms of aesthetics makes it possible to turn the colonial gaze against itself to highlight the barbarity inherent in dominant modes of media production.

We have organized this book into three main parts to highlight the influence representations have on the reality we experience in relation to one another. Part One explores the impact non/human imagery has on the non/humans being represented in a literal sense. The chapters attempt to craft strategies of resistance by reading against the grain in animation, blockbuster films, and science fiction. The chapters emphasize how non/human animal narratives serve human actors and audiences, while pardoning humans from acknowledging the dangers of anthropocentrism and ensuing violence. The first chapter, written about *The Hobbit*, explores the illusory compassion felt for non/human animals on the screen while ignoring their (mis)treatment when the cameras cease to roll. In doing so, J.L. Schatz demonstrates how the wall put between fiction and reality serves to further distance humans from the very others they relate to. This then sets the stage for Jennifer Polish's chapter that explores the intersection of non/human oppression and queerness to elucidate how contemporary film uses representational strategies to promote an anthropocentric heteronormativity. In doing so, they look at how Disney-Pixar's film *Maleficent* (2014) convinces moviegoers to regard the heroine's abusive relationship with non/human animals as admirable rather than exploitative. The next chapter by Matthew Lerberg addresses the cultural legacy of the film *Jaws* (1975) and seeks to counter the overly negative view of sharks that persists in Western culture today. He compares the cultural impact of *Jaws* with the popular cartoon *Jabberjaw* by Hanna-Barbera that, while representing sharks in a positive light, nevertheless constructs a speciesist frame that still ensures human supremacy. Afterward, Stella Hockenhull's essay explores the binary relationship and communication between the non/humans and their human trainers in Steven Spielberg's *War Horse* (2011). Her chapter contends that the very method of training—as well as the means by which it gets represented—continues to ignore non/human interests even as emotional bonds are established as a means to create empathy. Amber E. George's essay concludes Part One by describing how Looney Tunes' depiction of Bugs Bunny leads some humans to accept a very narrow understanding of pet rabbits's complex needs and interests. Instead of merely accepting the harmful portrayal of rabbits in the media, she argues that consumers ought to reevaluate cartoons, pet keeping, and the interests of rabbits in captivity.

Part two of this book surveys the relationship between human and non/human animals, and their deployment on the screen based on how humans understand "the animal" in reality. The first chapter in this part, by Carter Soles, explores *I Am Legend*'s (2007) portrayal of human and non/human animals within the ideological terrain of race in the post-9/11 era of the War on Terrorism. He argues that the protagonist's position is as a mediator between the properly white, civilized, imperial world (to which he used to belong as a scientist and military officer) and the bestial, savage, colonized world. In his analysis, Soles suggests that the film *I Am Legend* re-inscribes a firm boundary between the human and the non/human as a representational effort to restore U.S. hegemony. In the next chapter, Sean Parson reveals how *The Planet of the Apes* films are based on human understandings of ape culture. He argues that on the surface, these films seem to promote non/human rights and revolution; however, upon deeper reflection, they actually solidify an anthropocentric worldview by using human-based ontology. Next Anja Höing considers non/human animals in Martin Rosen's *Watership Down* (1978) and *The Plague Dogs* (1982), suggesting that unconventional cinematic approaches could develop alternative understandings that may cause viewers to internalize the films differently. This chapter creates alternative readings of problematic representations while remaining cognizant of the violence that manifests itself in the real world. In the last chapter, Fernando Pagnoni Berns and César Marino examine non/human and human relationships within the genre of "nature-run-amok" films. The authors suggest that the films *Frogs* (1972) and *Orca* (1977) represent an influential template for the genre because both emphasize modern ecological issues and support non/human animal revolt against human exploitation. These representations are then paralleled with the ecological fears of reality.

The chapters in Part Three explore the complexity of non-feature-length media messages that conspire to exploit non/humans. Topics in this section range from advertisements to online marketing as well as social networking and Internet-disseminated documentaries alongside short films. This section begins with an analysis by Joseph Anderton of animals in cyber culture. Using Jean Baudrillard's pronouncement in "Simulacra and Simulation" that the image has replaced reality, Anderton argues that nonhuman animal depictions in electronic media create distortions in perception that lead to superficial relationships between species. The interest in repeatedly viewing these copies might foreground a vague desire to connect with the animal, but ultimately contributes to the loss of the real in preference to virtual substitutes. In the following chapter, Fiona Yuk-wa Law discusses how pet ownership and adoption within human-animal relationships are riddled with dialectics of alienation in Hong Kong, Taiwan, and the People's Republic of China. She argues that the increase in concern regarding animal abuse and animal welfare by the local media and non-governmental organizations is compounded by urban development and shelter politics that simultaneously deny intrinsic value to non/human lives. Next, Guilherme Nothen and Michael Atkinson demonstrate the urgent need for critical animal perspectives on the use of non/human animals as mascots in professional sports. The authors show how seemingly disparate struggles of Native Americans against mascotry and non/human animals are fundamentally entangled. The authors advocate merging the two campaigns to strengthen the fight against domination and oppression in the realm of professional and amateur sports. The final chapter in this book, by Christina V. Cedillo, focuses on how bee images are used in campaigns to promote awareness of bee death. Using visual examples, Cedillo argues that they promote flawed managerial logics of species preservation and encourage viewers to accept counterproductive ideologies. Cedillo maintains that such trophic associations are based on notions of human embodiment that we must interrogate in order to ever solve pending ecological disasters.

In the end, we firmly believe that if the logic of speciesism goes unchallenged, and large-scale animal agriculture continues unchecked, it will become impossible to tackle problems like global warming, food insecurity, and inequity (Carrington 2014). The world may no longer sustain itself if modes of production continue to poison the air, waterways, and soil (Carus

2010). A critique of the speciesism inherent in media could prevent us from going down a path of self-destruction by awakening human awareness to the representational strategies that give so much weight to notions of dehumanization. Altering representations would make revising the world's trajectory for future generations possible. Undoubtedly, the first step to solving any problem is to identify the underlying difficulties that need to be addressed. By paralleling the fictional imaginings of our world with the concrete reality, this book collectively seeks to expose not only the current ordering of society but also imagine what society could become. Rather that imagining exclusionary and violent futures, our investigation into the non/human aims to craft a competing vision of what our world could be when we leave categories of "the human" and "the animal" behind.

Ultimately, by the book's end, we hope to fully demonstrate the cultural constructions that transpire to oppress others both on and off the screen. The interconnection between cultural studies, identity politics, and critical animal studies assists in articulating how processes of normalization dehumanize and exterminate entities and beings. These representations, if not challenged, will continue to stigmatize those who cannot fit universalized constructs of what it means to be a "human" citizen in a "civilized" world. Without these constructs, dehumanization will lessen, and its impact will diminish. The transformation will be complete only when total non/human liberation is achieved, not in terms of rights, but in terms of moral and social consideration. Beyond the question of non/humans's rights, we should give pause to consider how cultural representation affects the way humans relate and construct the world in oppressive ways. Through doing so it is possible to theorize solutions that don't replicate other forms of oppression via the discursive practices we deploy. To be fully moral beings living in this society, we must be able to justify the actions we take that affect others. We have a responsibility to share with each other how our interlinked networks of power perpetuate forms of domination based on individual subjectivity—human and non/human alike. We must learn from one another, be willing to fail, but keep struggling to produce the liberation necessary to end violence upon all living things. Humans are capable of choosing to live a life in nonviolent harmony with other humans, non/humans, and the ecosystem. We must, as critical animal studies scholars, take unapologetically radical revolutionary action for total liberation from teach-ins, workshops, boycotts, sit-ins, protests, rallies, civil disobedience, liberation, property destruction, and armed struggle. But we must first imagine the world this way in order to make it happen.

REFERENCES

Bach, Steven. 2008. *Leni: The Life and Work of Leni Riefenstahl.* New York: Vintage Books.

Beers, Diane L. 2006. *For the Prevention of Cruelty: The History and Legacy of Animal Rights Activism in the United States.* Athens, OH: Swallow Press/Ohio University Press.

Best, Steve, and Anthony J. Nocella II. 2006. *Igniting a Revolution: Voices in Defense of the Earth.* Oakland, CA: AK Press.

Best, Steve, Anthony J. Nocella II, Richard Kahn, Carol Gigliotti, and Lisa Kemmerer. 2007. "Introducing Critical Animal Studies." *Institute for Critical Animal Studies.* http://www.criticalanimalstudies.org/wp-content/uploads/2009/09/Introducing-Critical-Animal-Studies-2007.pdf.

Bogdan, Robert. 1988. *Freak Show: Presenting Human Oddities for Amusement and Profit.* Chicago: University of Chicago Press.

Carrington, Damian. 2014. "Giving Up Beef Will Reduce Carbon Footprint More Than Cars, Says Expert." *The Guardian,* July 21. http://www.theguardian.com/environment/2014/jul/21/giving-up-beef-reduce-carbon-footprint-more-than-cars.

Carus, Felicity. 2010. "UN Urges Global Move to Meat and Dairy-Free Diet." *The Guardian,* June 2. http://www.theguardian.com/environment/2010/jun/02/un-report-meat-free-diet.

Collins, Patricia Hill. 2011. "It's All in the Family: Intersections of Gender, Race, and Nation." In *The Meaning of Difference: American Construction of Race, Sex, and Gender, Social Class, Sexual Orientation, and Disability,* edited by K. E. Rosenblum and T-M. C. Travis, 245–254. New York: McGraw-Hill.

Davis, Lennard. 2002. *Bending Over Backwards: Disability, Dismodernism and Other Difficult Positions.* New York: New York University Press.

Doty, Roxanne. 1993. "Foreign Policy as Social Construction: A Post-Positivist Analysis of US Counterinsurgency Policy in the Philippines." *International Studies Quarterly* 37.

Edwards, Jim. 2012. "Before Dr. Seuss Was Famous He Drew These Sad, Racist Ads." *Business Insider,* March 23. http://www.businessinsider.com/before-dr-seuss-was-famous-he-drew-these-sad-racist-ads-2012-3.

Fancione, Gary. 2000. *Introduction to Animal Rights: Your Child or Your Dog?* Philadelphia: Temple University Press.

Institute for Critical Animal Studies. 2016. "Mission." http://www.criticalanimalstudies.org/about/.

Lorde, Audre. 1984. *Sister Outsider: Essays and Speeches.* Trumansburg, NY: Crossing Press.

Spiegel, Marjorie. 1996. *The Dreaded Comparison: Human and Animal Slavery.* New York: Mirror Books.

Stubblefield, Anna. 2007. "Beyond the Pale: Tainted Whiteness, Cognitive Disability, and Eugenic Sterilization." *Hypatia* 22(2): 162–181.

West, Cornel, and Tavis Smiley. 2008. *Hope on a Tightrope: Words and Wisdom.* Carlsbad, CA: Smiley Books.

Wilderson III, Frank. 2010. *Red, White & Black: Cinema and the Structure of U.S. Antagonisms.* Durham, NC: Duke University Press.

Wollstonecraft, Mary. 1792. *A Vindication of the Rights of Women.* Boston: Peter Edes for Thomas and Andrews.

I

The Truths Behind the Fiction

Chapter 1

The Brown Wizard's Unexpected Politics: Speciesist Fiction and the Ethics of *The Hobbit*

J.L. Schatz

Entertainment is not a neutral event. It is a political one. Going to the movies is a social act that expresses community. What tops the box office to a large degree reflects what a society is, what it values, and what it's willing to exploit. What we choose to consume on the screen shapes our cultural norms and discourse, as well as the consequences for those put on screen. When those individuals are non/human animals it becomes imperative to consider the consequences that impact them.

> As Stuart and Elizabeth Ewen emphasize in *Channels of Desire*: The politics of consumption must be understood as something more than what to buy, or even what to boycott. Consumption is a social relationship, the dominant relationship in our society—one that makes it harder and harder for people to hold together, to create community. At a time when for many of us the possibility of meaningful change seems to elude our grasp, it is a question of immense social and political proportions. (hooks 2006, 376)

Whether it is going to a movie or reading a book, the act of consuming fiction implicates the non-fictional identity of the consumer. Unlike books whose characters are entirely imagined, films require non-fictional actors to appear on the screen. When films make use of non/human animals to tell stories, they inform the consumer what it means to be human. "As Cary Wolfe argues: . . . the figure of the 'animal' in the West . . . [is] at the very heart of the constitutive disavowals and self-constructing narratives enacted by that fantasy figure called 'the human'" (Kendall 191). Thus, regardless of the genre, once the lights go down, it is always already more than just a movie. Rather, the non-fictional performances of human and non/human actors help (re)create the fictional stability over what it means to be human.

As Joan Scott, professor at the School of Social Science at Princeton University, argues,

> Fantasy is at play in the articulation of both individual and collective identity; it extracts coherence from confusion . . . and reconciles illicit desire with the law. It enables individuals and groups to give themselves histories. . . . Fantasy can help account for the ways subjects are formed, internalizing and resisting social norms . . . that endow them with agency. (2001, 289–290)

Perhaps fantasy is even more informative than other genres since the imagination can run wild without the hindrance of real world representations. However, eschewing reality in both constructing and consuming fantasy is not without cost in the physical environment. Indeed, "to be ethical means resisting the temptation to relate to the world as if we were directors of our own personal Hollywood films, forcing others to play prescribed roles or reducing them to depthless characters in pursuit of our predetermined but, from others' perspectives, fictional ends" (Smith 2011, 41). To be sure, fiction helps to imagine ethics. Simultaneously, when acting ethically we must not understand ethical relationships fictionally even if those relationships happen exclusively on the screen. As with meat eating and the purchasing of sweatshop clothing, just because the other before us is not present doesn't mean there isn't an-other beyond those representations. It is paramount that those others are remembered when situating ethics to cut against the dismembering process. Otherwise non/humans will continuously be reduced to consumable goods that vanish when the clothing is thrown away, or when the lights come back on after the movie ends.

This chapter examines the 2012 global box-office smash *The Hobbit: An Unexpected Journey*, directed by Peter Jackson, alongside its sequels and the novel by JRR Tolkien that inspired it. While the filming process and plot are profoundly anthropocentric, the ethical orientation of the Brown Wizard, and to a lesser extent Bilbo Baggins and other secondary characters, provides a window to revamping human relationships to the non/human world. This film serves as an excellent example of how the fantastic creation of fictional universes has political impacts in the real world for at least two reasons. First, the film was aptly renamed by the People for the Ethical Treatment of Animals (PETA) as an *Unexpected Cruelty* once it was discovered that at least 27 animals "died because they were housed on a treacherous farm full of 'death traps,'" while many more were injured (Cooke 2012). Jackson denied all allegations, saying that "no mistreatment . . . [or] abuse" occurred while filming since many of the deaths happened when the cameras weren't rolling (Lonaz 2012). Jackson's response abdicated the responsibility of his cast and crew by blaming the farm where the animals were housed. In doing so, he created a distinction between the fictional production of the film and the non-fictional facilities used to house the non/human actors. Second, Tolkien "gave us a critical framework for understanding . . . the study of . . . what has been called secondary world fantasy" (Northrup 2004, 816).

> For fantasy to succeed it must be formed out of the Primary World and refer the reader back to the Primary World. Flieger comments, "[t]he particular skill of the writer of fantasy, especially in devising a sub-created Secondary World, lies in . . . maintaining that delicate balance between fantasy and reality that will lead us to the underlying truth." And at this, she notes, Tolkien was the master . . . [since] "if examined closely, one finds that for a major fantasy it has surprisingly few actual fantastic elements," especially when compared to many of the fantasies that have followed. . . . "Tolkien's 'fantasy' is both attractive and powerful not because of its fantasy but because of its reality, because his world shows us that things are 'so' in our own world." (Northrup 2004, 818–819)

The same holds true for Jackson's cinematic trilogy that transformed Tolkien's work for the screen. This transformation enabled the ethical orientations of the characters in the films to parallel the orientations of the cast and crew. Thus, to read *The Hobbit* critically requires making the "hard recognition" that the world of Middle Earth is of humanity's design, and that the characters' mistakes and triumphs are outgrowths of society's own making.

Sadly, the popular response to PETA's claims of animal abuse, much like Jackson's, was largely dismissive. "The American Humane Association, which oversees animal welfare in the films, claims no animals were harmed during filming. But it also says . . . [that it has] shortcomings in its oversight system, which monitors film sets but not the facilities where the animals are housed and trained" (Perry 2012). Elijah Wood, who played Frodo, claims PETA's accusation "was the most ridiculous thing ever" despite admitting he "didn't even read the full report" and was only on set for a very limited amount of time (Child 2012). These sorts of defenses turn the fiction of the film (what the cameras actually captured) into being more important than the reality (what actually happened when the cameras weren't rolling) while denying a connection between the two. Severing the "hard recognition" of reality from Middle Earth is precisely what allowed Jackson's films to receive the AHA's seal of approval for animal treatment despite the mistreatment of non/human animals. *The Hobbit* is not the only movie to receive AHA's seal without deserving it (Wyatt and Walker 2013). In fact, the entire process of animal acting is fraught with abuse that often begins at birth with training and continues through adulthood without ever getting reported

(PETA 2015). As French philosopher Jean Baudrillard has explained, this disjunction between fiction and reality is particularly troublesome because

> an unreal event . . . is merely the expression of a—neither good nor bad, but quite simply immoral—collective will. . . . And we are not passive spectators of this fatal episode, but full-blown actors in it, playing our part in a lethal interactivity for which the media provide the interface. . . . There are no longer either actors or spectators; all are immersed in the same reality, in the same revolving responsibility, in a single impersonal destiny which is merely the fulfillment of a collective desire. (2001, 137–138)

From the patron in the movie theater to the characters on the screen, as well as the actors who play them, we are all responsible. Each film is a communal event that transcends the realms of Middle Earth and connects the collective desire of human and Dwarf alike. Purchasing a movie ticket and consuming popcorn means much more than the right to sit in a seat for three hours and snack. Rather, as consumers of cinematic culture, we must make ourselves culpable to what is on-screen as well as behind the scenes to ensure an-other being doesn't die for the price of admission.

THE ETHICS OF MIDDLE EARTH

The Hobbit: There and Back Again was originally written as a single book to serve as an introduction to *The Lord of the Rings* trilogy written by JRR Tolkien. After adapting Tolkien's trilogy for the screen, Peter Jackson decided to adapt *The Hobbit* as well. Unlike *The Lord of the Rings* trilogy, where each book got its own movie, Warner Brothers commissioned Jackson to make Tolkien's prologue into a trilogy of its own. As a result, there are story arcs and plot points in the films that are barely hinted at in Tolkien's original work. While diehard fans of the original novel may take issue with Jackson's adaptation, the integrity of translating the book for the screen is irrelevant to this chapter. Indeed, my argument is less about the accurate repetition of storytelling than it is about exposing what lurks beneath the text. This is not to say that differences between the films and the book aren't important. Certainly, significant departures from the original can signal a difference in ethical perspective. However, it is to say, as Joan Scott argues, that fantasy's power lies in how it operates like an echo in its ever changing repetition of remembrance.

> In either case the repetition is not exact since an echo is an imperfect return of sound. . . . The echo is a fantasy, the fantasy an echo; the two are inextricably intertwined. . . . There is no shortage of writing about history in these terms: history as the result of empathetic identification made possible either by the existence of universal human characteristics or, in some instances, by a

transcendent set of traits and experiences belonging to women or workers or members of religious or ethnic communities. In this view of things, fantasy is the means by which real relations of identity between past and present are discovered and/or forged. (Scott 2001, 287)

Hence, whether it is Jackson's or Tolkien's telling of the tale, *The Hobbit* persists in the viewer's imagination through what is remembered and expanded upon. Altering how one approaches the characters of Middle Earth will modify the ethical lens one uses to determine their identity. In this way, fantasy takes on a life of its own as it evolves with each active relationship people have when they consume its tale. Therefore, while the content might change, this echo is part of the natural evolution of fiction that gives fantasy its power to begin with.

What remains consistent through each reiteration of *The Hobbit* is the central plot of Bilbo Baggins, a hobbit from the Shire, helping a company of Dwarves retake their home from Smaug the dragon who stole it for its treasure. Narratively, the purpose of *The Hobbit* is to have Bilbo discover the ring, which is later inherited by Bilbo's nephew, Frodo, who attempts to destroy it in *The Lord of the Rings* trilogy. The first of Jackson's installments, *An Unexpected Journey*, opens long before Bilbo formally enters the tale. It begins with Smaug's attack on the Dwarves' home, Erebor. Reflecting, Bilbo narrates this history as he transcribes what will become his autobiography. He begins after Thror, king of the Dwarves, finds the greatest treasure of all time, known as the Arkenstone.

Thror named it the King's Jewel. He took it as a sign . . . that his right to rule was divine. All would pay homage to him, even the great Elvenking, Thranduil. . . . But the years of peace and plenty were not to last. . . . Thror's love of gold had grown too fierce. . . . Such wanton death was dealt that day [the dragon attacked], for this city of men was nothing to Smaug; his eye was set on another prize. For dragons covet gold, with a dark and fierce desire. (*An Unexpected Journey* 2012)

As the Dwarves flee Erebor, they witness King Thranduil and his Woodland Elves approaching Erebor. Thorin, Thror's grandson and the main focus of the film, calls to the Elves for aid. As the Elvenking turns away, Bilbo narrates, "Thranduil would not risk the lives of his kin against the wrath of the dragon. No help came from the Elves that day, or any day since" (*An Unexpected Journey* 2012). This history contextualizes the ethical landscape of Middle Earth. From the very beginning Bilbo forefronts how greed and an unwillingness to help others are the precursors to destruction. Was it not for Thror's greed, or Thranduil's turning away, Erebor may not have been lost, and the entire need for Bilbo's unexpected journey would have been irrelevant.

With the background to the film established, the story returns to the present day, where Bilbo and his nephew Frodo discuss relatives and prepare for Bilbo's birthday party. "In both cases—hobbit and dwarf—there is little about them that distinguishes them from humans. . . . If we can accept their size differences and their racial quirks, they are quite 'ordinary' in their desires and behaviors, except for the dragon" (Northrup 2004, 820). This is why viewers can readily connect with the characters and can understand how Thror's greed could lead to the demise of his kingdom. Outside of the film, Steven Best, professor of philosophy at the University of Texas, El Paso, points out how capitalist greed through the "profit imperative overwhelms the moral imperative. . . . In pursuit of the development and accumulation imperatives that drive its dynamic grow-or-die economy, capitalism devours nature, species, human lives, and indigenous cultures" (Best 2009). As wealth and self-interest grow, the moral consideration for others diminishes because self-preservation and accumulation becomes a stand-in for an ethical orientation. This is precisely why wealth is sucked up instead of trickled down. In the film, this self-interested mentality is why the seven Dwarf kingdoms tell Thorin that the quest for Erebor is his alone when he petitions them for help. In the third installment of *The Hobbit, The Battle of the Five Armies*, this mentality is also why Thranduil becomes involved only when it is possible for him to recover the jewels the Elves lost to Smaug when he captured Erebor. In each instance, the refusal to look out for the well-being of others over oneself is followed by violence.

The importance of caring for others as a guiding principle is apparent in the way the Dwarves greet Bilbo upon meeting him, with each saying, "At your service" (*An Unexpected Journey* 2012). The popularity of this common greeting can be witnessed in reality as well. The irony in both cases is that the saying rarely implies its literal meaning. In *The Hobbit,* the Dwarves appear at Bilbo's door exclusively for his service as a burglar for their quest to retake Erebor. When Bilbo reveals that he is not a burglar Dwalin remarks, "The wild is no place for gentlefolk who can neither fight nor fend for themselves" (*An Unexpected Journey* 2012). This observation reveals that despite valuing service to others, Middle Earth is built only for those who can fend for themselves. It becomes obvious as the film progresses that the protagonists can only succeed by bonding together and not by fighting alone. Thus, the discursive construction of the ethics of Middle Earth is very different from its reality and the morality ultimately put forth in its narrative. This becomes clearer when they discuss their plans. Balin tells Thorin, "You don't have to do this. You have a choice. . . . You have built a new life for us . . . that is worth more than all the gold in Erebor" (2012). Thorin responds to Balin, "There is no choice . . . for me" (2012). At this moment, the Dwarves decide to relinquish their lives, knowing they were worth more than gold, to satisfy Thorin's desire to rule Erebor as the rightful heir to the throne. This "non-choice" eventually drives Thorin to madness out of his obsession with wealth following in his grandfather's footsteps. Undoubtedly, in the second installment Smaug considers giving Bilbo the Arkenstone, remarking, "I am almost tempted to let you take it, if only to see Oakenshield suffer, watch it destroy him, watch it corrupt his heart and drive him mad" (*The Desolation of Smaug* 2013).

Wealth and power is constructed in these scenes as an inevitable choice even though acquiring such fortune will unavoidably result in demise. It is easy outside of the film to find people who hew to these views, and suggest they are inescapable. Slavoj Zizek, Senior Researcher at the Institute for Social Studies in Ljubljana, argues that "today's predominant form of ideological 'closure' takes the precise form of mental block which prevents us from imagining a fundamental social change, in the interests of an allegedly 'realistic' and 'mature' attitude" (2000, 324). These arguments of inevitability are often used by those who defend democratic capitalism, as Francis Fukuyama does in *The End of History and the Last Man*, and defenders of non/human exploitation. However, "to argue for the current system's preservation because the alternatives are imperfect is to dismiss a moral imperative in the name of short-term expedience. Normative reconfiguration never happens easily" (Cassuto 2007, 87). Likewise,

> it is absurd to say that capitalism is inevitable. This is really just an excuse for doing nothing to examine and promote improvements and alternatives. The way society is organised is due to the actions of people, and these actions can change. History shows a tremendous range of possibilities for human patterns of interaction. . . . Defenders of capitalism assume that there are only two basic options: either capitalism or some sort of system based on . . . dictatorship. . . . But of course there are more than these two options. (Martin 2001)

Thus, when searching for potential realities, it is important to remember there is always more than the status quo. Dominant representations can be overthrown just as easily as they can be maintained. It is vital that people do not merely resign themselves like Balin does when governing agencies say there is no choice. This is especially true as current global capitalist patterns are rapidly destroying the environment and countless species along with it. Put bluntly, "politics as usual just won't cut it anymore. . . . Narrow windows of opportunity are rapidly closing. The actions that human beings now collectively take or fail to take will determine whether the future is hopeful or bleak" (Best 2009).

Naturally, alternatives to capitalist production and speciesist orientations to the world exist both in reality and in Middle Earth. Not long after Bilbo leaves on his quest with the Dwarves he asks Gandalf about the other Wizards of Middle Earth. Gandalf explains that there are five wizards, including himself, Saruman, two Blue Wizards, and Radagast the Brown. While Tol-

kien's work only hints at the Blue and Brown Wizards, Radagast has a
significant presence in Jackson's trilogy. Bilbo asks Gandalf, "Is he a great
Wizard or is he more like you?" To which, looking slightly offended, Gandalf responds, "I think he's a very great Wizard, in his own way. He's a
gentle soul who prefers the company of animals to others. He keeps a watch-
ful eye over the vast forest lands to the East" (2012). Two points are noteworthy from this exchange. First, and most obvious, Radagast's connection
with non/human animals over other human-like beings is framed positively.
This is apparent when the camera immediately follows this dialogue by
cutting to Radagast rushing through the forest examining dying plants and
dead animals before finding a hedgehog he desperately works to save. Second, Gandalf defines greatness as relatively ordinary and not some super
power. While certainly Gandalf is a great Wizard, Bilbo has difficulty recognizing this greatness since there is nothing tremendously unusual about him.
In this way, much like how viewers must face their own similarities with
reality when confronted with fantasy, Bilbo must accept the normalcy within
the great Wizards whose everydayness is what makes them great.

Unfortunately, this everyday compassion was not the orientation that the
AHA used when giving *An Unexpected Journey* its seal of approval. In fact,
even after

> an animal trainer working on the film informed an AHA official of the fatal-
> ities in 2012 . . . [he was] told the lack of physical evidence would make it hard
> to investigate the claim further. When the trainer replied that he had buried the
> animals himself and knew of their location, the AHA representative told him
> that because the deaths had taken place off-set, it could not officiate. (Wyatt
> and Walker 2013)

Worse still, "*The Hollywood Reporter* [accurately] accuses the American
Humane Association . . . of not only failing to protect animals on set, but also
of covering up those lapses" (Wyatt and Walker 2013). Eventually, the AHA
acknowledged the deaths that took place while filming *An Unexpected Journey*. However, in doing so they still denied responsibility and placed blame
elsewhere. The president and CEO of AHA, Dr. Robin Ganzert, went on
record stating that the AHA is "currently only empowered to monitor animal
actors while they are working on production sets. . . . We do not have either
the jurisdiction or funding to extend that oversight to activities or conditions
off set or before animals come under our protection" (AHA 2012). Given
Radagast's struggles to save every creature he encounters regardless of their
nature or relation to him, it is shocking that the filmmakers did not extend
this same care to the non/human animals who made the film a success.
Warner Brothers supported Jackson when he "completely rejected" the accu-
sations and absolved the production crew of fault instead of admitting to the

deaths and taking preventative action to avoid future abuse (*Hollywood Reporter* 2012).

Shortly after Bilbo learns about Radagast, Gandalf leaves the party because he has had enough of Thorin's stubbornness. The remaining Dwarves along with Bilbo make camp for the night. In the book, "one of the baggage ponies bolts and is lost in the flood-swollen river before they can catch him. This particular pony was carrying most of their food . . . [so] when one of the lookouts sees a fire flickering in the distance . . . they decide to send the 'burglar' to investigate" (Northrup 2004, 820). In the movie, two ponies disappear and when Bilbo is sent to investigate he discovers that three trolls are preparing to cook them for dinner. It is ironic that the ponies's lives are spared in the film after being rescued at the same time the filmmakers allowed the animals used in the production to die. It is also interesting that in the book Bilbo's purpose is to steal food instead of preventing non/human animals from being turned into food. In both cases, the trolls are ultimately defeated after Gandalf returns. The Dwarves then discover the trolls' cache. It is there that Bilbo is united with Sting, his sword. When Bilbo remarks that he "never used a sword in my life," Gandalf reassures him by saying, "And I hope you never have to. But if you do, remember this: true courage is about knowing not when to take a life, but when to spare one" (*An Unexpected Journey* 2012). These words echo the ethical framework for the film since once again true heroism comes not from killing others but for looking out for the individuals most likely to be killed by others. Interestingly, these are the words Bilbo hears in his head while being attacked after obtaining the ring and is presented with the opportunity to kill Gollum. And, while some viewers may think that it was the wrong choice due to Gollum's appearance and nature, it is worthwhile to remember that in the last installment of *The Lord of the Rings* trilogy Frodo also spares Gollum's life for exactly that same reason. Had Bilbo or Frodo killed Gollum he wouldn't have been alive to enable the destruction of the ring at the end of Tolkien's trilogy. Ultimately, time and time again the narrative returns to the necessity of looking out for others even when it might not be in one's best interest, or when it is far easier to simply look away.

It is not coincidental that in the following scene Radagast informs Gandalf about dark forces gathering in the forest. He is quickly interrupted by a Warg's howl, signaling that a pack of Orcs are nearby. Instead of joining the fight against the Orcs, Radagast offers to distract them so the party can escape. In doing so, the Brown Wizard aligns himself with Gandalf, the Dwarves, and Bilbo without sacrificing his ethics since he simultaneously abstains from killing both Warg and Orc. While many of the Wargs and Orcs do die by the end of the scene, it is not accidental that the Dwarves and the Elves, who arrive on the scene, do the killing. After the Dwarves and Elves encounter each other, Gandalf goes to great lengths to get Thorin to accept the Elves' help. Later, Gandalf goes to a similar length to get Elrond, the leader of the Elves, to help the Dwarves. As a result, even as Gandalf sides with the Dwarves he remains critical of their pride. This sentiment is echoed in the second installment when the party meets a skin-changer named Beorn. While picking up and gently holding a small mouse, Beorn declares, "I don't like Dwarves. They're greedy and blind, blind to the lives of those they deem lesser than their own" (*The Desolation of Smaug* 2013). Another character, Bard, shares a similar view of the Dwarves, stating, "The blind ambition of a mountain-king so driven by greed, he could not see beyond his own desire" (*The Desolation of Smaug* 2013). In short, even as the Dwarves' quest to recapture their home is portrayed as a noble ambition, the greed that inspires Thorin to act is a despicable trait in Middle Earth that many characters remain highly critical of.

The Dwarves' greed and pride is juxtaposed when the party takes refuge with the Elves. There Gandalf discusses the future of Middle Earth with Elrond, Saruman, and Galadriel, a powerful Elf priestess. While Elrond and Saruman believe the world is at peace due to the absence of war, Gandalf reads the prior events in the film as components of war. Gandalf believes the smaller everyday instances of violence constitute war, whereas Elrond and Saruman believe war occurs only during armed conflict. Sadly,

> Neglecting the omnipresence of militarism allows the false belief that the absence of declared armed conflicts is peace, the polar opposite of war. It is particularly easy for those whose lives are shaped by the safety of privilege, and who do not regularly encounter the realities of militarism, to maintain this false belief. . . . Antiwar resistance is then mobilized when the "real" violence finally occurs, or when the stability of privilege is directly threatened, and at that point it is difficult not to respond in ways that make resisters drop all other political priorities. . . . Seeing war as necessarily embedded in constant military presence draws attention to the fact that horrific, state-sponsored violence is happening nearly all over, all of the time, and that it is perpetrated by military institutions and other militaristic agents of the state. (Cuomo 1996, 31–32)

Galadriel ultimately sides with Gandalf, telling him, "You are right to help Thorin Oakenshield. But I fear this quest has set in motion forces we do not yet understand." She then asks, "Why the Halfling?" Gandalf responds, "Saruman believes that it is only great power that can hold evil in check. But that is not what I have found. I've found it is the small things, everyday deeds of ordinary folk, that keeps the darkness at bay" (*An Unexpected Journey* 2012). Hence, it is unsurprising that during the council meeting Saruman rolls his eyes at the mention of Radagast's name while Gandalf and Galadriel hold the Brown Wizard in high regard.

Gandalf and Galadriel are not alone in recognizing how everyday violence and a lack of compassion are acts of war. As mentioned earlier, Beorn is another character who holds a similar belief that more mundane cruelties are every bit as violent as the military clashes that Saruman fears. Before the party takes refuge from the Orcs with him in the second film, Thorin asks if he's "friend or foe," to which Gandalf responds, "Neither" (*The Desolation of Smaug* 2013). Much like Radagast, while he clearly aligns himself with the Dwarves, he doesn't do so by killing their enemies despite sufficient motivation to do so. Shortly after taking refuge, Beorn explains how he knows the leader of the Orcs, Azog the Defiler. "My people were the first to live in the mountains, before the Orcs came down from the north. The Defiler killed most of my family, but some he enslaved. . . . Not for work, you understand, but for sport. Caging skin-changers and torturing them seemed to amuse him" (*The Desolation of Smaug* 2013). This sentiment of horror carries itself over to reality in the same way humans enslave and enable the death of non/humans for their own amusement, for example in things like the filming of *An Unexpected Journey*. However, it is imperative that humans not be turned into enemies who should be killed or imprisoned. No doubt,

> fighting for human animal rights is fighting for nonhuman animal rights. . . . Workers at slaughterhouses and fast food restaurants are often poor or living just above the poverty line . . . and dealing with police profiling and minimum wage jobs at the very McDonald's or slaughterhouse that animal advocates seek to dismantle. . . . This means that we must stop talking and writing about so-called alliance politics and solidarity and get involved in struggles to end racism, poverty, sexism, ableism, and heterosexism, while also working for animal justice. (Nocella 2012)

Moreover, humans must recognize that true courage comes not from attacking others but from forming alliances with those who initially may be our adversaries. Only then is it possible to truly care for others regardless of whether others' viewpoints and ethics align with our own. Put simply, "whether we defend the violation of another's life through our denial of reality which makes us uncomfortable, or through outright enthusiasm for oppressive power relations, the results are devastating" (Spiegel 1996, 80).

Even the Woodland Elves had individuals who argued against the evil spreading across Middle Earth outside of their borders. In a scene that takes place after the Dwarves leave Beorn and venture into the Woodland Elves's domain, Thranduil tries again to bargain for his kin's jewels. After Thorin turns him down, Thranduil talks with another Elf named Tauriel over the state of Middle Earth. He instructs her to "keep our lands clear of those foul [spider] creatures" (*The Desolation of Smaug* 2013). When she asks, "And when we drive them off, what then? Will they not spread to other lands?" Thranduil responds, "Other lands are not my concern. The fortunes of the world will rise and fall, but here in this kingdom, we will endure" (*The Desolation of Smaug* 2013). Later still, Tauriel tells Legolas, Thranduil's son, "It is our fight. It will not end here. With every victory, this evil will grow. If your father has his way, we will do nothing. We will hide within our walls, live our lives away from the light, and let darkness descend. Are we not part of this world?" (*The Desolation of Smaug* 2013). While Tauriel resorts to killing, unlike Radagast and Beorn, her willingness to argue against the isolationism of the Woodland Elves proves that her ethical purview extends beyond her own interests and those of her kin. Her resistance to Thranduil's command continues into *The Battle of the Five Armies*. While Thranduil gets involved only for the sake of his jewels and people, Tauriel furthers her involvement in the war for the benefit of others even to the point of sacrificing her own life to save a Dwarf she loved. Thus, her words and actions align with the fundamental message that greatness can come from protecting the lives of others even at the cost of one's self-interest to survive.

Of course, challenging the status quo is not always limited to literal protest, rallies, sit-ins, and strikes in the streets and direct personal one-on-one confrontation. Rather, it can also grow out of a profound understanding of solidarity with those who are marginalized and silenced, and those who appear only off-screen. Such an understanding can serve as an entry point to developing a positive ethical orientation of caring for others beyond limited circles of self-interest. As part of an audience, the viewer experiences a literal silence imposed by the theater when the lights go down that deliberately shields the viewer from the behind the scenes abuse. In turn, there is a responsibility to theorize against such abuse. These actions are far from meaningless in much the same way Radagast struggling to save a single hedgehog while other non/human animals die around him is anything but fruitless. Baudrillard argues,

> What is essential is that nothing escape[s] the empire of meaning, the sharing of meaning. . . . They, the animals, do not speak. In a universe of increasing speech . . . only they remain mute, and for this reason they seem to retreat far from us, behind the horizon of truth. But it is what makes us intimate with them. It is not the ecological problem of their survival that is important, but still and always that of their silence. In a world bent on doing nothing but making one speak, in a world assembled under the hegemony of signs and discourse, their silence weighs more and more heavily on our organization of meaning. (1994, 137)

If viewers pay attention to their relationship with non/human animals in film, they can become an ally to non/humans in reality. This awareness can also foster a deeper appreciation of the fictions that inform their lives. While many may see this as a trivial act, it is important to remember Gandalf's words that "it is the small things, the everyday deeds, that keeps evil in check." Put simply, it is these unexpected alliances between moviegoers, the cast, and crew that can help prevent violence from repeating itself by forming a truly compassionate relationship with the non/human animals who become alive on the screen.

In responding to the abuse that occurred during the filming, PETA suggested that Jackson should delve even deeper into the illusion of fiction instead of clinging to non/human actors. They claimed, "He is the CGI master and has the ability to make the animals and other interesting creatures in his movies 100% CGI" (Child 2012). While this may not end all non/human animal abuse—undoubtedly not all cast and crew members would instantly shift to veganism—it would give meaning to the silence many expressed when animals were unnecessarily injured and killed to tell its story. The ongoing retelling and rereading of Tolkien's work provides the perfect opportunity to alter the course of history if we are willing, like Bilbo, to step outside our holes despite all the dangers in doing so. Nevertheless, to build alliances with others—especially those entirely removed from the self—forces one to engage in an endless journey that spawns new imaginations and realities for generations to come. Our fictions are the ideal place to start because they are always subject to reinterpretation, and hence change. In short, no site of resistance or creature is too small to matter once we begin to perceive consumption and entertainment differently. Differences between the book and films show that our narratives and ethics can and do evolve. There is no reason we cannot do the same to our reality by looking at fictions such as *The Hobbit* politically. Ceding the fictional world for only a strict discourse on reality ignores the way we must evolve our imaginations to confront ethical considerations from another light.

REFERENCES

American Humane Association. 2012. "American Humane Association Calls Animal Deaths on 'The Hobbit' Unacceptable." November 19. http://www.americanhumane.org/about-us/newsroom/news-releases/aha-the-hobbit-animal-deaths.html.
Baudrillard, Jean. 2001a. *Impossible Exchange*. London: Verso.
———. 1994b. *Simulacra and Simulation*. Ann Arbor: University of Michigan Press.
Best, Steven. 2009. "The Rise of Critical Animal Studies: Putting Theory into Action and Animal Liberation into Higher Education." *Journal for Critical Animal Studies* 7(1). http://www.stateofnature.org/theRiseOfCriticalAnimal.html. Last accessed September 5, 2015.
Cassuto, David. 2007. "Bred Meat: The Cultural Foundation of the Factor Farm." *Law and Contemporary Problems* 70:59–87.
Child, Ben. 2012. "Hobbit Animal Abuse Claims: Warner Bros Backs Peter Jackson." *The Guardian*, November 23. http://www.guardian.co.uk/film/2012/nov/23/hobbit-animal-abuse-warner-bros.
Cooke, Sonia. 2012. "27 Animals Died During Making of *The Hobbit*, Say Handlers." *Time*, November 19.
Cuomo, Chris. 1996. "War Is Not Just an Event: Reflections on the Significance of Everyday Violence." *Hypatia* 11(4): 30–45.

The Hobbit: An Unexpected Journey. DVD. Directed by Peter Jackson. Warner Brothers Pictures, 2012.

The Hobbit: The Desolation of Smaug. DVD. Directed by Peter Jackson. Warner Brothers Pictures, 2013.

The Hobbit: The Battle of the Five Armies. DVD Directed by Peter Jackson. Warner Brothers Pictures, 2014.

Hollywood Reporter. 2012. "Warner Bros. Responds to 'Hobbit' Animal Cruelty Allegations." November 20. http://www.hollywoodreporter.com/news/hobbit-animal-abuse-warner-bros-393486.

hooks, bell. 2006. "Eating the Other." In *Media and Cultural Studies*, edited by Meenakshi Durham and Douglas Kellner. Malden, MA: Blackwell Publishing.

Loinaz, Alexis. 2012. "The Hobbit Controversy: Animal Cruelty Allegations Cast Shadow Over Premiere as Peter Jackson Again Denies Claims," *E! Online*, November 28. http://www.eonline.com/news/366567/the-hobbit-controversy-animal-cruelty-allegations-cast-shadow-over-premiere-as-peter-jackson-again-denies-claims.

Martin, Brian. 2001. *Nonviolence versus Capitalism*. London: War Resisters International.

Nocella, Anthony. 2012. "Challenging Whiteness in the Animal Advocacy Movement." *Journal for Critical Animal Studies* 10(1). http://www.criticalanimalstudies.org/volume-10-issue-1-2012/.

Northrup, Clyde. 2004. "The Qualities of a Tolkienian Fairy-Story." *Modern Fiction Studies* 50(4): 814–837.

Perry, Nick. 2012. "Hobbit Animal Deaths: Up To 27 Die as Wranglers Blame Production Company." *The Huffington Post*, November 19. http://www.huffingtonpost.com/2012/11/19/hobbit-animal-deaths-wranglers_n_2158198.html.

PETA. n.d. "Animal Actors." http://www.peta.org/issues/animals-in-entertainment/animal-actors.aspx.

PETA. n.d. "'The Hobbit': Unexpected Cruelty." http://www.peta.org/features/the-hobbit-unexpected-cruelty.aspx.

Scott, Joan. 2001. "Fantasy Echo: History and the Construction of Identity." *Critical Inquiry* 27(2): 284–304. http://www.culturahistorica.es/scott/fantasy.pdf.

Smith, Mick. 2011. *Against Ecological Sovereignty: Ethics, Biopolitics, and Saving the Natural World*. Minneapolis: University of Minnesota Press.

Spiegel, Marjorie. 1996. *The Dreaded Comparison: Human and Animal Slavery*. New York: Mirror Books.

Wyatt, Daisy, and Tim Walker. 2013. "27 Animals Died During Filming of Hollywood Blockbuster 'The Hobbit.'" *Independent*, November 26.

Zizek, Slavoj. 2000. *Contingency, Hegemony, Universality: Contemporary Dialogues on the Left*, edited by Judith Butler, Ernesto Laclau, and Slavoj Zizek, New York: Verso.

Chapter 2

The Passing Faerie and the Transforming Raven: Animalized Compulsory Re-covery, Endurance, and Dis/ability in *Maleficent*

Jennifer Polish

Hailed by critics for challenging the heteronormative rape culture narrative of *Sleeping Beauty's* "true love's kiss," Disney's *Maleficent* (2014) broke through some long-standing gender molds. As one reviewer noted, "[a]s the final, spell-breaking kiss demonstrates, it is the love between women—not a sexual/romantic love, exactly, but a non-heteronormative kind to be sure—that is most powerful, most "true" love in this universe" (Lowder 2014). While fair and refreshing, this critical reaction elides the ways in which the film narrativizes the triumph of the restoration of (compulsory) able-bodiedness and what I call compulsory re-covery. When Maleficent's violently sliced-off wings magically return to her body at the end of the movie, her able-bodiedness is compulsorily restored. She can then continue to enact able-bodiedness both despite and because of her dually animalized and racialized otherness. This compulsion toward able-bodied performance involves "covering over, with the appearance of choice, a system in which there actually is no choice" but to perform able-bodied(ness) (McRuer 2006). Thus, the film follows the embodiment of this compulsion in the faerie Maleficent, played by Angelina Jolie. This chapter will review her journey from being an optimistic, wide-eyed, high-flying child into a wingless "tyrant," then back into a renowned, compassionate faerie. The classic "happily ever after" ending firmly embodies the differential burdens that compulsory re-covery places on racialized and animalized people, humans and non/humans alike.

The film begins shortly before young Maleficent befriends a human boy, Stefan, who courts her in her youth. In adulthood, Stefan (Sharlto Copley) betrays Maleficent by drugging her and cutting off her wings as a present for the dying human king so that he can become king himself. The species-based dis/ablement of losing her wings subsequently shapes the entire narrative of the film, as she collapses into anguish and anger after this traumatic event. After saving her from human violence and employing the raven Diaval (Sam Riley) as her servant, Maleficent learns that Stefan is the king and that his wife is with child. In her new role as leader of the non/human land the Moors, Maleficent curses Stefan's newborn, Aurora (Elle Fanning). However, after carefully watching her grow up, Maleficent bonds with the blond child and tries in vain to reverse the (classically recognized) spinning-wheel curse placed on her in infancy. In the midst of attempting to save Aurora from cursed sleep, Maleficent and Diaval confront King Stefan, who attempts to infiltrate the Moors to kill Maleficent. When all seems lost, Maleficent's wings triumphantly return to her, and with King Stefan's threat and her curse both eliminated, all rapidly collapses into a "happy ending."

In the opening narration, an older Princess Aurora states of Maleficent that, "You might take her for a girl. But she was not just any girl. She was a faerie." This narration overlays a beautiful shot of Maleficent as a child, reclining in a tree, panning over her horns, her wings, and the golden magic she passes joyfully between her fingertips. Similarly marked by potential misrecognition, the passing faerie, upon meeting her first human—a young Stefan—is greeted by the remark, "And you're just a girl. *I think.*" This statement questions both her species-being and gender based on the presence of her wings and horns and the abilities they bring her. He almost coyly reveals that he likes her wings, marking the beginning of their cross-species, cross-race friendship, and eventual courtship. One film reviewer notes this interest in her wings—and indeed, their relationship generally—as Stefan's passing, fetishizing interest in Maleficent's "exoticism" (Lowder 2014).

As narrated by Aurora, *Maleficent* presents at first from an unapologetically human perspective, despite the ending's portrayal of a unification of the non/human and human king(queen)doms. Aurora-as-narrator and Stefan "thinking" Maleficent is a girl immediately establish a human gaze. It also constructs a dichotomy between, as the narrator says, "folk like you and me [narrator Aurora] with a vain and greedy king to rule over them" and "the other kingdom, the Moors, [in which] lived every manner of strange and wonderful creature, and they needed neither king nor queen. They trusted one another." This immediate otherification of non/humans simplifies non/human affect and agency by both exotifying ("strange") and romanticizing ("wonderful") them. The fantasized racialization of non/human creatures as exotic others embodies the parallel deployments of dehumanizing racist structures and agency-stripping speciesism.

Maleficent is consistently referred to by humans like murderous King Stefan as the "winged creature" and mocked for her otherness. King Stefan asks her, "How does it feel, hm? To be a faerie creature without wings? In a world where you don't belong?" In this instance, Maleficent is othered as a racialized non/human animal by humans. This fantasy-realm portrayal of non/human creatures as a different *race* than humans makes plain the real-world connections between racism and speciesism, as Cary Wolfe (2003) elucidates:

> As long as it is institutionally taken for granted that it is all right to systematically exploit and kill nonhuman animals simply because of their species, then the humanist discourse of species will always be available for use by some humans against other humans as well, to countenance violence against the social other of whatever species—or gender, or race, or class, or sexual difference. (8)

When the faeries categorize Maleficent as an "other" to both non/humans *and* humans because of her human size and large wings, it is clear she is a human-passing faerie.

However, her passing as a human other is not complete until her gender is enacted. Early in the film, soon-to-be King Stefan drugs Maleficent and while she is sleeping, cuts away her faerie wings. This scene can be read as a metaphor for, or direct instance of, sexual assault and rape. Indeed, Jolie confirmed that this climactic scene is an intended rape scene (Rich 2014). While it is certainly a scene of horrific gender-based violence, the wing cutting is also an instance of speciesist violence. Maleficent is being targeted, not (only) as a woman, but as a "winged creature" whom the king preceding Stefan had demanded be killed. Here, Maleficent is both racialized as other and othered by her species-being. The particular violence inflicted upon her would not have been possible or desired had she not been other-than-human. Stefan targets Maleficent for rape-esque violence, and dis/ables her precisely *because* she is a non/human "winged creature" with abilities that humans do not have. Ironically, the process of dis/abling her strips most of her visible non/human abilities, allowing her to pass easily as a human. However, it costs her the ability to fly, which was a critical part of her non/human existence.

Precisely because of her animality, King Stefan targeted Maleficent for the dis/abling violence of slicing off her wings. The subsequent magical restoration of her able-bodiedness at the end of the story was a heroic defense of animal(ized) life. Thus, the viewer may believe that human dis/abilities must be heroically "cured" via compulsory re-covery. Thus, compulsory re-covery is one facet of compulsory able-bodiedness. While compulsory able-bodiedness is assumed to be the norm in dominant spatial and temporal frames, compulsory re-covery is forced upon dis/abled bodies and minds after impairment is acknowledged. Compulsory re-covery forces a "cure" (or prostheticization if a "cure" is not available) onto people with dis/abilities. In so doing, compulsory re-covery re-covers—hides—dis/ability, rendering it invisible or less visible and thus less threatening to able-bodied superiority.

Compulsory re-covery places differential demands on bodies that experience multiple layers of gender-, race- and species-based violence. Furthermore, Maleficent experiences these demands as a racialized woman juxtaposed with dual animalization and humanization. This racialization and animalization throughout the film create a distinct interaction between compulsory re-covery and *compulsory endurance.* In other words, animalized, racialized beings are expected to *endure* dis/abilities and traumas inflicted by speciesist and racist structures. This does not allow *recovery* because animalized, racialized subjects are considered *inherently* dis/abled and targeted for perpetual dis/ablement by human white supremacist structures. Maleficent—though targeted for violence because of her "otherness"—passes as human just enough to achieve the "triumph" of compulsory re-covery.

Furthermore, the bodily traumas and dis/abilities of non/humans represent compulsory endurance because non/humans serve as mere prosthetic devices to reduce the dis/abling effects of wing-amputation of the human-passing protagonist. Movie magic is used to demonstrate what is perhaps only implicit in real-world film and cosmetics industries. That is, when non/humans aren't used as prosthetics for humans with dis/abilities or visible differences, their bodies are mined for "cures" to human "imperfections" (as racialized human bodies have been violently used throughout U.S. history) (Washington 2006). The film situates these "imperfections" as something to be heroically "cured" or at least hidden—compulsorily *re*-covered—to complete a positive emotional and human physical transformation. By nonconsensually changing her raven servant Diaval's body to suit her needs on a regular basis, she makes him "[her] wings." Maleficent re-perpetuated Diaval's lack of control over his body through forcibly silencing his animalized protests.

COMPULSORY RE-COVERY OF DIS/ABILITY: RAPE AND NETTING

Race- and gender-based acts of violence in *Maleficent* are intimately linked to dis/abling acts of violence against non/human animals. The dis/abling impacts of this violence perpetuate speciesism *because* they serve as prosthetic devices and are "saved" when their dis/ability is "healed" by an able-bodied, white human savior. Furthermore, scenes of non-consent and violence toward Maleficent are terrifying and awful while similar scenes toward Diaval are amusing and poignant. Comparing these scenes highlights the differing expectations of compulsory able-bodiedness placed on animalized subjects.

Moreover, silence and non-lingual communications are critical vehicles through which to understand these differential expectations, which are made explicit in the film's climactic scene of compulsory re-covery. Able-bodiedness is positioned as a saving grace for ending violence that non/humans are compulsorily expected to endure. This violence was made literal by the hidden violence against non/humans deployed by both the production and advertisement of the film. The silenced nature of this violence, however, reveals the ways that non/humans—like many racialized human groups—are relegated to compulsory *endurance*: persistently defined by dis/ability, so much so that dis/ability becomes an unspoken, assumed default position of non/human and/or racialized identities.

However, dis/abling violence against Maleficent is not hidden, nor are her animalized responses devalued. Nonlinguistic communication in *Maleficent* is privileged and admired in Angelina Jolie's (human) facial expressions but otherified in her non/human servant Diaval. This directly mirrors the ableist and racist assumption that being influent and inarticulate of a dominant verbal language means one is "dumb." Perhaps ironically, Maleficent's most animalized moments occur during two torturous scenes portraying, respectively, the rape that stripped her of her wings and the horrific hunt for non/humans. Maleficent's nonverbal agony was extremely articulate as she was netted, beaten, and had her wings stripped from her. Viewers were encouraged to empathize with her non-lingual language in those moments of speciesist and misogynistic violence. Her compulsion to endure such violence and its repercussions ended only with the magical restoration of Maleficent's able-bodiedness as her wings returned to her body. Aurora, who explicitly embodied the ableist, patriarchal, racist norms of beauty, facilitated this return.

After the very pale, blond, embodiment of white beauty, Aurora freed Maleficent's wings from the cage, they flew to rejoin Maleficent's body just before Stefan dealt her the final blow. Meanwhile, Diaval, in dragon form, was chained, tortured, and almost killed nearby. The restoration of Maleficent's wings to her body allowed her to end this horrific, torturous violence against both her and Diaval. This triumph, ultimately resulting in Stefan's death, marks the celebrated restoration of her able-bodiedness (Bahr 2014).

After the return of her wings, her subsequent escape and overthrow of King Stefan's violent reign, compulsory re-covery is necessary to ensure a happy ending. Compulsory re-covery, as an extremely temporal configuration of compulsory able-bodiedness, demands that someone who is dis/abled be "cured" of their dis/ability (recover) or, at the very least, re-*cover* it. This covering of dis/ability protects able-bodied privilege because it forces dis/ability to hide, making people pass as (or become) able-bodied as to seem unthreatening to able-bodied-dominated spaces and institutions. Compulsory re-covery also emphasizes individual "healing" rather than interlocking systems of oppression that actively dis/able people's bodies and psyches daily. Structural violence creates dis/ability, and to be sure, action against, preventing, and reversing this particular damage is desirable. However, compulsory re-covery focuses on individualized "recovery" and "cure", thus individualizing dis/ability and divorcing it from structural oppressions that create dis/abilities (or at least, position impairments as dis/abilities).

Without her wings, Maleficent could threaten able-bodied spaces by existing as a person with a dis/ability who was not tyrannical as a result of the dis/ability. The restoration of her wings and the "healing" of her dis/ability, however, negated any threat to able-bodied supremacy. Along with this recovery of dis/ability, Maleficent win(g)s over the hearts of the people of her queendom again and restores a positive relationship with the community. The process of compulsory re-covery is victorious and portrays able-bodiedness as the restorer of peace and heals trauma inflicted on animalized beings. Thus, ableism and speciesism represents two distinct systems that operate against each other when they are actually mutually beneficial.

The restoration is enacted by the animality of her wings themselves. In response to Maleficent's proximity, or perhaps to the danger she finds herself in, her wings, encased in glass, desperately flap and struggle to get free before Aurora intervenes. Positioned as creatures or as non/humans of their own, intent on rejoining their human-esque figure, they cannot free themselves and need Aurora's help to escape their confines.

When the wings re-fuse with her body, light pours out of Maleficent—who had donned black attire and physically darkened the Moors after her disablement—as she takes flight for the first time in years. This intentionally evokes in audiences a visceral response of triumph and celebration, woman-powered and, subtly, able-bodied-powered victory. However, as Judith Jones of the online feminist of color website Crunk Feminist Collective argues,

> Her wings were a source of power and strength and they are taken early on in the movie. And as a result she is left alone and to an extent othered by her community. Her "dirty" body is then paired with darkness and she is perceived as evil and witchy. This often happens to women of color in films. She is then positioned next to a blonde, blue eyed, pure "pretty" girl making Maleficent's ways more apparent. The image of darkness juxtaposed with light has always had light as the saving grace, as if the image of darkness (in this case, Maleficent) could not save itself. In a variety of movies and shows a white character is the savior to the women of color and the voice of reason, while the person of color adds excitement and spice to the white character person's content life. This white "savior complex" reinforces racist ideals of women of color lacking ability to run their own life and as a result need the guidance of a white

woman. Sleeping Beauty is Maleficent's white savior. She is only redeemed
by loving this innocent blonde girl. (Jones 2014)

This racialization is a critical component of the ways that compulsory re-
covery operates. Maleficent is healed psychically by "loving this innocent
blonde girl," however, her restoration is incomplete. For the film cannot end
until she achieves a physical re-covering of her dis/ability as well. The racialization intertwines with and mutually reinforces Maleficent's animalization,
which makes her a target for dis/abling violence.

Thus, Maleficent cannot re-cover or recover from her dis/ability without
help from an able-bodied, white human or the prostheticized assistance from
an animalized creature. Her wings, becoming lively in their glass cage, are
shown to be themselves perhaps non/human creatures. Her wings position as
an intimate part of her body *and* as themselves almost separate, animalized
beings. Without determination on the part of the wings to be reunited with
Maleficent's body, Aurora tipping and breaking the cage would not have
reunited the wings with her larger body. It was their performance of eager-
ness to return to Maleficent that enabled her compulsory re-covery and,
therefore, her survival.

Emphasizing performance is critical; however, Judith Butler's development of performativity in the context of gender ironically limits itself to
humans. This is ironic because performativity, as articulated by Butler, dramatically unsettles the very meanings of gender and sex (1988). This unset-
tlement can also be extended to unsettle the very meanings of human and
non/human. Indeed, Karen Barad encourages us to think of humanity and
animality, like womanhood and manhood, as being created by performance.
She implores us to query, "[h]ow did language come to be more trustworthy
than matter?" and in so doing, encourages posthumanist thought to direct
itself to pay attention to non/human (here, non-lingual) forms of performativity (Barad 2003). Performance is particularly crucial to thinking about non/
humans because of how easily human assumptions are projected onto non/
humans. Emphasizing performativity is a way to unsettle the supremacy of
human "knowledge" in assuming that all forms of communication and expression are comprehensible in human ways.

The non-consensual control of Maleficent and Diaval's body during the
scene of triumphant recovery is an intimate, yet torturous example of non/
human suffering. Stefan rigs an iron net (iron burns faeries) to fall on Maleficent, netting and trapping her as Diaval had been caught earlier in the film.
He then has his soldiers surround and beat her through the net. Maleficent
represents as a non/human animal, as prey hunted for the utility and perhaps
even the sadistic pleasure of male perpetrators, just as Diaval had been targeted, hunted and tortured almost to death earlier in the film.

A human had netted Diaval and beaten him with a pole as two dogs looked on and barked. Fresh from experiencing rape and the destruction of her wings, Maleficent saves Diaval from his capture and almost fatal beating. Instead of simply sending the aggressors away from him to save him as a raven, however, Maleficent saves Diaval by transforming him into human form. Naked and covered in dirt, Diaval in the shape of a human man arises from the net. Maleficent circles him slowly, surveying him silently until he asks, "What have you done to my beautiful self?" She dismissively responds, "Would you rather I let them beat you to death?" Diaval turns his neck around to view his back, taking in his new lack of wings, and tells her, "I'm not certain." She responds, again dismissively, by telling him to "Stop complaining. I just saved your life." Maleficent's body was transformed non-consensually in an ironic act of "saving her life," when Stefan raised a dagger to kill her, but in sparing her life, he took her wings instead. Maleficent repeats that pattern with Diaval, non-consensually taking his wings as he gains human form so that he would not die. She could have chosen to save him another way, just as Stefan could have chosen to not violate her.

Diaval accepts her logic and agrees that he will be Maleficent's "servant," asking what she needs him to do. After informing him that she needs him to be her wings, she transforms him back into raven form. He immediately flies to the palace, knowing she seeks information about Stefan. Diaval's wings thus serve as Maleficent's prosthetic, her able-bodiedness-by-extension. All of her magic could not give her what the non/human, Diaval, could—the ability to fly and all the power that comes with it. Diaval becomes her wings, and a little more. Throughout the film, Maleficent gracefully flicks her wrist, sometimes giving minimal verbal commands such as "Into a dragon," for example, and transforms Diaval's body into whatever form *she* chooses. That is, whichever form is convenient for her and will serve her best.

The harm of losing control over one's body to another was a silent subtext, portrayed as less important than the growth of Maleficent and Diaval's bond. Similarly silent was Diaval when he was in many of his non/human forms. In this way, the use of non/human beings for human ability restoration effectively dis/abled non/humans. In their non/human existences, animalized forms of communication are portrayed as either comical or tragically pathetic. Diaval is shown to develop strong relationships with both Aurora and his "Mistress," Maleficent—indeed, the film ends with the latter two soaring above the clouds together. The film does not address the underpinning violence and coercion of Diaval and Maleficent's relationship. Given the ways that perpetual non-control of one's body is dis/abling, Maleficent perpetually dis/ables Diaval through controlling his body.

Indeed, Maleficent completely disregards Diaval's traumatic history with dogs when she transforms him into a wolf so he would assist with rounding up some of Stefan's soldiers. After they dispose of the threat, she turns him back into human form, and he rages, "How could you do that to me?" Mildly, she reminds him, "You *said* anything I need." He objects, "Yeah, but not a dog!" Maleficent tells him, "It was a wolf, not a dog." This use of "it was" rather than saying "you were" indicates that, despite transforming into different creatures at the nod of Maleficent's head or the flick of her wrist, Diaval does not *become* that which she transforms him into. He maintains his *self,* that which is raven, during his transformations. These transformations are traumatizing for him, and despite Maleficent making light of his pain, viewers are encouraged to focus on the budding relationships with Maleficent and Aurora instead. In human form, Diaval articulates with verbal language that dogs are "dirty, vicious, *and* they hunt birds!" He is not speaking in the abstract since two dogs were present at his near-death experience. Maleficent herself acknowledged the dogs' assistance with his capture and torture when she asked whether she should have let "them" beat him to death (there was only one human present). Despite knowing he carries the burden of such distress, Maleficent cuts off his objections midsentence with the flick of her wrist, which transforms Diaval once again into a raven, ultimately silencing him.

This silencing is highly significant because non-verbal and non-lingual communication—both in humans and in non/humans—are rendered illegitimate, ineffective modes of communication. Emily Clark (2012) focuses on J. M. Coetzee's fictional female characters who "speak for those who cannot speak for themselves" (in respective cases, a dis/abled human and factory farmed non/humans). She argues that Coetzee's texts promote "voicelessness" as a "force" rather than a passive object, something that "voiceness" cannot hope to represent accurately (29). Using this interpretation, Diaval's caws and abrupt departure from arguing with Maleficent is an articulate performance of anger, indignance, pain, and protest of her transforming him into a wolf. The film, however, undermines this "force" and renders it "voicelessness" by encouraging viewers to laugh at Diaval and Maleficent's bickering as relationship-building (Fernandez 2014). Since he cannot speak human language, Diaval's expression of trauma and resistance is not forced on the viewer.

Kari Weil (2006) similarly frames human language as an obstacle rather than a portal to comprehension. She unsettles the ableist and speciesist notion that non-lingual communication is indicative of "lower-level" communication. Weil joins Wolfe (2013) in promoting the theoretical intersections between ableism and speciesism from the writings of dis/abled humans like Temple Grandin (2006), who argues that some dis/abilities can serve as an *ability* to enhance communication with non/humans.

Maleficent's dis/ability, however, does not provide insight into her power over Diaval's body and her ability to trigger his traumas (by turning him into a dog, for instance). Instead of recognizing the commonality in their experiences and fostering empathy between them, she focuses on how to use his body as a prosthetic to offset her dis/ability. She manipulates his body at her pleasure to maintain his animalized silence and refuses to centralize his raven-esque behaviors as fully articulate.

In a deleted scene, Diaval intervenes (as he does throughout the film) as Maleficent's conscience. He asks her permission to speak freely, which she declines. When he begins to speak, she moves her arm up. He catches her forearm in his hand, and she looks accosted. He says softly, "any time you don't like what I have to say, you change me." Her wrist flicks despite his grasp on her arm, and he becomes a raven again. Even when Diaval gives a human voice to the problem, Maleficent insists on silencing him by animalizing him.

Interestingly, Maleficient's nonverbal communications, however, are honored as worthy modes of expression. Reviewers perceived Maleficent's performance and presence, with her silences (facial expressions, wrist flicks, and the like) as "commanding," articulate and forceful (Gettell 2014 and Rich 2014). In the powerful and much-anticipated curse-casting scene, King Stefan begs Maleficent to spare his daughter. She tells him, "I like you begging. Do it again." She slowly lowers her eyes to the ground before returning them to his face. He gets the message and kneels though she did not direct him. Her non-lingual communication, then, moved a king to his knees in front of his wife and his entire court.

However, Maleficent's animalized non-lingual communication is perhaps most forceful in scenes where her traumas are most visible. Her wrenching screams, racked body, and agonized, terrified facial expressions during the wing ripping and netting/torture scenes are poignantly articulate. These scenes give emotional force to non-lingual pain and acknowledge animalized silence or non-linguistic expression can communicate complex concepts. Ultimately, this deconstructs the dually ableist and speciesist erasures of non/human and dis/abled non-lingual expressions. Maleficent's refusal to verbalize thoughts and emotions in words makes her use gestures, facial expressions, and vocal intonations to develop an intimate relationship with animality. She then enters the world of animalized "pure body," and this performance *does* things to audiences, holding ethical force over the narrative arc of the film (Gibbs 2014).

Maleficent's performance of animality is validated through her non-lingual communication and enabled by her primarily human appearance. Since she can pass as mostly human, her animalized forms of communication are privileged as articulate speech that *does* things in the world. Diaval's caws in raven form, conversely, are rendered as either background noise or the disgruntled butt of one of Maleficent's dismissive jokes. This privileging of Maleficent's human-passing animality above Diaval's animality facilitates the privileging of Maleficent's traumas over Diaval's. Thus, her silences are dramatic, and her injuries are recognized and addressed as such. Diaval, on the other hand, is portrayed *as* non/human animal rather than as *performing* animality. He is known only through Maleficent's words and actions, has no control over the form his body takes, and thus is *truly* just a raven. Diaval does resist this lack of control, through his verbal and nonverbal protests and by bonding with Aurora when Maleficent was intent on destroying her. In this way, Diaval—non/human though he may be—performs acts of humanity as acts of resistance against his dis/ablement and lack of control of his body.

Despite these resistances, however, Diaval's nonverbal expressions are not (as described above) as forceful as Maleficent's. Jolie's mere facial expressions, conversely, aren't just positioned as *saying* things, but as *doing* things. *Maleficent*, then, makes a tremendously anti-speciesist and anti-ableist intervention by rendering nonverbality as articulate, legitimate, and incredibly forceful. However, this is only the case when Maleficent—someone who passes as a human and, therefore, passes as able-bodied is the one articulating herself nonverbally. Diaval's nonverbal expressions are not forceful and are therefore ignored, which perpetually reinforces the harm inflicted upon him. This harm is a silent subtext, portrayed as less important than the growth of Maleficent and Diaval's bond.

Accordingly, Maleficent and Diaval's relationship to dis/ability is treated differently. Maleficent's traumas (bodily and psychic) represent a triumphant space of compulsory re-covery. Her silences and non-lingual screams give forceful expression to her traumas, and she consequently is compulsorily re-covered from her dis/ability through the celebration of her newly restored wings and able-bodiedness that ends the film. Diaval, however, does not even have his traumas legitimized enough by the film's narrative to have the ableist burdens of compulsory re-covery placed upon him. Instead, non/humans like Diaval—like many racialized, dehumanized human subjects (Spears 2010)—are relegated to the unsung, perpetually performed, unacknowledged *compulsory endurance.*

Compulsory endurance is the forced survival through persistent, repeating, structural violence that is not acknowledged by dominant systems as traumatizing and/or dis/abling. Non-control of one's body is an *expected* attribute of non/human life (as well as non-white human life), so non-lingual or silent articulations of the agonies caused by this trauma are *not recognized as articulations of trauma* (Mollow 2006). They are silenced, like non/humans themselves. Non/humans, then—like people of color who are treated as non/humans in white supremacist societies, such as the one in which *Maleficent* was produced and consumed (Meadows 2010)—are not afforded the triumphant celebrations that accompany the (white) human achievement of compulsory re-covery.

This invisibility of non/human articulateness is reflected not only in the film's narrative but also in its production and advertisements as well. Non/

humans sometimes experience fatal harm in film production, as during the production of *The Hobbit* (2012) (Perry 2012). However, while no non/humans were killed in producing *Maleficent*, the use of non/human (specifically, horse and chicken) labor in the production of this film re-inscribes the invisibility of the non-consensual use of non/human beings to further human ends (American Humane Association 2014). In the film, this end goal was the restoration of compulsory able-bodiedness for Maleficent. In production, this end goal was the creation of background non/humans to heighten the drama of potential battle scenes.

Similarly, when the end goal was advertising and capitalizing on the film's potential success, non/humans were tremendously and silently exploited. MAC Cosmetics makeup created a *Maleficent*-inspired line of non-vegan, non-cruelty free makeup (Combs 2014; Cruel 2014). The damage inflicted upon non/humans for makeup production is tremendous (featuring a broad range of unanaesthetized, painful tests that end in the neck-breaking, asphyxiation, and decapitation of the non/humans) (Humane Society International 2013). Yet, the violent dis/abling exploitation is ignored in mainstream discussions through the silent erasure of trauma against non/human bodies.

Just as the film and cosmetic industrial complexes convince consumers to ignore the exploitative and deadly uses of non/humans, moviegoers may regard Maleficent and Diaval's relationship as humorous rather critique it as harmful. The narrative silencing of Diaval's perpetual trauma runs parallel with how the production and marketing of the film fail to recognize the "voices" of the "voiceless." Maleficent's voicelessness, however, was understood as a reflection of Jolie's "commanding presence" (Gettell 2014). The differential standard demonstrates how bodies that can consistently pass as more or less human are burdened "only" with compulsory re-covery. Meanwhile, non/humans must undergo uncelebrated compulsory endurance, which refuses to acknowledge the systemic and dis/abling violence inflicted upon and resisted against them.

CONCLUSION

Despite passing as human *enough* to appeal to moviegoers, Maleficent was targeted throughout the film because of her animalized and othered body. Maleficent was racialized and otherified by the narrative's bringing her into "darkness" upon becoming dis/abled. Ironically, her dis/ability—the loss of her wings—brought her closer to appearing (and "acting") human. This enactment of humanity enabled one form of ableism—compulsory re-covery—to dictate the narrative structure of the film, giving Maleficent a triumphant, transformative ending that "healed" her from her dis/abling traumas. With the return of her wings to her body, ableism was positioned as a pro-animal mode of embodiment. Compulsory able-bodiedness and anti-speciesist violence ironically colluded to end violence against an animalized victim (Maleficent). Compulsory re-covery works, then, to "save" animalized victims but in so doing, produces animalized creatures helpless on their own. For example, Maleficent and Diaval were helpless in their netting scenes, and Maleficent's animalized wings could not rejoin her body without help from an able-bodied human. This reinforces the manipulation of non/human bodies, the control that human/human-passing figures have to commit (or not commit) violence against non/human bodies. Even though compulsory re-covery may produce favorable outcomes for non/humans, it does not change non/human animal agency.

This perceived lack of agency is embodied by Diaval, as his body is read as being unable to articulate non-lingually with the same ethical force that Maleficent is. The non-consensual manipulation of his body throughout the film was the butt of jokes rather than considered as a perpetual trauma not much unlike those experienced by Maleficent. The force ascribed to Maleficent's silence undoubtedly works to deconstruct speciesist and ableist misunderstandings of the articulateness of silence, but the refusal to recognize this agency and force to Diaval's expressions counteracts the potential power of this portrayal. Denied the ableist "triumphs" of compulsory re-covery, Diaval—like other non-humans (and racialized, dehumanized humans)—is racialized and animalized as *naturally* dis/abled and suffering, enforcing unacknowledged, unsung *compulsory endurance* onto his body and others like him.

Furthermore, non/humans are portrayed in *Maleficent* as targets of dis/abling violence, as tools to commit dis/abling violence, or as helping humans or non/humans passing as human re-cover from and prostheticize their dis/ability. Whatever the case, non/human animal bodies are persistently defined with dis/ability, their very species-beings irrevocably connected to the impositions of the various modalities and differential expectations of compulsory able-bodiedness. While *Maleficent* intervenes in speciesism and ableism in critical ways, it also re-inscribes ableist, racist, and speciesist assumptions, such that non-lingual or non-dominant modes of expressions are invalid, and relatedly, erase the dire significance of traumas that structurally enforced violence inflicts on animalized and racialized people. As we in this book critique the ableism, racism, and speciesism in movements through multiple theoretical frameworks, we must also organize together in communities to educate one another beyond this book and engage in activism for social change, else the words on this page will be nothing more than another academic inquiring into intersectional oppression.

REFERENCES

Annamma, Subini Ancy, David Connor, and Beth Ferri. 2013. "Dis/ability Critical Race Stud-
ies (DisCrit): Theorizing at the Intersections of Race and Dis/ability." *Race Ethnicity and
Education* 16(1): 1–31.
Bahr, Robyn. 2014. "Why Maleficent Is the Rape Revenge Film That We Need." *Women and
Hollywood: IndieWire,* June 24.
Barad, Karen. 2003. "Posthumanist Performativity: Toward an Understanding of How Matter
Comes to Matter." *Signs* 28(3): 801–831.
Barker, Clare, and Stuart Murray. 2010. "Disabling Postcolonialism: Global Disability Cultures
and Democratic Criticism." *Journal of Literary & Cultural Disability Studies* 4(3):
219–236.
Bell, Christopher M. 2011. *Blackness and Disability: Critical Examinations and Cultural Inter-
ventions.* East Lansing: Michigan State University Press.
Butler, Judith. 1988. "Performative Acts and Gender Constitution: An Essay in Phenomenolo-
gy and Feminist Theory." *Theatre Journal* 40(4): 519–531.
Clark, Emily. 2012. *Voiceless Bodies: Feminism, Disability, Posthumanism.* Ph.D. diss., Uni-
versity of Wisconsin, Madison.
Combs, Tashina. 2012. "MAC Cosmetics Is No Longer Cruelty Free." *Logical Harmony,*
March 15.
Cruel, Jessica. 2014. "See the Entire MAC Cosmetics x Maleficent Makeup Collection." *Pop
Sugar,* May 1.
Fernandez, Leanette. 2014. "My Maleficent Interview with Sam Riley A.k.a. Diaval." *Teach
Me 2 Save,* May 29.
Frozen. 2013. Directed by Jennifer Lee and Chris Buck. Buena Vista Home Entertainment.
DVD.
Gettell, Oliver. 2014. "Maleficent Reviews: Angelina Jolie, at Least, Is Bewitching." *Los
Angeles Times,* May 30.
Gibbs, Adrienne Samuels. 2014. "Women Everywhere Are Talking About the Maleficent
Assault Scene." *Chicago Sun Times: Voices,* June 9.
Grandin, Temple. 2006. *Animals in Translation.* London: Bloomsbury.
Hartnett, Alison. 2000. "Escaping the 'Evil Avenger' and the 'Supercrip': Images of Disability
in Popular Television." *Irish Communications Review* 8: 21–29.
Humane Society International. 2013. "About Cosmetics Animal Testing." March 6.
Jones, Judith. 2014. "Maleficent Unpacked: A Black Feminist Review." *Crunk Feminist Col-
lective,* July 24.
Lowder, J. 2014. "Maleficent: As Queer as It Is Kid-Friendly." *Slate,* June 5.
Maleficent. 2014. Directed by Robert Stromberg. Buena Vista Home Entertainment. DVD.
"Maleficent." 2014. *Humane Hollywood: American Humane Association,* May 30.
"Maleficent." 2014. *M·A·C Cosmetics.*
"Maleficent - Diaval Asks about the Curse (Deleted Scene)." 2014. YouTube video, 0:51,
posted by "MrArtemissCat." September 29.
McRuer, Robert. 2006. "Queer/Disabled Existence." In *The Disability Studies Reader Second
Edition,* edited by Lennard J. Davis, 301–309. New York: Routledge.
Meadows, Tashee. 2010. "Because They Matter." In *Sistah Vegan: Black Female Vegans
Speak on Food, Identity, Health, and Society,* edited by A. Breeze Harper, 150–154. New
York: Lantern Books.
Mollow, Anna. 2006. "'When Black Women Start Going on Prozac': The Politics of Race,
Gender, and Emotional Distress in Meri Nana-Ama Danquah's *Willow Weep for Me.*" In
The Disability Studies Reader 2, edited by Lennard J. Davis, 283–299. New York: Rout-
ledge.
Muñoz, José Esteban. 2006. "Feeling Brown, Feeling Down: Latina Affect, the Performativity
of Race, and the Depressive Position." *Signs* 31(3): 675–688.
Perry, Nick. 2012. "'Hobbit' Animal Deaths: Up To 27 Die as Wranglers Blame Production
Company." *Huffington Post,* November 9.

Puar, Jasbir K. 2009. "Prognosis Time: Towards a Geopolitics of Affect, Debility and Capacity." *Women & Performance: A Journal of Feminist Theory* 19(2): 161–172.

Rich, Katey. 2014. "How Angelina Jolie Included a Rape Scene in *Maleficent*." *VanityFair.com*, June 12.

Sleeping Beauty. 1959 (2008). Directed by Clyde Geronimi, Les Clark, Eric Larson, and Wolfgang Reitherman. Walt Disney Home Entertainment. DVD.

Spears, Mary. 2010. "Eyes of the Dead." In *Sistah Vegan: Black Female Vegans Speak on Food, Identity, Health, and Society*, edited by A. Breeze Harper, 80–81. New York: Lantern Books.

Washington, Harriet A. 2006. *Medical Apartheid: The Dark History of Medical Experimentation on Black Americans from Colonial Times to the Present*. New York: Doubleday.

Weil, Kari. 2006. "Killing Them Softly: Animal Death, Linguistic Disability, and the Struggle for Ethics." *Configurations: A Journal of Literature, Science, and Technology* 14(1–2): 87–96.

Wolfe, Cary. 2003a. *Animal Rites: American Culture, the Discourse of Species, and Posthumanist Theory*. Chicago: University of Chicago Press.

———. 2013b. "Learning from Temple Grandin, or, Animal Studies, Disability Studies, and Who Comes After the Subject." In *Re-Imagining Nature: Environmental Humanities and Ecosemiotics*, edited by Alfred Kentigern Siewers, 91–106. Lewisburg, PA: Bucknell University Press.

Chapter 3

Jabbering *Jaws*: Reimagining Representations of Sharks Post-*Jaws*

Matthew Lerberg

Humanity's fear of shark attacks extends far back into history. The first recorded shark attack occurred in 429 BC and subsequent records extend through various cultures (Crawford 2008, 153). American history also includes records of shark attacks. In fact, the recognition of the possibility of shark attacks exists in famous texts such as *Moby-Dick* or *The Narrative of Arthur Gordon Pym* and artworks such as *Watson and the Shark* or *The Gulf Stream*. While fictional, these works demonstrate a cultural awareness of shark attacks prior to American independence. However, according to Michael Capuzzo, the mass concern and popularity of sharks is a more recent phenomenon. In fact, the 1916 shark attacks off the coast of New Jersey (the focus of Capuzzo's *Close to Shore*) and the release of Steven Spielberg's 1975 adaptation of Peter Benchley's 1974 novel *Jaws* (inspired by the 1916 attacks) have exacerbated this fear. Capuzzo illustrates the media flurry surrounding Americans' increased fear through extensive documents and anecdotal testimony. According to Capuzzo, the overwhelming data suggests Americans were skeptical that the 1916 attacks were perpetrated by a shark. Experts, such as Dr. John Treadwell Nichols, viewed shark attacks as rare or nonexistent because sharks were "too timid to threaten a live human being" (Capuzzo 2001, 154). The revelation that a shark could be responsible precipitated an increase in shark hunting as a preemptive "safety" measure (Capuzzo 2001, 271–72).

The fear of sharks reignited with the release of *Jaws* (Capuzzo 2001, 296–97). As a result of its release, "*Jaws* launched a thousand ships, or at least a thousand charter fishing boats [and] . . . captains like Frank Mundus, the model for Quint [the shark hunter in the film], saw their bookings explode" (Crawford 2008, 75). Renowned shark expert George Burgess states that following the film, "a collective testosterone rush certainly swept through the East Coast of the U.S. It was good blue-collar fishing. You didn't have to have a fancy boat or gear—an average Joe could catch big fish, and there was no remorse, since there was this mindset that they were man-killers" (Choi 2010). Yet, data from the late sixteenth century to the twenty-first century indicates that "sharks inspire terror out of all proportion to their actual threat" (Crawford 2008, 7). According to the Florida Museum of Natural History's ichthyology page, 1,100 shark attacks on humans occurred from 1837 to 2014. Despite the data and efforts of scholars such as Burgess, Americans still view sharks as a high threat to human safety. For instance, the rhetoric for reporting shark attacks uses evocative language that often reproduces the type of numerical inaccuracies that underlie misplaced fears about sharks. The *New York Times* ran an opinion piece highlighting the language used in news stories about shark attacks in the summer of 2001. The authors of the stories use language like a spate, wave, and summer of shark to imply "that there is something more than coincidence at work, and it is that something more, as well as the sharks themselves, that we tend to worry about attacks" (*New York Times* 2001). These terms suggest to readers that shark attacks are far more frequent than data indicates.

Yet, while humans fear sharks, the number of sharks killed by humans each year is staggering. "The UN Food and Agriculture Organization estimates that 100 million sharks are caught and killed per year, many of them slaughtered for shark fin soup" (Crawford 2008, 132). The wholesale slaughter of sharks for their fins flourishes because of the high profit margins, the economic feasibility of long-line fishing, and the fear of shark attacks on humans. In an interview in the film *Sharkwater*, William Goh, the managing director of Rabbit Brand Shark Fin, implies that the finning benefits mankind because sharks are "very vicious" (*Sharkwater* 2006). Also in the film, infamous Australian shark hunter Vic Hislop states he has saved countless lives by killing sharks. In fact, Hislop embraces his mission with fervor. In his book *Shark Man* he states that God placed him on this earth to restore "the balance and justice for all the gentle creatures of the sea" (Monkeyfist 2011). Hislop believes white sharks are responsible for many of the missing people who go swimming or surfing and do not return. He even believes, similar to the plot of *Jaws*, that white sharks have evolved to have a taste for human flesh (Thomas 2009). His beliefs echo many of the fears of people who post on blogs that "the only good shark is a dead one" (Monkeyfist 2011).

Since the release of *Jaws* consumer culture has capitalized on the fear of sharks by marketing this fear as a type of commodity. This paradoxically leads to sharks having a high popularity with American audiences despite remaining afraid. Thus, while Americans still fear sharks, rather than run in panic, they flock to spot sharks from the safety of boats or the shore. Tom

Keane highlights this trend in New England when he states, "The frightened folks on Amity Island—the fictional location of the film *Jaws*—desperately tried to deny the existence of the great white shark in their midst. 'You yell shark, we've got a panic on our hands on the Fourth of July,' worried the town's mayor. He was wrong. This is Shark Summer on Cape Cod, and rather than fleeing, the crowds are flocking" (Keane 2013). The excitement sharks generate for the public hinges on what Cynthia Chris titles "Fang TV." She argues the increase in popularity of wildlife programming stems from works that "feature top predators such as sharks, tigers, crocodiles, and grizzly bears, [because viewers enjoy] the violent natures" of these species (Chris 2006, 105). The reliance on sensationalism and the popularity of *Jaws* extends to other "documentary" and "educational" series such as the widely popular Shark Week. Similar to *Jaws*, Shark Week has greatly increased the interest in sharks. It "has drawn as much as a 100 percent increase in viewers, and the network invariably schedules it during the sweeps" (Casey 2006, 8). However, " instead of seeking to educate or to promote environmental conservation, these shows focus only on presenting graphic, sensationalized animal violence" (Palmer 2012). Shark Week programming also focuses on these issues through titles such as "Air Jaws," "Ocean of Fear," "Top 5 Eaten Alive," "Blood in the Water," and "Killer Sharks."

The collision of fear and admiration places sharks in a paradoxical position where they remain one of the most maligned, yet captivating, animals in art and film. However, many contemporary portrayals of sharks are not only reductive in scope, but also in their aesthetic approach. These representations of sharks risk reducing all sharks to "Shark" and then subsequently to fin and jaws, which equals *Jaws*. The fin, bite, and death become the dominant sign of their character. In this respect, proponents of shark finning literally and figuratively eliminate the danger for humans by killing sharks and removing the symbol of impending doom (the fin). To alleviate the totalizing representation of sharks as physical embodiments of the widely popular fictional shark from the *Jaws* films, viewers must seek out and produce counternarratives that mitigate the singular vision that circulates around contemporary representations of sharks. Such counternarratives serve as potential sites to unseat the misinformed representations of sharks that stem from *Jaws*' cultural potency.

Yet, the ethical and political imperative of rethinking sharks post *Jaws* remains an enormous task. The film is one of the most iconic American movies, making it the American Film Institute's second greatest "thrilling American film" of all time. The film spawned a franchise of three other films, a Universal Studio Orlando amusement ride, and remains the most popular cultural work where a shark has a significant role. Disregarding the cultural impact of *Jaws* for the representations of sharks would be an error. At the same time, recasting the cultural impact of the film remains difficult without addressing the normative paradigm that underlies it. Hence, one must be careful in producing counternarratives based on a single movie or even the entirety of Shark Week. To do so it becomes imperative to untether some of the reductive qualities that go into the making of the "Shark."

The cultural transformation of sharks to the overly reductive "Shark" relies on casting the material semiotic relationship between shark, jaws, and fins with a singular aspect of their behavior, feeding. The practice serves as a normative paradigm that much like the film *Jaws* casts the human as hero and the Shark as villain. Similarly, the relationship relies heavily on an anthropocentric logic whereby human opposes the Other. The film not only reflects this binary construction in its plot, but also in its trailer, which states: "there is a creature alive today who has survived millions of years of evolution without change, without passion, and without logic. It lives to kill. A mindless eating machine, it will attack and devour anything. It is as if God created the Devil and gave him jaws." The evocative language relies on fairly common Cartesian logic as the Shark (the Other) must be mindless because only humans possess thought. Sharks' identifying characteristic is their jaws, melding materiality and semiotics where the flash of teeth indicates an unspeakable evil. The literal (material) jaws of sharks become imbued with meaning (semiotics) whereby the biological and historical meaning (feeding) becomes overshadowed by a cultural meaning (intent on locating and killing humans).

By focusing on a particular physical attribute and associating it with loaded cultural terms (such as evil) the film follows a similar cultural normative structure criticized by both disability and animal studies scholars, where attributes, whether physical, cognitive, or metaphysical separate the norm (in this case humans) from the Other (non/humans). Rosemarie Garland Thomson makes a similar claim while analyzing the history of freak shows. She notes:

> Freak shows framed and choreographed bodily differences that we now call "race," "ethnicity," and "disability" in a ritual that enacted the social process of making cultural otherness from the raw materials of human physical variations. . . . In freak shows, the exhibited body became a text written in boldface to be deciphered through normative structures ensuring anthropocentric values. (Thomson 1997, 60)

While *Jaws* does not make the otherness of the shark from "human physical variations" it does construct an otherness from physical difference between species (shark jaws and fins) and cognitive ability (mindless eating machine). Furthermore, the physical characteristics serve to exhibit the message of not only the plot, but also the cultural normative structure inherent in anthropocentric and humanist paradigms. The shark becomes wholly other, reduced to an evil and mindless killing machine devoid of any complexity. The normative structure of the film reproduces, "on some level, the semiologically normative signs surrounding the reader, that paradoxically help the reader to read those signs in the world as well as in the text" (Davis 1995, 41–42).

In this respect, the title, *Jaws,* literally (through eating) and figuratively (through representations of them) reproduces future sharks and the fear humans have of sharks. In this respect, the jaws of the great white shark represent a double death—the potential for death of humans who venture into shark waters and of the species itself from human paranoia and commercialism. The title, *Jaws,* is doubly troubling for shark populations as shark jaws have become emblematic of one of the more memorable lines in the film where Hooper indicates "what we are dealing with here is a perfect engine, an eating machine. It's really a miracle of evolution. All this machine does is swim and eat and make little sharks, and that's all." The adherence to mechanical desires makes sharks easily classified as something primal and monstrous. The connection between normative practices in the film and those that Davis highlights is even more apparent as he notes, "If people with disabilities are considered anything, they are or have been considered creatures of disorder—monsters, monstrous" (Davis 1995, 143). Just as Thomson and Davis highlight a physical feature as indicative of otherness in normative paradigms the very title of the book and film encapsulates their arguments. For example, in the "Making of *Jaws*" feature contained on the *Jaws* DVD released in 2000, Peter Benchley states that while struggling to title the novel he and his editor agreed "the only word we even think means anything, that says anything, is jaws, call the book *Jaws.*"

However, recognizing this material semiotic normative message only serves as a starting point for formulating counternarratives. A potent one, but a starting point nonetheless. Cary Wolfe argues that

> the larger philosophical and ethical challenge of speaking *for* non/humans animals, speaking *to* our relations with them, and how taking those relations seriously unavoidably raises the question of who "we" are, of the notion of the "human" . . . that may be answered quite indirectly not in the manifest content of the artwork or its "message" but in its formal strategies. (Wolfe 2010, 146)

Similar to Davis, Wolfe argues these formal strategies rest on a foundation of a specific type of human, excluding those, humans and non/humans, who do not fit the established criteria. This creates a paradoxical relationship as the Other defines what is "human" while simultaneously being defined by humans. Wolfe provides an example of how this logic remains problematic, even when well intentioned. He argues that addressing rights for marginalized beings "reproduce[s] the very kind of normative subjectivity—a specific concept of human—that grounds discrimination against nonhuman animals and the disabled in the first place" (Wolfe 2010, xvi–xvii). These types of normative practices use a particular type of human as the point of comparison, basing concepts such as rights off the "norm." For sharks post-*Jaws*, a similar problem arises: all sharks risk becoming Shark—the cultural reverberation of *Jaws*. The underlying cultural normative structure ensures that sharks are "read" in a particular manner, whether in the ocean or on the screen. Collapsing sharks into Shark ignores the vast diversity of the shark species that exist. For instance, both the World Wildlife Foundation and Oceanic.org identify the number one myth about all sharks is that "sharks are all man-eaters" (Edmonds). Yet, there are "over 460 known species of sharks, ranging in size from the gigantic whale shark to the miniature dwarf shark, and they come in all manner of shapes, each adapted to its own peculiar niche in the sea" (Bright 2002, 5). Moreover, out of the 460 species of sharks, "only about 30 have been reported to ever attack a human. Of these, only about a dozen should be considered particularly dangerous when encountered" (Florida Museum of Natural History). The primary problem of casting all sharks as human predators centers on the overwhelming power of fiction on reality. Modern society, as Xavier Maniguet claims, "is in the end less well equipped to separate myth from facts with regard to a film like *Jaws* than was the society of the nineteenth century with regard to the novel *Moby Dick*" (Maniguet 1991, 32). More specifically, he argues that whalers often knew "that whales could kill their hunters" but that they did not "devour a man deliberately." The fiction of *Jaws* continues to instill a fear of sharks deliberately preying on human flesh. Imbued with this baggage, the term shark without a modifier becomes a signal of horror, whether the shark is a whale shark or a tiger shark.

Yet as early as 1976 the popularity of sharks produced counternarratives to the simplistic vision firmly rooted in the consciousness of the majority of Westerners who saw *Jaws*. Three such narratives are *Jabberjaw* (1976–1978), *Finding Nemo* (2003), and *Shark Tale* (2004). While all three are animated and generally classified as children's shows, they offer moments that attempt to erode the overly general vision that resonates in America from *Jaws*. These representations offer an alternative to understanding sharks as the reductive Shark/*Jaws*.

Jabberjaw was created by Hanna-Barbera and first aired in September 1976. The show aired shortly after the release of *Jaws* and followed the formula of one of their most popular creations, *Scooby-Doo, Where Are You?* The series follows an anthropomorphized white shark and his human companions, who live in a futuristic underwater world. Jabberjaw is a large talking shark who can breathe both in and out of water. He and his companions play music in the domed underwater towns as the team solves crimes or prevents political problems while on tour. Only a few anthropomorphic non/humans exist in the series. At the same time, the underwater cities have a strict "no sharks allowed" policy. Mechanical "shark ejectors" police the cities, keeping the citizens "safe" from the dangers sharks pose despite the peaceful nature of Jabberjaw, who is one of the only sharks ever featured on the show.

Part of the marketing strategy for *Jabberjaw* rested upon the perception of danger that sharks represent. However, the reality of the immediate popularity of sharks is the danger for sharks from human attacks, who were increasingly inspired to kill sharks due to the supposed danger they represented. The series illustrates the significant divide between reality and fiction where danger is overrepresented in order to be more marketable to audiences. At the same time, Jabberjaw is in far more danger of being attacked by humans and the shark ejector machines than the various humans in the series are of being attacked by him. In doing so the show reaffirms the danger of sharks even while making light of that danger in a children's cartoon.

The series also poses a critical question immediately in the wake of *Jaws*—can humans imagine a radically different version of "Shark?" The choice of the white shark for the companion animal so shortly after *Jaws* signals a strong response to the shark hysteria the horror movie helped engender. While the choice of the Great Dane as a character in *Scooby-Doo* is consistent with prevailing cultural attitudes toward and relationships with animals, the choice of a shark as a companion is not. The choice of a white shark to stand in place of the Great Dane not only challenges the portrayal of white sharks in *Jaws*, but also eschews the prevailing human preferences for sea "companions" during the 1960s and 1970s, which would have been a dolphin in large part due to the popularity of *Flipper*. By 1976 Americans afforded both dogs and dolphins legal protection (see the Animal Welfare Act of 1966 and the Marine Mammal Protection Act of 1972). Yet, throughout the series Jabberjaw states he "gets no respect," a not so subtle comment on sharks, who were afforded no legal protection at that time.

In the world of *Jabberjaw* the disrespect the shark experiences stems from shark ejectors programmed primarily to prohibit shark/human interaction. The normative structure of this advanced underwater human culture hinges on visual recognition of species markers, ensuring "proper" separation of species and eliminating the perceived threat to humans. Similar to their mechanized programming, the "shark ejectors" follow fairly rigid programming to locate and eliminate threats. Unable to discern difference outside highly taxonomical species lines, the robots attempt to remove Jabberjaw because, as per their programmed logic, all sharks pose a significant threat to human safety. This threat, however, proves to be nonexistent as Jabberjaw tours the undersea communities with his human companions in order to solve social and political problems. In turn, Jabberjaw tirelessly protects the very structure that excludes him. The series deems him "the most futuristic shark" yet he still experiences exclusion and persecution based on species designation. Jabberjaw's trials of persecution highlight the material consequences for sharks post-*Jaws* because, even in a technologically advanced society a talking, air breathing, and erect walking shark is feared via deep-seated perceptions of his species. It is important to note that the robots are shark ejectors, not white shark ejectors, lending credence to how all sharks are perceived. In fact, Jabberjaw's material body becomes a text by which normative society "reads" him via cultural understandings of sharks and then excludes him.

In order for Jabberjaw to "participate" without persecution he frequently must pass via cross-species-dressing in order to evade the robots, thereby allowing him to stay with his companions. These moments of cross-species-dressing illustrate the folly of normative structures, which delineate supposedly rigid species boundaries. In Episode 3, Jabberjaw and his companions stumble upon a political plot by a prime minister to overthrow her majesty of Atlantis. In order to notify her of the impending demise they must evade recognition by the prime minister and his lackeys by dressing as dancing girls to entertain the queen. Jabberjaw's disguise consists of a veil, which is fairly transparent, and a wig. His shark shape, fins, and pointed teeth all remain visible. Yet, the guard pauses only briefly, noting that "the big one looks familiar." The prime minister stops Jabberjaw upon entering, declaring, "I've never seen you dance here before." Jabberjaw assures him that this is "her" debut. Still skeptical, the prime minister wants to see what is under the veil. The prime minister pulls the veil only to reveal another one. He is interrupted by one of Jabberjaw's companions before the shark's identity is revealed. The veil serves as a metaphor for the cultural normative importance of visual "human" markers. The literal and figurative meaning of this type of exchange circulates throughout the series as comic relief. In Episode 6 Jabberjaw and the gang infiltrate the Brotherhood of Evil by wearing the group's garb. However, similar to his disguise in Episode 3, Jabberjaw's shark physiology remains quite apparent. Yet, he passes unnoticed until he gives a tribute of worthless items to the leader while the real members of the Brotherhood of Evil give tributes of riches. The leader looks at the odd tribute and asks, "Who are you?" Jabberjaw responds, "What do I look like?" This brief exchange highlights this duality of meaning because at once Jabberjaw appears as a member of the Brotherhood of Evil because of the garb but at the same time the leader recognizes something is slightly off.

These sorts of exchanges that continue throughout the entirety of the show as a repeat gag also figuratively highlight the misconception of white sharks in 1976. Both questions (who are you and what do I look like) identify key problems in shark representations. Outside of the cartoons Burgess argues data recording shark attacks must be used carefully as many species of sharks are difficult to identify, thereby leading to misidentification (Florida Museum of Natural History). While he states the white shark is easily identifiable in appearance and bite, the questions (who are you and what do I look like) also align with calls for more white shark research to better be able to discern the difference. Also, researchers still have a lot to learn about white shark behavior and habitat (Martins). These questions also signal a larger disconnect, as the visual identification of a white shark (what do I look like) leads to perceptions based on the misinformation and cultural baggage of white shark behavior (who are you).

The marker of human in the series rests solely on physical markers, yet both the shark ejectors and humans frequently fail to identify Jabberjaw as a shark when he cloaks himself in human apparel. The material symbolic power of this transformation—his ability to pass by wearing a wig and dress—demonstrates the absurdity of taxonomical singularity as his fins, sharp teeth, and enormous size are readily apparent. He passes even though he is unable to "conceal [his] impairment" (Linton 2006, 166). Yet, by adhering to a singular "human" characteristic, such as wearing a wig or a hat, he alters the perception of those he encounters. The very physical characteristics that encode "human" come under scrutiny as Jabberjaw eludes detection until his disguise falls.

Changing his appearance in order to garner acceptance signals the type of ingrained theoretical and ethical conundrum Wolfe highlights since to pass he must adopt the "normative subjectivity" that excludes him. Moreover, rather than solve the foundational issue for sharks this logic aligns with the problem of "treat[ing] the condition and the person with the condition rather than 'treating' the social processes that constrict disabled people's lives" (Linton 2006, 162). Therefore, Jabberjaw will continue to lack the respect (closely aligned with "rights" in the series) he desires because as Wolfe argues the very foundation of these rights rests on the type of normative subjectivity that discriminates against him. More specifically, to gain rights Jabberjaw must adhere to the normative rules that govern them. He must appear human to have rights associated with being human. His cognitive and linguistic abilities do not factor in his ability to gain rights since throughout the show Jabberjaw's intelligence alone does nothing to stop him from exclusion.

Jabberjaw's prevailing counternarrative reveals the profound lack of shark "respect," which stems from the hysteria of *Jaws*. This not only refers to the cultural perceptions of sharks, but also to the type of legal protection afforded to dogs and dolphins but not sharks. If Jabberjaw was an earnest attempt to reconsider the image of white sharks shortly following *Jaws*, it failed to resonate as it took almost two decades after the show for white sharks to gain legal protection when California initiated protection in 1993 (Martin). Since *Jaws* appeared on the silver screen, countries with legislation to protect white shark populations include:

South Africa (1991), Namibia (1993), the United States of America (1997), Australia (1998), Malta (2000) and New Zealand (2007). These conservation plans were not based on scientific evidence about the White Shark population, but mostly on the observed decline in the number of large sharks caught by fishermen. White Sharks have been listed on the Appendix II list of CITES in October 2004. (White Shark Trust)

Sadly, these legal protections remain tenuous as occasional shark attacks continue to hamper the image of white sharks and lead to calls for repealing the laws. For example, Australian surfer Ben Linden was recently killed in a white shark attack, which caused "Western Australia [to call] on the federal government to lift a ban on hunting Great Whites after the fifth death in its waters in a year" (Reynolds 2012).

Despite the statistics, surfers continue to enter waters white sharks and their prey frequent (Florida Museum of Natural History). One of the prevailing theories for the number of attacks on surfers is the "mistaken identity" theory. The bio-semiotic field in shark attacks on humans relates directly to perceptual and environmental markers. The human paddling on a surfboard triggers the visual markers white sharks associate with seals, their favorite prey. This theory only holds true when the shark is offered a choice between a seal-shaped object and an object with a shape not associated with the shark's environment. If offered a single object not shaped like a seal, sharks will still attack. In these cases, sharks are unsure about the object so they "test" bite it. The overwhelming percentage of attacks are not fatal, which indicates that once sharks realize the misidentification, they stop their attack (Florida Museum of Natural History). The problem directly relates to the absence of a more complex aesthetic for how sharks perceive and are perceived by humans. Instead of being viewed as test bites or misidentifications, white sharks are perceived as deliberately and viciously targeting humans.

Jabberjaw challenges this semiotic normative sign (jaws/*Jaws*) of white sharks' insatiable hunger for human flesh. His jaws "jabber" rather than bite, a powerful rhetorical choice so immediately after *Jaws*. The shift in the meaning of his jaws from killing to speaking attempts in earnest to shift the negative public perception of white sharks. In fact, the outlandish backlash humans in the show have toward Jabberjaw illustrates the significant hold myths about sharks have on humans, even in a futuristic society. Jabberjaw, unlike real sharks, addresses those who vilify him. The series provides Jabberjaw with a voice to respond in a manner that should include him in normative culture, rather than exclude him. Yet, the structure in place to exclude Jabberjaw is so deeply entrenched that most of the humans in the series revile him despite his ability to think and speak.

Disney-Pixar's *Finding Nemo* (2003) and DreamWorks's *Shark Tale* (2004) fill an important void that the character of Jabberjaw does not. This concerns his literal existence as an apex predator. Unlike Scooby-Doo, who is constantly eating, Jabberjaw generally avoids eating on the show. *Finding Nemo* and *Shark Tale* explicitly address the gastronomic drive of sharks, and the fear of being a shark's prey. In fact, for *Shark Tale*, the eating habits of the film's protagonist shark, Lenny, are central to the plot and to the overall message of acceptance. In *Finding Nemo*, the sharks provide comic support, as well as the urge to resist biological determinism by opting to never eat fish.

As with *Jabberjaw*, both films reference *Jaws*. Bruce, the white shark attempting to forgo eating fish in *Finding Nemo*, is also the name of the Spielberg animatronic shark used to film close-up scenes in *Jaws*. Moreover, *Finding Nemo*'s Bruce states he didn't know his father, creating a comical allusion to the animatronic Bruce from *Jaws* that is violently killed at the end of the film. The reference is both literally and figuratively important. Literally, Bruce (jr.) attempts to overcome his biological determinism, struggling to not kill and eat other non/humans. Figuratively, Bruce (jr.) attempts to move from out of the shadow of his famous father by going vegetarian and trying to counter the image of horror the great white shark has come to represent for all sharks.

Shark Tale also references *Jaws* as it opens with the iconic John Williams score playing as a worm on a hook dangles in the ocean. A shark appears in the distance, eventually appearing behind the worm with jaws open. Suddenly Lenny, says, "Hi, I'm Lenny. Did I scare you?" As Lenny leaves his brother joins him singing the theme song. Lenny interjects that the song "gives me the creeps." His brother replies, "What do you mean, it's our theme song." Similar to the allusion to *Jaws* in *Finding Nemo*, the reference serves as a literally and figuratively important message for sharks post *Jaws*. Literally, the song provides a visceral reminder to Lenny about his aversion to fish and the expectations of him to be a "killer" by his family. Figuratively, the simplification of the species to a "theme song" signals the overly reductive representations of sharks and the entertainment value of them post *Jaws*.

In this respect, the image of sharks post *Jaws* as mindless eating machines becomes the central conflict in both films. For Bruce and his cohorts (including a shark named Chum) in *Finding Nemo* this idea explicitly moves to the forefront as the sharks pledge that "I am a nice shark. Not a mindless eatin' machine. If I want to change this image, I must first change myself. Fish are friends. Not food." Scientific inaccuracies aside, the implications of the pledge are clear. Sharks do not have to eat fish. This is an addiction, something that given the proper support and work can be overcome. Yet the film pokes fun at this idea as well when Chum continuously "slips up." Similarly, the normative structures outlined by Wolfe, Thomson, Davis, and Simi employ a similar logic. The sharks, not those who perceive them, must change.

They need to fix themselves, overcome *their* problem. The rhetoric of overcoming stems from the normative conceptions of rights, whereby "deviations" must aspire to return to normalcy. However, in this paradigm "the problem" is defined through normative structures. For example, on the one hand, following a humanist paradigm, it is the non/human that must change (become more human/civilized), not the human (in this case fish and the other undersea creatures) who must change their singular vision of sharks. On the other hand, this well could be a very strong and decisive critique to the human audience. The unwillingness to see sharks in any other manner, despite evidence of their complex behaviors, means that the shark must change because humans are too arrogant, stubborn, or short-sighted to do so. The overwhelming parallels to addiction and biological determinism indicate the former humanist message probably prevails, whereby the message becomes overcoming biological drives/desires via reason and transcendence. This is not a narrative of acceptance—but of transformation from "base" desire, a strong vertical hierarchy with reason as its apex and material drives at its base.

The opposite is true in *Shark Tale*, where a white shark named Lenny finds eating meat revolting. Unlike Bruce, Lenny isn't trying to suppress his desire to eat fish, he is trying to be accepted for NOT eating fish. For Bruce, not eating fish is something to aspire toward; for Lenny it is a source of ridicule. The overt message in *Shark Tale* emphasizes the pressures of normativity—veiled in biological determinism. In fact, Lenny's father Don Leo emphatically informs his son, "You see something, you kill it. You eat it. Period. That's what sharks do. It's a family tradition." Lenny, however, literally cannot stomach the taste of fish. When trying to save the other main character, his friend Oscar, he "eats" Oscar's love interest. Really, he intends to protect her by hiding her inside his mouth until they can escape. Before they can escape he vomits her up, revealing the deception. Lenny, as his father protests, must "learn how to be a shark."

While white sharks are almost solely carnivorous, a real six-foot nurse shark, also primarily carnivorous, is an example of "life imitating art." Similar to Lenny, the nurse shark, named Florence, stopped eating meat after an operation to remove a rusty fish hook trapped in her mouth. Like Lenny, Florence was subjected to national ridicule. While primarily a jest, Graham Burrows, the curator of the shark exhibit where Florence now resides, noted that "we just weren't expecting her to go completely veggie. We wouldn't want her to be an embarrassment to the other flesh-eating hammerheads and black-tipped reef sharks in the ocean tank" (Wrenn 2012). Burrows's statement bolsters the vision of sharks as only a killing machine. Scientifically, Florence is unique, both in her diet, and because she has "learned" to associate meat with the pain she suffered. However, like Lenny, her uniqueness is framed as a lack rather than a positive transformation. The normative structure that categorizes shark as Shark does not tolerate deviation. Florence, like Lenny, must come back into the fold by adhering to normative culture via the rhetoric of overcoming.

Ultimately, recasting the image of sharks in the wake of *Jaws* also requires overcoming the fictional shark that informs people's perceptions of sharks. These animated films and real-world examples, such as Florence, are a means of addressing this issue. However, disseminating information about the diversity of the species, their varied behaviors and habitats, as well as the significant impact that diminished shark populations will have on the ocean's ecosystem must remain a priority. White sharks are classified as macropredators and are valuable members of their ecosystems. Martins and Knickle highlight the need for protection because neither white shark populations nor reproduction rates are certain. Yet humans kill a high number of white sharks for commercial purposes. Despite the need for more information about white sharks, researchers agree that populations will decrease without better protection for the species (Martins). Advocating for projects that challenge these troubling perceptions of sharks could help to increase shark conservation efforts. For example, currently eight states have passed laws "outlawing the possession, sale, trade and consumption of shark fins," and another six have laws pending (Keledjian 2015). While positive, this is still a small number considering the staggering amount of sharks killed each year for their fins. Scholars, activists, journalists, filmmakers, and social media organizers can help change the negative perception of sharks through education and protest. If the perception of sharks does not change, they will continue to get no respect, as Jabberjaw frequently states.

REFERENCES

Bright, Michael. 2002. *Sharks*. Washington, DC: Smithsonian Institution Press.
Capuzzo, Michael. 2001. *Close to Shore*. New York: Broadway Books.
Casey, Susan. 2006. *The Devil's Teeth*. New York: Holt Paperbacks.
Choi, Charles Q. 2010. "How 'Jaws' Forever Changed Our View of Great White Sharks." *Live Science,* June 20. http://www.livescience.com/8309-jaws-changed-view-great-white-sharks.html.
Crawford, Dean. 2008. *Shark*. London: Reaktion Books.
Chris, Cynthia. 2006. *Watching Wildlife*. Minneapolis: University of Minnesota Press.
Davis, Lennard J. 1995. *Enforcing Normalcy: Disability, Deafness, and the Body*. London: Verso.
Edmonds, Molly. n.d. "Shark Facts vs. Shark Myths." World Wildlife Fund. http://www.worldwildlife.org/stories/shark-facts-vs-shark-myths.
Finding Nemo. 2013. Written and directed by Andrew Stanton. Walt Disney Studios. DVD.
Florida Museum of Natural History. n.d. "Ichthyology." http://www.flmnh.ufl.edu/fish/.
Jaws trailer. YouTube. https://www.youtube.com/watch?v=U1fu_sA7XhE.
Jabberjaw: The Complete Series. 2011. Written by Ruby, Joe, and Ken Spears. Directed by Charles A. Nichols. Warner Home Video. DVD.
Jaws: Anniversary Edition. 2000. Directed by Steven Spielberg. Universal Studios. DVD.

Keane, Tom. 2013. "Tourists Flock to the Cape for More Than Beaches and Clams." *Boston Globe*, August 18.

Keledjian, Amanda. 2015. "Texas Just Banned Sales of Shark Fin, Will Other States Follow?" *Live Science*, June 25. http://www.livescience.com/51343-texas-bans-shark-finning.html.

Linton, Simi. 1998. "Reassigning Meaning." *The Disability Studies Reader* 2nd ed., edited by Lennard Davis, 161–172. New York: Routledge.

Maniguet, Xavier. 1991. *Jaws of Death: Sharks as Predator, Man as Prey*. New York: Crescent Books.

Martin, Aiden R. n.d. "White Shark Ecology and Conservation." ReefQuest Center for Shark Research. http://www.elasmo-research.org/education/white_shark/conservation.htm.

Martins, Carol J., and Craig Knickle. n.d. "White Shark" under "Ichthyology." Florida Museum of Natural History. http://www.flmnh.ufl.edu/fish/Gallery/Descript/Whiteshark/whiteshark.html.

Monkeyfist. 2011. "Renegade Shark Hunter Vic Hislop; On a Mission From God to Search and Destroy." *Scuttlefish*. http://thescuttlefish.com/2011/08/rogue-shark-hunter-vic-hislop-on-a-mission-from-god-to-search-and-destroy/.

Oceana.org. n.d. "Shark Myths vs. Facts." http://usa.oceana.org/shark-myths-vs-facts.

Palmer, Chris, and Peter Kimball. 2012. "Shark Week—Education or Just Entertainment?" *Huffington Post*, August 13. http://www.huffingtonpost.com/2012/08/13/shark-week-2012-air-jaws-apocalypse-video_n_1772142.html.

Reynolds, Emma. 2012. "Hunt for Killer Shark after Australian Surfer Is Bitten in HALF by 15ft-long Great White Nicknamed Brutus." *DailyMail*, July 16. http://www.dailymail.co.uk/news/article-2174265/Australia-shark-attacks--Hunt-killer-shark-surfer-bitten-HALF-24ft-long-Great-White.html.

Shark Tale. 2006. Directed by Vicky Jenson, Bibo Bergeron, and Rob Letterman. DreamWorks Home Entertainment. DVD.

Sharkwater. 2006. Directed by Rob Stewart. Warner Home Video. DVD.

"The Statistical Shark." 2001. *The New York Times*, September 6. http://www.nytimes.com/2001/09/06/opinion/the-statistical-shark.html.

Thomson, Rosemarie Garland. 1997. *Extraordinary Bodies: Figuring Physical Disability in American Culture and Literature*. New York: Columbia University Press.

White Shark Trust. n.d. http://www.whitesharktrust.org/pages/index.html.

Wolfe, Cary. 2010. *What Is Posthumanism?* Minneapolis: University of Minnesota Press.

Wrenn, Eddie. 2012. "Meet Florence, the World's First Vegetarian Shark Who Prefers Celery Sticks and Cucumber to Fish." *Mail Online*, May 18. http://www.dailymail.co.uk/science-tech/article-2146340/Worlds-vegetarian-shark-shuns-meat--bemused-Sea-Life-staff-hide-fish-inside-cucumbers-protein.html.

Chapter 4

Horseplay: Beastly Cinematic Performances in Steven Spielberg's *War Horse*

Stella Hockenhull

Steven Spielberg's 2011 film adaptation of the Michael Morpurgo novel, *War Horse* (1982), is set in the First World War and follows the adventures and misfortunes of a horse named Joey (mainly played by two horses: Finder and Abraham). Purchased by a Devon farmer, Ted Narracott (Peter Mullan), and broken to harness by Ted's son, Albert (Jeremy Irvine), Joey forms a special bond with Albert until he is sent to serve as a front-line cavalry mount. Eventually, in an emotional sequence, horse and rider are reunited and both return to the safety of Albert's home in the English countryside. Throughout Spielberg's sentimental drama, the language of the film makes it seem as though the horse experiences different feelings, and subsequently is able to make decisions as a result. Joey seems fearful at being broken to saddle or trained to harness, and is playful and cunning on the Devonshire moors with the young Albert. When the horse is conscripted for active duty in the local village, he gives the impression that he wants to break free to return to his owner. Later in the film, he saves a fellow horse's life who is unable to work in harness until aided and guided by Joey's actions. The above description is an anthropomorphic analysis, a common and, at times, unethical reading, prevalent particularly in the medium of film.

Historically, non/human animals have appeared in the movies under a variety of guises: routinely they are personified and given human traits, including speech and agency, to propel the narrative. While denying their difference, non/humans such as Lassie, Trigger and, more recently, Uggie in Michel Hazanavicius's 2011 film, *The Artist*, became Hollywood stars. Indeed, as Margo DeMello suggests, these non/human manifestations "became part of the American cultural vocabulary" (2012, 333). Sometimes these non/human animals pose a threat, such as in *Jaws* (Spielberg 1975) and *The Fly* (Neumann 1958). Occasionally, they provide a moral message, such as in *Babe* (Noonan 1995), the film adaptation of the Dick King-Smith novel *Sheep-Pig* (1983). All the above characterize the non/human and attribute them human traits. Not only does this mode of analysis overlook the particularization of a species, as theatre scholar David Williams (2000, 36) suggests, it fails to affirm otherness and, therefore, does not deliver a positive relationship between human and non/human animal. This chapter argues that going beyond the classic anthropomorphic reading of film provides deeper insight into non/human behavior, and could result in greater non/human moral consideration. Deploying a variety of theoretical frameworks from performance studies, film studies and critical animal studies, this chapter examines the screen performance of the horse(s) used to portray Joey in Steven Spielberg's *War Horse*.

As is the case with celebrity non/human animals, Joey is bestowed with a stellar personality that, when coupled with a spectacular theatrical performance, garners critical acclaim (Gardner 2011; Suddath 2012). Indeed, the film encourages sentiment and requests that the spectator identify with the horse as a key humanized narrative agent. This occurs through the human emotions attributed to him and is supported partly by the film's stylistic vocabulary. Indeed, anthropomorphic interpretations, dependent on digital means, editing, and cinematography, make the non/human animal appear to perform and operate as a conscious intending subject. This is a state termed "disnification" by Steve Baker, which, is problematic because it follows,

> a kind of pattern: when the animal is put into visual form, it seems somehow to incline towards the stereotypical and the stupid, to float free from the requirements of consistency or of the greater rigour that might apply to other non-visual contexts. The image of the animal seems to operate here as a kind of visual shorthand, but a shorthand gone wrong, a shorthand whose meanings intermittently veer from or turn treacherously back upon that of the fuller form of the text. (Baker 2001, 175)

Thus, disnification makes the narrative lens lean toward sentimentality, a concept that is problematic and incompatible with scientific discourse. For Baker, disnification imbues non/human animals with human characteristics in an oversimplified fashion that means they are not taken seriously. As he suggests, "Popular culture . . . sees only itself in the eyes of its animals" (2001, xxi). Further, as Baker affirms, non/human animals are trivialized by this medium and are hence "forced to become for us merely 'images' of what they once so beautifully expressed" (Baker 2001, 175).

It is not only the film's cinematography and editing that mobilize disnification: the trainer/non/human animal relationship also facilitates this concept. This is an argument reinforced by Paul Bouissac, a theoretician of live circus presentations. For Bouissac, narrative is primarily produced by the trainer; the non/human animal responds to the trainer who then frames the presentation for the spectator. To illustrate his point, Bouissac uses the Clever Hans Phenomenon. Clever Hans was a horse that allegedly could understand arithmetic and undertake complex tasks, such as answering questions about geography and general knowledge (Bouissac 1981). It was later discovered that he was not capable of such independent thought processes, but was observing and responding to his trainer's involuntary and entirely unintentional expressions and movements. Bouissac applies this theory to circus acts and argues that the audience comprehends non/human conduct through trainer/non/human animal interaction. This forms part of an overall narrative, the circumstances of which are constructed within the framework of the presentation. As he suggests,

> by thus manipulating both the animal's behavior and the context of this behavior the trainer utilizes, at the same time, two different semiotic systems. As a result, such manipulation generates for the public, and to a lesser extent for the trainer, the illusion that the relevant context is the one they perceive and that the animals share this perception of the situation that is constructed in the ring. (Bouissac 1981, 19)

According to Bouissac, the trainer makes the audience believe they and the non/human animal share this acuity, even though it is impossible to know if this is true (arguably it is not). He argues that such presentations are a bilateral process, and the art of training creates an illusion akin to performances, noting that,

> [p]erforming animal acts are indeed patterned events that are two-sided. On the one hand, the trainers interact with their charges on the basis of their sociobiological competence, on the other hand they frame these interactions in particular situations relevant to the system of social interactions shared by the public for which they perform. (Bouissac 1981, 19)

Accordingly, because of this arrangement, the non/human animal appears to display a set of character traits that deceive the spectator into believing s/he has reasoning powers akin to humans. Therefore, the relationship between human and non/human animal characters appears cooperative and mutual, which is not necessarily the case. Consequently, a believable set of circumstances is presented as part of the performance, albeit this is an illusion, and the non/human is erroneously coerced rather than operating as a free collaborator. Bouissac concedes that the non/human animal must operate within its innate genetic system: as he purports,

> [i]n addition to the situation constructed for the audience and the one per-
> ceived and manipulated by the trainer interacting with the animals, there ex-
> ists . . . a situation that is experienced and negotiated by the animals within
> their own semiotic system, i.e., the system provided by the structure and pro-
> grams of their brain. (Bouissac 1981, 23)

Even though the trainer may frame the performance using educed movements and mannerisms, according to Bouissac, non/human actions are never
performed out of the innate structures of their species (1981, 24).

To some extent, Bouissac's arguments provide an interesting lens for
analyzing non/human animal performance in *War Horse*. For example, in
one sequence in the film, Joey appears to perform actions that suggest play-
fulness and cunning. Albert is teaching him tricks on the Devonshire moors,
an area that forms the setting for the early and latter parts of the film. The
boy and horse enter the frame from the left, Albert at Joey's head leading
him. Joey's schooling is observed by Albert's friend, Andrew Easton (Matthew Milne), who sits on a rocky outcropping. Andrew comments to Albert
that the horse is playing the game of deception known colloquially as
"Grandma's Footsteps." Every time Albert walks forward, the non/human
animal follows but stops when the boy turns around. Albert is attempting to
instruct Joey to remain motionless while he walks away from him, the purpose of which is unclear. Film vocabulary leads the viewer to believe that
Joey is disobeying orders as he quietly follows his owner, only ceasing his
pursuit and halting when Albert turns around to face him. The narrative
suggestion is that the horse is duping Albert in a playful and intelligent way
to convince him that he strategically remained motionless. This scene is
presented from a sideways perspective, and the camera is placed at a medium
distance to display both human and non/human animal in the frame together.
Finally, appearing to succeed in this aspect of his training, Albert encourages
him to respond to a particular whistle. Seen in close-up, the boy crouches on
the ground and, kneeling, emits the hooting sound of an owl. The spectator is
informed this whistle is an ancient Indian means of summoning horses from
a distance; narratively, this is the signal that will eventually save Joey's life
later in the film.

At this point, Finder, the horse who plays Joey in this instance, with ears
pointing forward, looks toward the camera, and indeed, toward the position
where Albert stands. The boy explains to the horse what his expectations are,
and subsequently jumps up and runs to crouch some fifty yards away. Joey
canters toward the boy and stops before him, and the spectator infers that
Joey has understood Albert's intentions and explanations. As Albert says,
"he's just puzzling it through." This comment personifies the horse and is
crucial to the sentiment of the film, along with spectator identification with
Joey as a character.

Apart from one instance, Joey and Albert do not appear in the frame together during this "training" period. However, through editing and cinematography, a relationship is implied between boy and horse. One assumes that Joey mindfully participates in a game with his new owner and the two develop mutual understanding. Instead, Finder executes his movements, presumably responding to a reward from his trainer, who, along with Spielberg, constructs the personification that the horse is astute and playful.

This manipulation of bodily interaction between boy and horse frames the performance, creating what Bouissac describes as an illusion within the context of the narrative. The suggestion is that the horse shares the same experience as the spectator. However, this analysis is inaccurate and dissuades the individuality of the species, a crucial aspect of human-to-non/human interaction. It also elicits a response from the spectator that does not acknowledge full comprehension of equine conduct. The horse is neither participating in a game in any knowledgeable way nor solving a puzzle, even though this is the inference. Further, his behavior is framed by his trainer and the film language to appear to produce meaning and to create emotion. Thus, the exchange is a form of coercion, predicated on non-consent and lack of negotiation between trainer and non/human animal.

Such an anthropomorphic reading denies the recognition of non/human innate (non-verbal) language and results in a reduction to sub-human status. This is a point reinforced by Mary Trachsel, who argues that anthropomorphism is a product of humans venerating vocabulary as a measure of status in a hierarchical structure. She reasons, "Our reluctance to recognize wordless animals as speaking subjects stems largely from our reverence for words as the hallmark of human mind, a species of mind that is not merely unique but also, because of its uniqueness, intellectually *advantaged* over other minds" (2014, 31–32). For Trachsel, anthropomorphism is not only demeaning, but it prioritizes, ranking human species at the top while demoting non/human animals to a substantially lower level. If these arguments are acknowledged, then the above-discussed sequence from *War Horse* not only homogenizes the equine species but also suggests limited training can produce fantastic results. In consequence, this disregards any notion of individuality or the permission of non/human otherness.

In terms of an ethical mode of training, and an acknowledgment of idiosyncrasy, Mary Trachsel is an influential advocate of horse whispering. This is a moral methodology for communication that supports an interspecies dialogue based on "caring and respectful relationships with members of other species [which] are morally desirable goals" (2014, 34). Emanating from an ethical and philosophical perspective, Trachsel's arguments express the requirement for "an *attentiveness* [original italics] to other animals that is grounded in 'attitudes and aptitudes such as openness, receptivity, empathy, sensitivity and imagination'" (2014, 35). This requires humans to develop listening skills so they can discern non/human intentions "behind wordless cries, postures, gestures, movements, facial expressions, odors, touches, and behaviors" (Trachsel 2014, 35). Trachsel calls for human and non/human communication to be generated, not as species representatives or en masse, but from "a familiarity with them as individual subjects of 'unique needs and wishes' and this familiarity depends upon relationships of embodied presence" (2014, 35). It is impossible to develop this interaction merely through training. For this to happen, humans must learn equine language and "the communication system natural to the horse, thereby joining the horse's 'linguistic community' rather than requiring the horse to join ours" (Trachsel 2014, 41).

Hence, from a moral standpoint, it is imperative that the viewer comprehend this necessity for language and interaction, along with considering the relationship between the trainer and non/humans. As noted, the "language" that Trachsel refers to is not linguistic in human terms as the film implies; rather it is spatial, "its primary units consisting of bodily postures, touches, movements, and directional orientations instead of words" (Trachsel 2014, 41). For Trachsel, "whispering" requires the horse to be the center of intentionality, where gentle persuasion and negotiation is favored over commands. Although this aspect is not clearly explicated in the sequence, one can infer that verbal and aural commands are essential. As Michael Allen Fox and Lesley McLean argue, there should be a moral imperative to

> open up a phenomenological and conceptual space within which to establish a human/nonhuman world of interaction [and] delineate[s] an opening that allows animals to guide us in how we should interpret and understand what they are telling us—by means of their expressions, behaviour and psychological abilities. (2008, 147)

Trachsel's points are, however, to a certain extent, underpinned by Bobby Lovgren, the head horse trainer for Spielberg's film, and the sequence mentioned above demonstrates Lovgren perceives each horse as an individual. When describing Finder, the key horse used, he reveals that "[h]e's got one of the most unique personalities of any horse I've trained. Horses have specialties, just like [human actors]" (in Suddath 2012). Interestingly, Finder was only one of fourteen horses chosen for the part of Joey, albeit he was used for most of the sequences. Previously, Lovgren had known the horse and worked with him on *Seabiscuit* (Ross 2003); he subsequently purchased him as a three-year-old when filming commenced.

Undeniably, both Lovgren's and the characters' participation in Spielberg's film is important when considering inter-species relationships based on care and respect. Although the trainer's primary objective is to frame the performance for the spectator, he must also recognize Finder's individuality, and as Gardner suggests, "the secret of Lovgren's success is the closeness he shares with Finder" (2013). In a newspaper article, Lovgren explains this unique affiliation, "It is very subtle. Ninety-nine percent of the time you don't even see me doing anything and the horse reacts. The only way I can explain it is that it's like having a dance partner. He duplicates what I do . . . I really teach the horse to have confidence in me and his surroundings" (in Gardner 2011). Thus, rather than coercing Finder into submission, Lovgren uses a system whereby he works alongside him to gain his confidence. Commenting on Finder's distinct characteristics, he suggests that "horses like Finder cannot be made to obey . . . Finder had a personality that he brought to the table" (in Gardner 2011). Thus, ethical consideration of the non/human requires an evaluation of the personal experience of the horse, acknowledging the existence of such training and full awareness of these influences on the spectator.

Throughout the film, the narrative arc focuses on the relationship between Joey and Albert over a period of many years. Initially, Joey is represented as wild and unbroken to harness or saddle, but Albert appears to possess a magic touch to which the horse responds. Superficially, this is demonstrated early in the film when Albert attempts to train him for work on the family farm. His father, Ted Narracott, purchased Joey as a work horse, despite advice that he is unsuitable for the heavy duties that farm work entails. Ted was trying to outdo his landlord, Lyons (David Thewliss), with whom he was quarrelling, and outbidding him at auction meant he paid an unnecessarily high price. Narratively, it is imperative that Albert break him to saddle and harness, otherwise his family will be unable to cope financially and repay their debts. There are hindrances and impediments along the way that create a series of cause and effect relationships. Further, Albert's difficulties in training Joey also contribute to the possibility that financial problems might arise for the family. Eventually, and inevitably to create sentiment and encourage audience identification, a bond is formed between the two. The spectator is finally reassured that the horse has responded to training, a credence facilitated through the editing, mise-en-scène (lighting, setting, figure expression and movement, and costume and makeup), cinematography, and sound.

The way in which the breaking to harness sequence is filmed suggests that Joey has been cajoled into cooperative behavior. By selecting the images for the editing process and framing them in such a manner, the director enables the belief that Joey is evasive and obstructive. Joey first canters to the left, then veers to the right, before coming to a halt. The camera subsequently cuts to Albert, who tries to entice him further with food. Apparently tempted, Joey advances, but then whinnies as though afraid, and shakes his head, before galloping away. Whereas the spectator is led to believe that Joey is initially cunning and untrainable, the process of habituation appears manageable in an incredibly short time frame.

The non/humans used in this film are already trained horses and, as noted, it is the work of the director to construct scenes through various framing devices and editing. Further, to return to Bouissac, it is the trainer/non/human relationship that manipulates the situation to create the illusion that the relevant context is the one they perceive. The horse in this case is named Abraham (trained by Zelie Bullen) and does not share the deception. Additionally, his own non/human achievements/performance are disregarded, which is arguably a form of speciesism. In the above sequence, Abraham responds to his trainer and ignores the food until the correct signal is given. During this process, he produces bodily movements that offer his individual temperament and characteristics regardless of the film language. From a moral standpoint, this should be carefully monitored to decipher his moods and feelings, and avoid the peripheralization of the horse that might occur through an anthropomorphic appraisal.

This is a notion pursued by performance scholar David Williams. On the training of horses, he proposes a symbiotic affiliation, one that affirms a mutually beneficial connection between human and non/human animal. Such a bond would allow the viewer to gain a real understanding of the performance. As he suggests, sometimes this is "a world he [*sic*] is able to inhabit with 'pleasure,'" although non/human performance is sometimes limited when a trainer is involved because the interaction may erase species otherness, a status frequently derided (Williams 2000, 34).

Williams uses the example of Théâtre Zingaro, a performing horse troupe owned by French equine trainer Bartabas, to illustrate his point. Frequently cited as one of the best trainers in the world, Bartabas creates positive relationships with the horses in his show, achieved through their shared theatrical performances. Although Williams admits that some sequences in Bartabas's act reflect Bouissac's model "of overlapping socio-biological frames constructing anthropomorphic images and narratives for spectators' pleasure" (Williams 2000, 35), the subtleties of Abraham's and Finder's behaviors in this sequence and intricacies of the performance cannot be ignored. For Williams and Trachsel, accepting that performance is entirely framed by the trainer occludes aspects of species peculiarities which are, as he notes, "based on the circuits and intensities of an unpredictable energetics, and a poetics of lightness" (Williams 2000, 36). Bartabas reinforces this argument by acknowledging that "the theatrical subject is only a pretext" (in Williams 2000, 31). For Bartabas, each horse is treated as discrete and individual, and he calls for an inter-species inter-subjectivity between trainer and non/human animal.

Drawing on the work of three philosophers, Mikhail Bakhtin (1895–1975), Emmanuel Levinas (1906–1995), and Gilles Deleuze

(1925–1995), Williams questions the ordinariness of interactions between human and non/human. Bakhtin, for instance, attempts to articulate accountability by following a Kantian agenda. He suggests that an interconnection between art and life necessitates "answerability . . . the name for individual responsibility and obligation that leads to action for ourselves, of course, but also on behalf of other" (Haynes 2013, 41–42). Based on art, morality, and outsideness merging with empathy, these assertions make answerability possible. It takes into account the necessary separation between persons as, although we might empathize with another, there are boundaries that separate consciousness, and this disconnection enables greater connectivity with the individual. Bakhtin's model relies on observing the other's experience, that which they cannot see themselves, thus prompting ethical action. Deborah Haynes interprets Bakhtin's work thus: "One may feel pain or outrage but effective action, especially the ability to act on behalf of another to alleviate suffering, is the result of the complex interplay of cognitive, moral and aesthetic decisions" (Haynes 2013, 44). Bakhtin's arguments can be translated into human non/human relationships and, for Williams, both answerability and responsibility conceive identity as "act, verb, multiple becoming," resulting in intersubjectivity and sociality (Williams 2000, 29).

It is, therefore, important that answerability and responsibility be acknowledged when animals appear onscreen. Undeniably, Lovgren and Bullen work with Finder and Abraham on an intimate basis, the trainers perceiving a distinctiveness and eccentricity about the horses. Not only are the horses operating alongside Jeremy Irvine, the results of which create a barely discernible frisson in their movements and actions, but they also observe the finer details of their trainers' signals and bodily mannerisms. All represent another facet of the intimate communication, thus adhering to Bakhtin's moral concepts—essential ethical principles. This stance is linked to corporeality, yet non/human animals are erroneously defined as lacking "reason, memory, imagination, free will, conscience, language and so on" (Williams 2000, 30). Furthermore, they are homogenized and categorized on a sliding scale according to degrees of humanity and animality, with humans customarily privileged in this hierarchical structure. On this occasion, the horses are enabled their individuality. In combination with their trainers, equine corporeal action is evident, culminating in the acknowledgment of their barely discernible "micro-details of expression, mood shifts in skeleton-muscular tension, thermal skin patterning, olfaction"; to comprehend this "body language" is affirmative, both from a spectator's point of view and that of their trainers, and what is non/human about the creatures is therefore not erased (Williams 2000, 32).

The human and non/human animal as a result must forge a cooperative and mutually beneficial relationship. As Bartabas argues,

> A horse is a mirror; it reflects back at us our mistakes and our moods. Every
> horse must be approached in a different way, just like people . . . if intelligence
> is sensitivity to what is around us, then horses are far more subtle than us. The
> more one knows, the less one feels . . . equestrianism is a becoming-centaur for
> both rider and horse. (Bartabas in Williams 2000, 32–33)

Though the language of the film shapes how the spectator reads the situation,
the creaturely conduct of the horse has raised it to a higher level presenting a
non/human that might not be knowable in human terms in the same sense as
Joey. Finder and Abraham communicate a corporeal language and act like
horses determining their separateness through their own species behavior.
Their expressions and body movements signal their sensitivity as non/human
animals in what Williams terms "impulse-based dialogue through a step, a
shift in the angle of the head or gaze, a tension in the shoulders, a run, a
sound, a pulse" (Williams 2000, 38). Thus, Finder and Abraham invoke
bodily affect beyond the patterns carefully constructed for spectator appeal.

In conclusion, attributing human characteristics to non/humans presents a
hierarchical structure that does not consider answerability and responsibility,
thus devaluing and restricting moral space. Further, if the trainer is not sensitive to bodily signs, and the audience is aware of the discrepancy, then the
horse's language remains unidentified. Even if the horse is domesticated and
seemingly happy, a film set can still feel like a zoo, or a circus, or a space of
confinement and separation that situates the horse within boundaries. As Fox
and McLean argue,

> Domesticated animals exist at our pleasure, within the spatial boundaries of
> the moral community, yet they are not *of* [original italics] it, except in the very
> weak sense that there are anti-cruelty or humane laws in effect in most juris-
> dictions. Hence, we have a communal life with (selected) animals, but it is a
> life whose quality is one-sidedly determined and very seldom influenced by
> reciprocal considerations. (2008, 156)

From a moral standpoint, in *War Horse* and other films with non/humans as
central motivating protagonists, an awareness and understanding of the language, and interaction between trainer and horse is pertinent. As noted by
Williams and Trachsel, the "language" is not linguistic in human terms as the
film implies; rather it is spatial, "its primary units consisting of bodily postures, touches, movements, and directional orientations instead of words"
(Trachsel 2014, 41). For Trachsel, "whispering" relies on the notion that the
horse is a center of intentionality, and gentle persuasion and negotiation is
favored over commands: this aspect is not clearly explicated in the film, the
inference being that verbal and aural commands are imperative. If, to return
to Bouissac, it is the trainer/non/human relationship that manipulates the
situation for the audience to create the illusion that the relevant context is the

one they perceive, then it is important to note that the horses in this case do not share the deception. Additionally, the horses' own non/human achievements/performances are disregarded—itself a form of speciesism. In the above noted sequences the horses are responding to their trainers, yet during this process they produce bodily movements that offer their own individual temperaments and characteristics regardless of the film language. This should be carefully monitored by the trainer to decipher their moods and feelings, and, moreover, to avoid the peripheralization of the horse: a marginalization which is likely to occur through an anthropomorphic appraisal. We must, in order to end speciesism, move beyond the relationship of trainer, or dominator, and trained, that is, dominated. This is an association not only depicted in this film, but throughout a world that is grounded in human supremacy over all elements and life on this planet.

REFERENCES

Allen Fox, Michael, and Lesley McLean. 2008. "Animals in Moral Space." In *Animal Subjects: An Ethical Reader in a Posthuman World*, edited by Jodey Castricano, 145–175. Waterloo, Ontario, Canada: Wilfred Laurier University Press.

Baker, Steve. 2001. *Picturing the Beast*. Urbana, Chicago: University of Illinois Press.

Barnard, Chris. 2004. *Animal Behaviour: Mechanism, Development, Function and Evolution*. Harlow: Pearson Prentice Hall.

Bekoff, Marc. 2007. *The Emotional Lives of Animals*. Novato, CA: New World Library.

Bouissac, Paul. 1981. "Behavior in Context: In What Sense Is a Circus Animal Performing?" In *The Clever Hans Phenomenon: Communication with Horses, Whales, Apes, and People*, edited by Thomas A. Sebeok and Robert Rosenthal, 18–25. New York: New York Academy of Sciences.

Budiansky, Stephen. 1997. *The Nature of Horses: Their Evolution, Intelligence and Behaviour*. London: Phoenix.

Butterfield, Max, Sarah Hill, and Charles Lord. 2012. "Mangy Mutt or Furry Friend? Anthropomorphism Promotes Animal Welfare." *Journal of Experimental Social Psychology* 48: 957–960.

Carlson, Marvin. 1996. *Performance: A Critical Introduction*. London, New York: Routledge.

Castricano, Jodey. 2008. *Animal Subjects: An Ethical Reader in a Posthuman World*. Waterloo, Ontario, Canada: Wilfred Laurier University Press.

DeMello, Margo. 2012. *Animals and Society*. New York, Chichester, West Sussex: Columbia University Press.

Fudge, Erica. 2002. *Animal*. London: Reaktion Books.

Gardner, David. 2011. "War Horse Superstar." *Mail Online*, December 17. http://www.dailymail.co.uk/news/article-2075302/War-Horse-superstar-The-Mail-tracks-unsung-star-Spielbergs-blockbuster--Hollywood-horse-whisperer-telepathic-bond.

Goffman, Erving. 1959. *The Presentation of Self in Everyday Life*. Garden City, NY: Doubleday.

Griffin, Donald. 1984. *Animal Thinking*. Cambridge, MA: Harvard University Press.

Haynes, Deborah. 2013. *Bakhtin Reframed*. London, New York: I. B. Tauris.

Levinas, Emmanuel. 2006. *Humanism of the Other*. Translated by Nidra Poller. Urbana, Chicago: University of Illinois Press.

Levy, Emanuel. 2011. *Steven Spielberg interview with Emanuel Levy in "War Horse: The Equine Cast,* http://www.emanuellevy.com/interview/war-horse-the-equine-cast/.

Lury, Karen. 2010. *The Child in Film: Tears, Fears and Fairytales*. London, New York: I. B. Tauris.

Packwood Freeman, Carrie. 2014. "Embracing Humanimality: Deconstructing the Human/ Animal Dichotomy." In *Arguments about Animal Ethics*, edited by Greg Goodale and Jason Edward Black, 11–29. Lanham, MD: Lexington Books.

Park, Sowon S. 2013. "'Who Are These People?': Anthropomorphism, Dehumanisation and the Question of the Other." *Arcadia* 48(1): 150–163.

Parker-Starbuck, Jennifer. 2006. "Becoming-Animate: On the Performed Limits of 'Human.'" *Theatre Journal* 58(4): 649–669. http://lion.chadwyck.co.uk.ezproxy.wlv.ac.uk/searchFulltext.do?id+R03957557&divL.

Peterson, Michael. 2007. "The Animal Apparatus: From a Theory of Animal Acting to an Ethics of Animal Acts." *TDR: The Drama Review* 51(1): 33–48.

Pick, Anat. 2011. *Creaturely Poetics.* New York, Chichester, West Sussex: Columbia University Press.

Sassani, Gino. 2011. "War Horse Interview with Horse Trainer Bobby Lovgren." http://upcomingdiscs.com/2011/12/27/war-horse-interview-with-horse-trainer-bobby-lovgren/.

Schechner, Richard. 2002. *Performance Studies: An Introduction.* New York: Routledge.

Sebeok, Thomas A., and Robert Rosenthal. 1981. *The Clever Hans Phenomenon: Communication with Horses, Whales, Apes, and People.* New York: New York Academy of Sciences.

Spielberg, Steven. 2012. "War Horse: Star One of Hollywood's Equine Elite." http://www.backstage.com/news/war-horse-star-one-of-hollywoods-equine-elite/.

Suddath, Claire. 2012. "Training the Horses in Steven Spielberg's *War Horse.*" *Time Entertainment.*

Tait, Peta. 2011. "Animal Performers in Action and Sensory Perception." In *Animal Movements: Moving Animals: Essays on Direction, Velocity and Agency in Humanimal Encounter,* edited by Jacob Bull, 197–211. Crossroads of Knowledge Skrifter från centrum för genusvetenskap, Uppsala University, Uppsala.

———. 2012. *Wild and Dangerous Performances: Animals, Emotions, Circus.* Basingstoke, New York: Palgrave/Macmillan.

Trachsel, Mary. 2014. "How to Do Things without Words: Whisperers as Rustic Authorities on Interspecies Dialogue." In *Arguments about Animal Ethics*, edited by Greg Goodale and Jason Edward Black, 31–52. Lanham, MD: Lexington Books.

Weil, Kari. 2012. *Thinking with Animals: Why Animal Studies Now.* New York: Columbia University Press.

Williams, David. 2000. "The Right Horse, the Animal Eye—Bartabas and Théâtre Zingaro." *Performance Research* 5(2): 29–40.

Chapter 5

Would Bugs Bunny Have Diabetes?: The Realistic Consequences of Cartoons for Non/Human Animals

Amber E. George

The first image for many people that comes to mind when imagining a cartoon rabbit is Bugs Bunny eating a carrot. From the moment American children begin watching television, they are taught that each cartoon species loves certain foods to the point of exclusivity and obsession. Occasionally, the stereotypes uphold the truth. Mostly, they are far from reality. For instance, unlike cartoon mice, real mice are not obsessed with cheese (Associated Newspapers Ltd. 2006). Americans experience such strong indoctrination of these false assumptions that it is difficult to imagine their untruth, let alone harm. The knowledge acquired from cartoons distorts the needs of non/ human animals, such as rabbits. This ultimately damages their health and safety. For example, when species such as rabbits are exclusively fed carrots they are more likely to develop nutritional deficiencies and chronic illness. Moreover, the dominant cartoon narrative of Bugs Bunny maintains simple representations that ignore the complex needs of non/humans. These realities underscore how urgently cartoon programming should be critiqued for its oppressive influence in order to promote awareness of the deepening crisis for non/humans and the irreversible harm that becomes a reality for those in captivity. This chapter explores the tangible suffering of rabbits that live in confinement and the logical consequences of treating them as though they are Bugs Bunny. Messages that contribute to the suffering of non/humans must be analyzed with the goal of bettering lives while demanding an end to pet keeping and speciesist media.

When I first mentioned critiquing cartoons for their health effects on non/ human animals, I was met with ridicule and confused faces. My peers ex-

59

imed, "That is what you are going to study?" "How can there be any connection between Bugs Bunny and chronic illness in rabbits?" "Aren't you taking this a little too far? After all, aren't cartoons just entertainment for children?" These responses are precisely why animation such as *Looney Tunes* and *Merrie Melodies* should be critically analyzed. Despite many years since their original creation, Warner Brothers continues to create products that reinforce a speciesist ideology. Although cartoons primarily exist as entertainment, they influence the way humans historically and culturally treat non/human animals. Sociologist Roger Yates labels this "easygoing speciesism," which he defines as "the easy assumptions humans tend to make about the rightful place and legitimate use of non/human animals" (2009). Speciesism, as defined by sociologist David Nibert, is more of an ideology than prejudice or discrimination based on species membership (2002). To resist speciesism, one must explore just how inundated the culture is in speciesist norms and values. Formulating a clear understanding of how cartoons inform reality may encourage humans to decisively act against perpetuating oppression.

Far from mere entertainment, animation is a serious field of critical cultural studies. Critical studies scholar John Berger has explored how humans "see" or fail to perceive knowledge (1973). Truth is analyzed according to media messages that present symbolic images, which over time and with enough repetition become associated with specific classifications. Baker suggests non/human animal representations in popular culture are based on stereotypes and ignorance (1993). Once a stereotype endures, it is nearly impossible to dislodge it from popular imagination. Such has been the case with rabbits obsessively eating carrots. This fixation has made distinguishing truth from falsity very difficult because preconceived notions always already impact the process of truth-making (Baker 1993).

Knowledge acquisition begins in early childhood when information about (in)appropriate relations with non/human animals is learned from parents, siblings, peers, and teachers. "Children are influenced by media—they learn by observing, imitating, and making behaviors their own" (2001, 1224). When individuals view unrealistic depictions of non/humans in animated media they put what they observe on the screen into practice. Animated media projects a credo of innocent childhood fun and pure entertainment. Cultural critic Henry Giroux characterizes this phenomenon as the "politics of innocence" (1994). He states, "Under the rubric of fun, entertainment, and escape, massive public spheres are being produced which appear too 'innocent' to be worthy of political analysis" (Giroux 1994, 28). Popular culture heavily informs its consumers in a passive and inauthentic way. Cartoons produced by Warner Brothers and Disney have a strong educational influence on children, implanting institutional frameworks that reinforce cultural norms in young minds. Giroux suggests that cartoons "inspire at least as much cultural authority and legitimacy for teaching specific roles, values, and ideals as more traditional sites of learning such as public schools, religious institutions, and the family do" (Giroux 1995, 99). Thus, viewers may be disinclined to analyze how media limits learning and presents itself as authoritative knowledge.

According to critical media scholar Renee Hobbs, many individuals lack "media literacy," or the ability to read messages that possess harmful and manipulative content related to non/human animals (1998). To avoid internalizing propaganda, Hobbs says media consumers "need a set of skills to ask critical questions about what they watch, see, listen to and read. Media literacy skills include the ability to analyze critically media messages and using different kinds of communication technologies for self-expression and communication" (Hobbs 1998). Furthermore, media literacy skills expose the difference between fact and fiction, enabling viewers to critique cartoons in a more discriminating fashion.

Even legendary philosophers from the Frankfurt School, such as Theodor Adorno and Walter Benjamin, analyzed animation. Walter Benjamin mentions Mickey Mouse in his essay "The Work of Art in the Age of Mechanical Reproduction" (1935). He also left behind among his possessions stacks of press clippings and notes about the famous mouse (Rollason 2003). In a personal letter written to Benjamin in 1936, Adorno criticizes Benjamin's reverence for Mickey Mouse. Adorno claims Disney animation produces an artificial escape that is disruptive and alienating, reflecting and subsequently reinforcing a growing sense of dissatisfaction with modern life (1977). Adorno directly challenges Benjamin in his text *The Dialectic of Enlightenment*, co-authored with Max Horkheimer (1972). They argue that industrially produced art like films or cartoons manipulates the masses into passivity. His famous culture industry analysis is summarized as follows, "The progressive technical domination of nature becomes mass deception . . . turned into a means for fettering consciousness. It impedes the development of autonomous, independent individuals who judge and decide consciously for themselves" (Adorno 1972, 85). The culture industry turns art into commodity that is produced en masse and sold through deceptive advertising and sales techniques. This spawns a populace driven to wasteful spending, which prevents a more sustained happiness. Thus, individuals are "colonized by mass consumption" and free time is spent working to merely consume and conform (Adorno 1972). Everyone sees the same films, listens to the same music, and all give up the opportunity to realize their interests or express individuality (Adorno 1972, 91).

Benjamin disagrees with Adorno insofar as he believes that cartoons provide a cathartic release from the tensions of living in the modern world. Harboring these tensions can produce a destructive energy that can lead to clinical psychosis. Accordingly, art forms such as cartoons and films provide "collective laughter [that] presents the timely and healing escape from such mass psychoses" (Caygill 1998). Benjamin regards "American grotesque films and the films of Disney as producing a therapeutic explosion of the unconscious" (Caygill 1998). Thus, Mickey Mouse is a symbolic figure in the debate between whether cartoons provide liberation or constraint. The Frankfurt School's interest in an animated icon coupled with the many brilliant histories on animation proves they are significant cultural productions worthy of critical analysis.

This analysis focuses on one of the most beloved and popular cartoon characters in the history of modern culture, Bugs Bunny. Since 1939, he has starred in more 175 films (both short and feature-length) with several cameos in non-animated films. He was nominated for an Oscar three times and won in the category of Short Subject (Cartoon) for his role in "Knighty Knight, Bugs" (Oscars 1959). In 1985, he earned a star on the Hollywood Walk of Fame, the second cartoon character ever given the honor (Commerce 1985). Additionally, Bugs is the first animated cartoon commemorated on a U.S. postage stamp (Smithsonian 1997). In 2002, *TV Guide* voted him the greatest cartoon character of all time. Interestingly, Mickey Mouse ranked number 19 on this same list (CNN 2002). He has had a long-lasting and far-reaching appeal to both children and adult audiences across the globe. Most film historians such as Michael Barrier site "A Wild Hare," the 1940s *Merrie Melodies* animated short film, as Bugs's first cameo on the big screen. It is considered his quintessential first feature because his general appearance, personality, and voice acting by Mel Blanc have not changed much since this inauguration.

Animator Bob Clampett cites observations from his daily life and films as the inspiration behind his animated characters, especially Bugs. When discussing Bugs's humble beginnings, Clampett says, "I loved Frank Capra's hit comedy *It Happened One Night* (1934) and went to see it a number of times" (Barrier and Gray 1970). Clampett was particularly drawn to Clark Gable's character Peter Warne. He recalls one particular scene in which Gable stands leaning against a fence, eating a carrot and talking with his mouth full. In hindsight Clampett says, "As I looked at this sequence, the thing that stuck in my memory was that all the time Clark Gable was talking, he was at the same time chewing on a carrot. As I looked at him, I didn't see Gable—all I saw was a big rabbit chewing on a carrot" (Barrier 2003). The film also features another character, Oscar Shapely, who coincidentally addresses Gable's character as "Doc." Gable's character attempts to intimidate Shapely by referencing an imaginary character named Bugs Dooley. Years later Clampett returned to this memory when drafting the original sketches for Bugs Bunny. Interestingly, the carrot almost didn't make it into the finished picture. Clampett explains, "The powers that be" thought "it would be too complicated and time-consuming for the editor to cut carrot sound effects in between the words in the dialogue" (Barrier 2003). Clampett recommended the carrot munching happen along with the dialogue, the way Gable had done it. This meant Mel Blanc had to eat many carrots, which he is known to despise (Barrier 2003). Animators and sound effects crew experimented with biting and chewing apples, celery, and other food. However, nothing generated the perfect crunch quite like a carrot (Barrier 2003). Thus, animators used these iconic traits along with other facets of *It Happened One Night* to create a character that audiences of the time would recognize as a parody (Barrier 2003).

Cartoonists like Clampett used stereotypes of rabbits to create Bugs. It is entirely possible their perceptions were influenced by historical accounts of essential rabbitness. "From Ancient Egypt and Mesopotamia through to India, Africa, China and Western Europe, hares have been portrayed as sacred, evil, wise, destructive, clever and, almost always sexy" (Mitchinson 2006, 151). Over the years, various art directors and animators infused these traits into the distinctive character that modern audiences have come to know and love. Bugs is a gray and white rabbit, with large front teeth, long ears, and sizable feet. He is wacky and wild, speaks in a hybrid of Bronx and Brooklyn dialects, and demonstrates his wisecrack antics by tormenting his opponents without mercy. Bugs is comedic and serious even toward his enemies who conspire to eat him, use him as a trophy, or make him a participant in experiments (Pendergast 2000).

Charles M. Young provides a useful reference for describing Bugs's essence when he compares him to Mickey Mouse. Young exclaims, Disney unceasingly denies Mickey Mouse's "essential mouseness" (Young 1975, 125). Mickey is not a prototypical mouse. He is not sneaky, nor does he live in a hole. He lives in a house. Additionally, he eats human food at a table and does not scrounge for cheese. In fact, Walt Disney hated the mouse and cheese stereotype. He has warm and loving relationships with his female companion Minnie Mouse, his best friend Donald Duck, and his yellow dog named Pluto. In short, Mickey is not a non/human metaphor for mouseness. Rather he's essentially a man who is highly anthropomorphized as a mouse. Adding to this analysis, animation theorist Paul Wells suggests Mickey's "mouseness" is more connected to a corporate brand rather than a true non/human animal identity (Wells 2009). Bugs Bunny is anthropomorphic as well, but as Young claims, he is "a rabbit who did not deny his essential rabbitness" (Young 1975, 125). This statement, however, is disputable. Bugs's rabbitness entails living and playing in the grasslands, occasionally popping out of a hole in the ground, eating a carrot, and posing the question, "Eh, what's up, Doc?" Perhaps Young is correct by saying Bugs does not deny his rabbitness. However, Bugs's representation is still a grossly inadequate description of a complex species. Added proof against Bugs possessing essential rabbitness is his reckless and disrespectful relationships with his cohorts when in reality rabbits are highly social creatures. His insolence is evident in the following monologue, written in the first person,

> Some people call me cocky and brash, but actually I am just self-assured. I'm nonchalant, imperturbable, and contemplative. I play it cool, but I can get hot under the collar. And above all I'm a very "aware" character. I'm well aware that I appear in an animated cartoon. . . . And sometimes I chomp on my carrot for the same reason that a stand-up comic chomps on his cigar. It saves me from rushing from the last joke to the next one too fast. And I sometimes don't act, I react. And I always treat the contest with my pursuers as "fun and games." When momentarily I appear to be cornered or in dire danger, and I scream, don't be consoined—it's actually a big put-on. Let's face it, Doc. I've read the script, and I already know how it turns out. (Barrier and Gray 1970)

Moreover, Bugs rarely hops, instead he bipedally walks, dances, and frolics as if it were actually possible. It is sufficient to say Bugs's personality and behavior is an inaccurate embodiment of rabbitness. Bugs's creators took a complex non/human rabbit form and reduced it to a cartoon image, which ultimately downgraded the species into simpler and misleading components. In this sense, reductionism assumes a complex phenomenon so an entire species is understood through interpretive, correlative, and causal relationships between the real and the imaginary (Rose 1997). When reductionism becomes ideology, one is more likely to deny non/human agency.

When one initially experiences Bugs, the cartoon production, and then meets a live rabbit thereafter, the latter may be perceived as "the original of the reproduction" (Berger 1973, 21). In this case, "it is no longer what its image shows that strikes one as unique; its first meaning is no longer to be found in what it says, but in what it is" (Berger 1973, 21). For a child (or adult) who has never met a live rabbit, and is only indoctrinated with knowledge of Bugs, the fictional anthropomorphized entity is what's real. This process produces minimal diversity or complexity in the meaning of rabbitness. Bugs Bunny is rabbit and rabbit is Bugs Bunny. Mass reproduction of Bugs has changed the way society perceives rabbits. Reductionism has a stronghold on rabbitness, and as explained before, without diversity of perspective and experience, rabbits will continue to be perceived in ways that lead to mistreatment and abuse.

The tendency to reduce non/humans to their cartoon image may be the result of non/human animals mostly disappearing from human lives due to extinction, confinement, and other segregationist practices. Berger argues human's spatial separation from non/human animals makes them difficult to imagine (1973). This severance, both real and imagined, causes humans to adopt an uncritical, indifferent stance toward non/human animals. Over time, spatial separation desensitizes humans to non/human pain and suffering. Feelings of apathy lead to inaction, inducing neglect, abuse, or general maltreatment. Berger writes, "The way we see things is affected by what we know and what we believe" (Berger 1973, 7–8). The authors of *Rabbit Behavior, Health and Care* suggest what humans know and believe is "based on comics and pictures from popular cartoons rather than an up-to-date knowledge of the rabbit's digestive system" (Buseth and Saunders 2015, 120). Put another way, "Animals have gradually disappeared. Today we live without them. And in this new solitude, anthropomorphism makes us doubly uneasy" (Berger 1980, 9). Images of real non/humans and their actual behaviors are replaced with images of what humans believe non/human animals typify. Since many humans cannot imagine non/humans, they rely upon exaggerated replications like cartoons as the standard for comprehending non/human behavior. Critical animal studies scholar Kay Peggs writes, "These imaginings do not center on the suffering of inflicted non/humans—rather they focus on romantic representations . . . [that] serve to hide rather than elucidate the reality of human-nonhuman animal relations" (2014, 40). Berger contends, "Animals are always the observed. The fact that they can observe us has lost all significance. They are the objects of our ever-extending knowledge. What we know about them is an index of our power, and thus an index of what separates us from them. The more we know, the further away they are" (1980, 16). Thus, perception is not based on the non/human itself. Rather it is based on the interests and characteristics of humans, who anthropomorphize live non/human animals with imagined representations. Consequently, what rabbitness means has been replaced with what humans imagine it should be.

Due to anthropomorphism, and the cute factor discussed in other chapters of this collection, humans tend to enjoy pet keeping. It is probably not coincidental that, in the early twentieth century, the rate of pet keeping steadily rose alongside an increase in anthropomorphized cartoon characters. According to the U.S. Pet Ownership and Demographics Sourcebook, there are roughly 6 million rabbits living in American households (AVMA 2012). The House Rabbit Society asserts that rabbits remain the third most commonly kept mammal after cats and dogs, in both the United Kingdom and the United States (Brown 2012). Pets are treated as children, grandchildren, spouses, and close friends. A pet is anything one desires it to be: a friend, lover, or someone to hang out with occasionally. Some animal advocates such as Gary Francione draw parallels between pet keeping and human slavery. In an interview for the Columbia University Press blog, Francione says, "We should take good care of the domestic animals we have brought into existence until they die. We should stop bringing domestic animals into existence" (Columbia 2008). Francione adopts an animal welfare approach, claiming we ought to treat non/human animals humanely. The Animal Welfare Institute mission statement best sums up the animal welfarist position, "We seek better treatment of animals everywhere—in the laboratory, on the farm, in commerce, at home, and in the wild."

In contrast to animal welfarists, animal liberationists such as Steven Best argue for a "new abolitionist" movement that rejects all forms of captivity. He claims humans should "seek not bigger cages, but rather empty cages" (Best 2016). To be sure, not a single non/human animal *ought* to be in captivity. When using language that insinuates care and responsible treatment is not a pure liberationist orientation as such, it is imperative to acknowledge non/human animals in captivity are unhealthy and discontent. However, we cannot ignore or take lightly that non/human animals *are* kept in captivity. As a result, many argue that a "new welfarist" approach is more desirable (Best). These individuals would support organizations such as the Institute for Critical Animal Studies, which advocates for animal liberation while simultaneously supporting sweeping welfare reforms that decrease the severity of non/human oppression. Idealistically, in a perfect world all non/humans would be self-determining and free to live as they choose. Conversely, releasing domesticated animals overnight might lead to perilous lives on city streets or rural landscapes that will result in miserable deaths. A viable option is to discontinue manufacturing pets and end the cycle that makes non/humans reliant upon humans for survival. Furthermore, acknowledging that non/human animals live in captivity does not insinuate they *ought* to live in exploitative or deprived environments. Since pet keeping affects animals directly, often in unrecognized and unintended ways, pet keepers have an even greater responsibility to be vigilant stewards of non/human care. It is morally unacceptable to inflict psychological and physiological suffering on non/human animals, especially if the treatment is overtly speciesist. These interactions can disrupt life-sustaining processes, impede quality of life, and lead to unnecessary suffering, illness, and death. The extent to which animals experience deprivation and suffering while in captivity requires humans to provide non/humans the benefit of shelter, proper diet, and health care. In short, so long as humans continue to keep animals confined, providing quality care must be a priority that can be achievable in both principle and practice.

The American Society for the Prevention of Cruelty to Animals states, "Our culture is so filled with images of children and rabbits together (think Easter Bunny and Peter Rabbit) that many parents see rabbits as low-maintenance starter pets for kids. Nothing could be further from the truth" (ASPCA 2015). The article explains that rabbits are "physically delicate and fragile" and require "specialized veterinary care" (ASPCA 2015). In an article on the popular pet adoption website Petfinder.com, an anonymous author exclaims,

> Rabbits have complex digestive systems, so it is very important that they receive a proper diet. Many health problems in rabbits are caused by foods incompatible with their digestive physiology. . . . Cartoons and other fictional portrayals of rabbits would lead us to believe that carrots are the basis of a

healthy rabbit diet. Many rabbits enjoy carrots, but they are a starchy vegetable and should only be given sparingly as a treat. (Petfinder 2015)

Non-domesticated rabbits rarely eat root vegetables such as carrots, nor do they eat certain fruits or lettuces. For instance, iceberg lettuce if ingested in large quantities can be fatal. As they are strict herbivores, their incisors and molars continually grow and are designed to tear and macerate dark green leafy foods such as collard and dandelion greens. Ideally, rabbits should graze on growing grass, eat regular portions of dark greens, and, most importantly, have a constant supply of hay, specifically Timothy grass hay. The fiber in the hay ensures proper gastrointestinal health and prevents health problems such as hairballs and diarrhea (Petfinder 2015). Administering improper dietary care can cause dental diseases such as malocclusion or overgrown teeth, obesity leading to diabetes, fatty liver disease, enterotoxemia or overgrowth of intestinal bacteria, and gastrointestinal stasis, which causes blockages due to lack of dietary fiber (McClure 2011). If left untreated, rabbits die a painful and miserable death from otherwise preventable illnesses.

Responding to several reports of neglect, the Royal Society for the Prevention of Cruelty to Animals launched the "What Bugs a Bunny" campaign to challenge common misperceptions (RSPCA 2015). The RSPCA commissioned the University of Bristol's School of Veterinary Sciences to survey pet keepers' knowledge of proper rabbit care. Rachel Roxburgh, an RSPCA animal scientist, states, "The RSPCA is trying to give rabbits Hay Fever! But not in a bad way—we want all pet rabbits to be eating hay as their main food." Furthermore, she adds, "People also think that their rabbits should eat carrots because that's what Bugs Bunny does. . . . But he's a cartoon—real rabbits don't talk, and they shouldn't be eating carrots too often either" (Bristol 2012). The results of the survey are sadly unsurprising. Participants believe a rabbit's diet should include commercially processed rabbit food or pellets (23 percent), carrots (19 percent), leafy greens (17 percent), fruit and vegetables (15 percent), and hay and grass (8 percent) (Bristol 2012). Another study, conducted by the People's Dispensary for Sick Animals, surveyed over 11,000 pet keepers to determine the quality of care pet rabbits receive. Some of the findings include:

Roughly 750,000 rabbits are not eating the recommended daily amount of hay or grass. Rabbits are eating less than their body size in hay or grass each day (42 percent). Rabbits not eating hay at all (3 percent). Pet keepers who give rabbits entire carrots on a regular basis (88 percent). Pet keepers who cite "common sense" (22 percent) or "past experience" (18 percent) to dictate how they feed their rabbit. Pet keepers who feed rabbits human leftovers such as cheese, cake, toast, chips, and chocolate (10 percent). Pet keepers who feed

artificial pellets or muesli (49 percent). Pet keepers who do not provide space/
time for exercise (56 percent). (PDSA 2011)

When rabbits live outside of captivity, they forage for food across an area
roughly the size of thirty tennis courts every day. Additionally, when not
properly cared for, they get bored, depressed, and angry (ASPCA 2015). Just
like their nondomesticated cousins, domesticated rabbits are social beings,
and prefer to live in large colonies with other rabbits where they can social-
ize, play, and be affectionate. To alleviate loneliness while captive, rabbits
commonly develop very close relationships with others such as humans,
dogs, and cats. If left to a life of solitary confinement in a cage either indoors
or outdoors, they are likely to exhibit signs of neglect or zoo-psychosis. This
condition includes symptoms such as chronic illness, aggressive tendencies,
and involuntary, repetitive movements or sounds. It originates from the trauma of being kidnapped, displaced, incarcerated, alienated, and bored to death
(Chaudhuri 2012). Ideally, when pet keepers learn these facts, they should
seek to develop new relationships with non/humans or perhaps give up pet
keeping altogether.

According to the Rabbit Welfare Association, "Most cases of cruelty and
neglect toward rabbits are from ignorance; people often don't realize they are
mistreating their rabbit because they haven't done enough research on rabbit
care and wellbeing before choosing to buy a pet rabbit" (Rabbit Welfare
Association & Fund). A pet keeper's continued wrongdoing and ignorance of
basic needs may be explained using Greek philosopher Socrates' understanding of "ignorance" to mean a lack of knowledge or flawed education. Education is a nurtured, lifelong upbringing in morality that teaches virtue. Although an individual materializes as a product of one's actions, and actions
are a product of choices, culture is also a nurturing force. If society remains
ignorant of proper rabbit care then the individual pet keeper reared in society
will have an increased probability of ignorance (Woodruff 2014). Though
certain segments of society may condemn the pet keeper's actions, informed
members of society can assist the individual by helping them recognize their
ignorance. An appropriate response is an intervention to uproot societal
wrongdoing and check the ignorance that remains unchecked in society. Of
course, wrongdoing can occur unintentionally or willfully. Certainly, media
outlets such as Warner Brothers may be unaware of its harm. Alternatively,
perhaps cognizant of its harm, it may be easier to justify perpetuating harmful representations by appealing to the expectations and desires of the viewing audience. Furthermore, appealing to the fallacy of tradition or antiquity
to justify wrongdoing simply means accepting the status quo. A viewer may
tell themselves, "It's always been this way" or "Bugs Bunny has been consumed for generations, where's the harm in that?" The common thread
among these statements easily leads back to a pet keeper's faulty or incom-

plete knowledge. If left unexamined, cultural ignorance allows the public, and by extension the pet keeper, to wrongfully harm non/humans without correction or condemnation.

This analysis would be remiss if it only focused on the role of individual forces, without exploring the structural influences that permeate non/human animal oppression. When criticizing the animation industry and pointing fingers at "bad" pet keepers, one may overlook the entire system of oppression operating on a structural scale. Drawing from Barbara Noske's work on the Animal-Industrial Complex, it is possible to contextualize how the relationship between non/human media entertainment and pet keeping accentuates oppression (1989). The intersectional overlap between these industries may seem unrelated at first. However, upon closer examination they cannot be analyzed as mutually exclusive since they contribute to each other in a self-perpetuating cycle. Just as Noske asserts, producers working within the Animal-Industrial Complex are often motivated by capital accumulation (1989). A media giant such as Warner Brothers compels consumers to buy into the cultural forms it creates, and perpetuates the ruse that using non/humans for entertainment is inevitable. The viewer, complicit with the speciesist cartoon ideology, reinforces the human as a consumer of the non/human other. Those benefiting from the Animal-Industrial Complex encourage rampant consumerism. This could be purchasing a *Looney Tunes* box set or winning a stuffed animal of Bugs and Porky Pig at Universal Studios or gifting a live rabbit to a child for their birthday. Thus, the Animal-Industrial Complex, when defined in intersectional terms, is a mechanism that generates immense capital through confinement in ideology and practice. Clearly, this is not to say that certain media outlets, pet stores, and pet keepers have secretly colluded in this endeavor. Rather, it underlines the socioeconomic power these constituents exert within the system.

Historical influence also has a substantial impact on the perception of rabbitness in cartoon images. "An image is a sight which has been recreated or reproduced" (Berger 1973, 9–10). Thus, images preserve ideology and perceptions that can potentially outlast what was initially represented. Using this analysis, one could argue the original parody of Bugs munching on a carrot and playacting as Clark Gable morphed into an unhealthy quality of how rabbits *should* be. In this sense, Bugs could be regarded as a historically produced image repeatedly replicated in the imagination. In *Ideology and Ideological State Apparatuses* Louis Althusser discusses how an ideology is unreal and comparable to a dream (1969). He states, "All its reality is external to it" (Althusser and Brewster 1971, 159). However, Fredric Jameson, in *The Political Unconscious*, opposes the notion that ideology exists in isolation from its reality (1981). He says that one's interpretation of reality is influenced by the ideology and categories adopted from cultural history and tradition (Jameson 1981). These concepts demonstrate how speciesist media from the past, if it continues unchanged, will translate for future audiences to consume.

To conclude, "To look is an act of choice" (Berger 1973, 106). Instead of using such ableist language of "looking," we should "perceive" images through all senses. Humans must actively choose what images will be allowed to linger unquestioned in the mind. Indisputably, what is perceived onscreen is often replicated in real life without care or concern of reproach. Human exploitation of non/humans exists on the praxis of ignorance and apathy. Hence, it is imperative to create spaces for critical dialogue to generate new forms of knowledge that spur people to act. In this historical moment, humans can choose to be critical thinkers and challenge the status quo rather than implement it as truth. If we recognize the harms of uncritically accepting media messages, and develop new relations based on an ethics of care and compassion, long-standing destructive cultural norms can be destroyed. To quote Roger Yates on the subject, "The changes nonhuman animals need are cultural, for it is widespread and mundane cultural activities, along with taught values and attitudes, that bring billions of them into existence for the purpose of exploitation" (2009). Likewise, we must comprehend that the harms of captivity outweigh the benefits and decisively end all practices that constrain freedom and ecological harmony. Humans will continually struggle to justify their choices and actions. Until we diagnose and then take radical revolutionary action the limits of media-imposed knowledge and pet keeping as a cultural practice we remain unprepared to challenge the injustices passively preserved from one generation to the next.

REFERENCES

Althusser, Louis, and Ben Brewster. 1971. *Lenin and Philosophy, and Other Essays*. New York: Monthly Review Press.
American Academy of Pediatrics, Committee on Public Education. 2001. "Children, Adolescents, and Television." *Pediatrics* 107(2): 423–425.
American Veterinarian Medical Association (AVMA). 2012. "U.S. Pet Ownership and Demographics Sourcebook." https://www.avma.org/kb/resources/statistics/pages/market-research-statistics-us-pet-ownership-demographics-sourcebook.aspx.
Animal Welfare Institute. n.d. "Mission Statement." https://www.awionline.org.
ASPCA. 2015. "Pet Care: General Rabbit Care." https://www.aspca.org/pet-care/small-pet-care/general-rabbit-care.
Associated Newspapers Ltd. 2006. "Mice Hate Cheese, New Study Reveals." *Daily Mail*, September 6. http://www.dailymail.co.uk/news/article-403925/Mice-hate-cheese-new-study-reveals.html.
Baker, Steve. 1993. *Picturing the Beast: Animals, Identity, and Representation*. Chicago: University of Illinois Press.
Barrier, Michael, and Milton Gray. 1970a. "Bob Clampett: An Interview." *Funnyworld* 12 (Summer).
———. 2003b. *Hollywood Cartoons: American Animation in Its Golden Age*. New York: Oxford University Press.

Benjamin, Walter, Harry Zohn, Hannah Arendt, and Leon Wieseltier. 2013. "The Work of Art in the Age of Mechanical Reproduction." In *Illuminations: Essays and Reflections.* New York: Schocken Books.

Berger, John. 1973a. *Ways of Seeing.* London: Penguin Books.

———. 1980b. *About Looking.* New York: Pantheon Books.

Best, Steven. 2015. "The New Abolitionism: Capitalism, Slavery and Animal Liberation." http://www.drstevebest.org/TheNewAbolitionism.htm.

Brown, Susan. 2012. *Small Animal Nutrition.* http://rabbit.org/small-animal-nutrition/.

Buseth, M. E., and R. Saunders. 2015. *Rabbit Behaviour, Health, and Care.* Malta: Gutenberg Press.

Caygill, Howard. 1998. *Walter Benjamin: The Color of Experience.* London: Routledge.

Chaudhuri, Una. 2012. "The Silence of the Polar Bears: Performing (Climate) Change in the Theater of the Species." In *Readings in Performance and Ecology*, edited by Wendy Arons and Theresa May. New York: Palgrave Macmillan.

Columbia University Press blog. 2008. "Interview with Gary Francione, author of *Animals as Persons: Essays on the Abolition of Animal Exploitation*," June 18. http://www.cupblog.org/?p=283.

CNN. 2002. "TV Guide's 50 Greatest Cartoon Characters of All Time." July 30. http://edition.cnn.com/2002/SHOWBIZ/TV/07/30/cartoon.characters.list/.

Giroux, Henry A. 1994a. *Disturbing Pleasures: Learning Popular Culture.* New York: Routledge.

———.1995b. "Are Disney Movies Good for Your Kids?" in *The Politics of Early Childhood Education: Rethinking Childhood*, edited by Lourdes Diaz Soto. New York: Peter Lang Publishing.

Hollywood Chamber of Commerce. 1985. "Hollywood Walk of Fame." December 21. http://www.walkoffame.com/bugs-bunny.

Horkheimer, Max, and Theodor W. Adorno. 1972a. *Dialectic of Enlightenment.* New York: Seabury Press.

———.1977b. "Letter to Benjamin." In *Aesthetics and Politics*, edited by Ernest Bloch. London: NLB.

Hobbs, R. 1998. "Building Citizenship Skills through Media Literacy Education." In *The Public Voice in a Democracy at Risk*, edited by M. Salvador and P. Sias. Westport, CT: Praeger Press.

It Happened One Night. 1934. (1999). Directed by Frank Capra. Columbia TriStar Home Video. DVD.

Jameson, Fredric. 1981. *The Political Unconscious: Narrative as a Socially Symbolic Act.* Ithaca, New York: Cornell University Press.

McClure, Diane. 2011. "Diseases of Rabbits." http://www.merckmanuals.com/vet/exotic_and_laboratory_animals/rabbits/noninfectious_diseases_of_rabbits.html.

Mitchinson, John, and John Lloyd. 2006. *The Book of General Ignorance.* New York: Harmony Books.

Nibert, David Alan. 2002. *Animal Rights/Human Rights: Entanglements of Oppression and Liberation.* Lanham, MD: Rowman & Littlefield.

Noske, Barbara. 1989. *Humans and Other Animals: Beyond the Boundaries of Anthropology.* London: Pluto Press.

Oscars. "The 31st Academy Awards." April 6, 1959. https://www.oscars.org/oscars/ceremonies/1959.

Peggs, Kay. 2014. "From Center to Margins and Back Again: Critical Animal Studies and the Reflective Human Self." In *The Rise of Critical Animal Studies: From Margins to the Centre*, edited by Nik Taylor and Richard Twine. Abingdon: Routledge.

Pendergast, Sara. 2000. *St. James Encyclopedia of Popular Culture* 1. Detroit: Gale Group.

Petfinder. 2015. "How to Care for Domestic Rabbits." https://www.petfinder.com/pet-care/rabbit-care/care-domestic-rabbits/.

Rabbit Welfare Association & Fund. "Main Page." http://www.rabbitwelfare.co.uk.

Rollason, Christopher. 2003. "'All Was to Play For': Review of Esther Leslie, 'Hollywood Flatlands: Animation, Critical Theory and the Avant-Garde,'" *Walter Benjamin Research Syndicate* site. www.wbenjamin.org/hollywood.html.

Rose, Steven. 1997. *Lifelines: Biology, Freedom, and Determinism*. New York: Penguin.

Save a Fluff: Finding Homes for Fluffies. 2015. "What Bugs a Bunny?" http://www.saveafluff.co.uk/what-bugs-a-bunny.

Smithsonian. "Looney Tunes: Bugs Bunny." May 22, 1997. http://postalmuseum.si.edu/artof-thestamp/SubPage%20table%20images/artwork/rarities/Bug%20Bunny/bugsbunny.htm.

Telegraph Reporters. 2012. "Carrots Are Bad for Rabbits, RSPCA Says." June 25. http://www.telegraph.co.uk/news/health/pets-health/9353529/Carrots-are-bad-for-rabbits-RSPCA-says.html.

The People's Dispensary for Sick Animals. 2011. "PDSA Animal Well-being (PAW) Report." http://www.pdsa.org.uk.

University of Bristol. 2012. "No-One Likes Grass, Except Rabbits." *Bristol News*, June 25. http://www.bris.ac.uk/news/2012/8594.html.

Wells, Paul. 2002. *Animation and America*. New Brunswick, NJ: Rutgers University Press.

Woodruff, Paul. 2014. "Plato's Shorter Ethical Works." *The Stanford Encyclopedia of Philosophy.* http://plato.stanford.edu/archives/win2014/entries/plato-ethics-shorter/.

Yates, Roger. 2009. "Easygoing Speciesism." *On Human-Nonhuman Relations: A Sociological Exploration of Speciesism*, May 11. http://www.Human-nonhuman.blogspot.com.

Young, Charles M. 1975. "Oryctolagus Cuniculus a.k.a. Bugs Bunny." *Village Voice*, December.

II

The Fictional Fashioning of Reality

Chapter 6

I Am Legend (2007), U.S. Imperialism, and the Liminal Animality of "The Last Man"

Carter Soles

I Am Legend (2007) addresses American fears of a viral apocalypse. This post-apocalyptic world includes an invasion of terrifying human Others, known as Dark Seekers, into the literal urban wilderness of New York City. Central to the film's articulations of racially tinged paranoia are Black pro- tagonist Robert Neville's (Will Smith) relationships with various non/human animals: the deer he hunts, the lioness he hunts alongside, his lab rats, and especially his dog Samantha (Sam). The once-human Dark Seekers are por- trayed as bestial animals, bereft of speech and likened in their movements to a swarm of monsters. Neville's survival hinges upon his prowess navigating the overgrown streets of Manhattan, defending himself against the infected, and maintaining his connection to Sam. *I Am Legend* explores the ideological terrain of post-9/11 America and the War on Terror via its soldier protago- nist's interactions with non/human animals against the backdrop of infection.

In its valorization of Neville's efforts, *I Am Legend* constitutes an ideo- logically conservative reworking of its source material. The novella the film is based on, by Richard Matheson, ends by showing Neville as the horrific monster. He is rightfully feared and despised by the supposed monsters he hunts. By contrast, the 2007 film adaptation reaffirms the post-9/11 ideologi- cal status quo, supporting U.S. anti-terrorist policies by re-positioning Ne- ville as a true hero and savior of humankind. In this way it echoes the conclusion of an earlier film adaptation, *The Omega Man* (1971), which depicts Charlton Heston's jaded scientist sacrificing himself so that a group of human survivors may obtain the vial of life-saving vaccine derived from his "pure Anglo-Saxon" blood (Nama 2008, 52). As philosopher and media

75

critic Slavoj Žižek has written, in the 2007 film the novella's "original para-
dox (the hero is now legendary for vampires, as vampires once were for
humanity) gets lost [and what] . . . gets obliterated . . . is the authentically
'multicultural' experience rendered by the title's original meaning, the realization that one's own tradition is no better than what appear to us as the
'eccentric' traditions of others" (2011, 63). What is doubly paradoxical about
the ideological regression across the adaptations of *I Am Legend* is that the
latest version is the one produced "precisely in our era, in which multicultural tolerance has been elevated into an official ideology" (Žižek 2011, 63). In
other words, what seems to be the most progressive version of the tale, with
its Black protagonist and its truly remarkable depiction of interspecies relations, is in fact the most ideologically regressive. *I Am Legend* conflates fears
of infection and attack by inhuman "zombies" with images reminiscent of
U.S. military operations in the real-life encounters with Othered terrorists.
The film culminates in a ringing endorsement of the U.S. War on Terror,
lionizing the nonwhite subjects who support its aims for the benefit of the
lighter-skinned characters they serve in times of war; but who must be ex-
punged before societal stasis is restored.

Horror films have always dealt with liminal monsters and Others who do
not adhere to the norms of gender, sex, race, species, and ideology (Wood
1985, 199–201). As in most horror (or action/horror) films, *I Am Legend*'s
protagonist, Neville, is likened to the monsters he fights. He has a special
bond with them and understands their ways by hunting and experimenting
upon them. However, the behavioral and visual parallels drawn between
Neville and the Dark Seekers highlight Neville's non-white racial status and
position him as a mediator between the properly white, civilized, imperialist
world (to which he used to belong as a scientist and military officer) and the
bestial, savage, colonized world (to which he now belongs, and which is
metaphorical for contemporary Third World sites such as Somalia and Af-
ghanistan).

Sam, Neville's dog, is presented in a non-speciesist way throughout *I Am
Legend* and is the main factor that keeps Neville in touch with his will to live.
In fact, immediately following Sam's death Neville attempts suicide. In doing so, the film portrays a complex relationship that fosters species interdependence between humans and companion species. This aptly illustrates
Donna Haraway's notion of "becoming with," a process that makes "a mess
out of categories in the making of kin and kind" (2008, 19). This manner of
"becoming with" emphasizes process and consorting with other species in
ways that acknowledge each other's subjectivity (Haraway 2008, 17). Neville achieves such a partnering with Sam. Yet the productive messiness
between them occurs within a larger narrative and visual framework that uses
Neville's closeness to animals to suggest his unfitness to participate in the
human civilization reestablished by the survivors who, thanks to his death,

make it safely to Vermont. If his animality and "becoming with" Sam benefit Neville in the early part of the film, these same qualities also necessitate his death so civilized humans can rebuild the American empire. Hence, *I Am Legend* re-inscribes a firm boundary between the human and the non/human, between the white colonizer and the non-white colonized, in order to restore U.S. hegemony.

The viewer first sees Neville driving his red Ford Mustang at high speed through the streets of post-apocalyptic Manhattan. He is hunting. A series of establishing shots show the eerily empty streets, overgrown with weeds and vines. Afterward a long overhead tracking shot depicts his car speeding down the empty road from above. A camera placed inside his car shows Neville clutching a high-powered rifle lying on the seat beside him. The camera then cuts to his passenger, a German shepherd named Sam. Already we know that Smith's Neville is fond of technologically induced speed, is heavily armed, and that his only companion is a dog. Point of view shots out the windshield invite the viewer to share the kinetic thrill of hurtling down the overgrown streets in this powerful vehicle. As Neville turns a sharp corner an exterior shot lingers on a series of weathered posters stuck to the sides of a military tank: "God Still Loves Us. And We Still Love God." Even before we learn that Neville is a military scientist and a religious skeptic, these conspicuous posters foreshadow his spiritual conversion and Christ-like self-immolation at film's end. This reference to his suppressed faith is one way in which his secular, Black masculinity is ultimately contained by his commitment to white, imperialist, Judeo-Christian values.

The hunt continues and the only sounds are the deep roar of the Mustang's engine and the occasional chirp of a bird. In response to Sam's suddenly alert expression, Neville asks, "What you see? What you see?" While this may seem an anthropomorphizing question to ask a German shepherd, who would more likely hear and/or smell something before she sees it, it is perfectly in line with Jonathan Burt's notion that films centered on non/humans tend to foreground "the *possibility* of animal understanding by emphasizing animal sight" (2002, 71). Images of non/human eyes and exchanged looks between human and non/human animals are privileged in order to convey interspecies communication. Neville's question, phrased quite matter-of-factly, sets up a dynamic in which Sam is understood to be Neville's partner and collaborator, not merely a pet to be talked down to or patronized. That said, there are later points at which Neville issues spoken commands to Sam, one moment in which he admonishes her for attempting to follow him into his laboratory, and several points at which he treats her as a surrogate child. He thus views her as a partner over whom he occasionally must assert authority, thereby attempting to reinstate a hierarchical relationship between them. In any case, the deep connection between Neville and Sam is one of the film's great strengths in terms of what it implies about human to non/human relations and interspecies ethics. It is also a means by which Smith's Neville, the last Black man on earth, is subtly animalized: his only family relation is a dog.

The car-bound hunting scene nears its climax when a deer leaps past the Mustang's windshield in a light brown flash. Neville swings the vehicle around to pursue the deer herd crossing his path. He draws up alongside the running deer and takes aim with his rifle. His shot is spoiled when the deer herd heads into a tunnel, and moments later his prey completely disappear over a barricade of police cars and concrete retaining walls. Neville's techniques here suggest an odd conflation of traditional hunting practices with those of an urban drive-by shooting: he hunts deer with the help of a dog in a car named "Mustang." Yet the type of military rifle he uses, his unsporting attempt to gun down a deer from a moving vehicle, and his being thwarted by parked police cars all evoke a gangland drive-by or a military action. Nevertheless, the presence of Sam and the deer mutually establish a key motif of the film: Neville is both a friend to and hunter of non/human animals.

The next shot reinforces this association, showing Neville stalking the deer on foot through the chest-high grass. Decrepit buildings loom in the background as Neville creeps through a patch of savannah-like grassland fringing Times Square, again placing him in a literal urban jungle. He stalks a buck, Sam at his side, but is stymied in his efforts by the sudden appearance of a lioness, who leaps upon the buck Neville is after. As the lioness pins the struggling buck to the pavement, her mate and cub appear, and they along with Neville and Sam watch as the lioness breaks the buck's neck. Neville considers killing the lioness, aiming his high-powered rifle at her, but relents after two sidelong looks at the male lion and cub. As with Sam in the car, the male lion returns Neville's look to suggest a mutual identification and understanding between them. However, the lion's look is also a challenge, from which Neville backs down. He is not the lion's equal here. Neville is a link in the local food chain, not the apex predator, which he acknowledges by retreating. Not until much later, after Sam's death, will Neville be jolted into fully releasing his animalistic, instinctive, predatory self. For now, Neville's wristwatch alarm beeps, alerting him that sunset approaches, and with it the Dark Seekers. Glancing fearfully over his shoulder at the setting sun, he leaves the lion family behind and, calling to Sam to follow him, returns to his car.

This sequence sets up two concurrent yet conflicting parallels: one between Neville and the lioness, both hunters seeking prey with which to feed their respective families, and a second between Neville and the dead buck, who, like Neville himself, serves as prey to a more dangerous predator species. Neville identifies with both hunter and hunted, caught in a liminal position between master/predator and colonized subject/prey. His oscillation between these two positions and their fluctuating relationship to animality marks the ideological parameters of this essentially conservative film. Akin to many post-apocalyptic protagonists, Smith's Neville stands at the juncture between the archaic and the modern, reduced to predatory, "tooth and claw" survivalism in a post-apocalyptic urban jungle abundant with wild animals while simultaneously possessed of modern technological gadgets (car, rifle, wristwatch), scientific acumen, and military discipline that mark him as an exemplary patriarchal imperialistic subject.

Viewer investment in Neville's tribulations is strongly bound up with his (and the viewer's) relationship to Sam, whose presence in *I Am Legend* demonstrates the visual animal's unique power to generate sympathy on-screen. The intimate bond between Neville and Sam is visually constructed via two tactics outlined by Jennifer Ladino in her discussion of non-species-ist camera: allowing human and non/human animals to co-inhabit cinematic space and showing non/human animals watching back and engaging in the interspecies look (2013, 131). We have already seen how the film opens with Neville and Sam sharing space. The opening hunt sequence sets a precedent to which the film adheres until Sam's demise: Neville and Sam are more or less constantly in frame together. The first half of *I Am Legend* abounds with shots of Neville and Sam as they eat together, sleep together, ride around town together, and hunt together. The only time Neville is seen apart from Sam in the first half of the film is when he ventures into his basement laboratory, a space from which Sam is forbidden until her death.

The most crucial of Ladino's anti-speciesist visual strategies is the inter-species look, which Burt claims is pervasively fetishized in animal-centered cinema to the point where "the exchange of the look is, in the absence of the possibility of language, the basis of a social contract" between human and non/human animals (Burt 2002, 64; 39). While the interspecies look in film can function as a means by which relations and identifications between spe-cies can be shown to break down, more often the interspecies look is not demystified. Most typically the look connotes "that the failure to under-stand . . . does not entail the breakdown of contact even if, as film sometimes suggests, the look is all we have" (Burt 2002, 64; 56). Significantly for *I Am Legend*, interspecies looking "can be a site of trauma or of healing," both of which apply to the looks exchanged by Neville and Sam (Burt 2002, 62).

I Am Legend first depicts this interspecies buddy pair in a series of two close-ups, one of each character, in which the eye line match makes clear that they are exchanging a knowing glance as they drive along together. In re-sponse to the glance, Neville lowers the passenger's side window so that Sam may stick her head out. Thus, the film makes clear from the outset that for these two bonded interspecies companions, the look is a conveyor of mean-ing and understanding. Immediately following this transaction there is a point of view shot looking straight out the front windshield of the car. The camera is positioned *between* Sam and Neville, in the middle and slightly

behind the front seat. This camera placement refuses to privilege either character's vision, instead suggesting parity or at least visual balance between
their two distinct points of view. It also functions as the film's first depiction
of these two sharing visual space, as the viewer sees both man and dog at
either edge of the frame.

A more tender exchange of interspecies looks features in a bathing scene
that takes place once Sam and Neville return from the opening hunt. The
sequence opens in long shot, with Neville sitting next to the bathtub in which
Sam stands, admonishing her for not eating her vegetables at dinner. This
dialogue suggests a parent/child dynamic, yet the subtle implication is that
Sam maybe never eats her vegetables and that this is one area in which
Neville's attempt to anthropomorphize her has failed. Nevertheless there is a
touching bond evinced between them as Neville rubs soap into her fur, turns
on his iPod, and sings along to Bob Marley's "Three Little Birds." It is as if
Neville is serenading Sam. The use of the Bob Marley song in this moment
of dog–human bonding marks Sam as a surrogate for Neville's deceased
daughter who, as we learn from subsequent flashback sequences, was named
Marley. In the present, Neville, in close-up, looks at Sam, massaging her
head, and in another close-up she looks up at him as he asks, "Doesn't it feel
good?"

This sequence not only establishes the more intimate side of the bond
between Neville and Sam, it also sets the stage for the most powerful and
disturbing scene in the film: Sam's surrender to the virus and subsequent
death in Neville's basement lab. Before discussing the death itself, a word
needs to be said about Sam's gender. The first fifty-three minutes of the film
give no hint of her sex. Neville refers to her only by the gender-ambiguous
name "Sam." However, once she is wounded and immobilized by the attack
of a Dark Seeker hound, Neville leans over her prostrate body in the street,
imploring, "Samantha! Samantha, look at me, girl!" Thus, *after* she is defeated in battle and infected with the virus, Sam's female sex is finally revealed.
Her femaleness, which aligns her with Neville's deceased daughter, both
reaffirms Neville's status as father/patriarch of his clan (also suggested via
the interspecies look Neville exchanges with the male lion in the film's
opening sequence) and simultaneously feminizes him, showing him to have a
female comrade in arms whom he cannot adequately defend. This sets up the
melodramatic basement lab scene in which Sam dies.

Up until this point in the film, Sam has not been allowed in the basement
lab, a secured space where the infected are quarantined. Thus Sam's presence
in the lab at the outset of the scene clearly signifies that she will be lost to the
infection, as have been all but one of the experimental rats currently kept
there. Sam's devolution and death begin with Neville vaccinating Sam on a
lab table, then holding her as he sinks to a sitting position on the floor. In a
long shot, which slowly tracks in toward them, we see Neville petting and

comforting Sam, singing "Three Little Birds" as he waits for the vaccine to take effect. His mournful singing continues as a close-up of their two faces close together starts slowly tracking in tight, gradually framing out all but Sam's right ear and Neville's face. An insert shows a clump of Sam's hair that has come loose in Neville's hand. He now knows that she is irrevocably infected.

Neville looks into Sam's eyes, as does the viewer in a lingering extreme close-up. What starts off as a possibly tender last look into the eyes of his closest friend soon takes a clinical turn as Neville pulls back the skin around Sam's eye socket to examine the white of her eye. He is confirming her infected status. He further confirms her transformation by pulling back her upper lip to reveal a bared fang suggestive of a Dark Seeker hound. This transition from the image of the eye, the privileged site via which interspecies communication and identification typically occur, to the gritted canine tooth, dramatically highlights the difference between a beloved companion animal and a bestial predator. It also foreshadows a similar change in Neville that subsequently occurs.

Once she turns into a Dark Seeker hound, Sam is framed out completely with a close-up of Neville's face as he strangles her while showing the pain it causes him. Although this is a mercy killing he performs without hesitation, he stares up at the ceiling throughout the ordeal and gives a look of devastating sadness once the deed is finished. He finally looks down, but rather than showing the viewer what he sees, the camera cuts to a long shot of Neville dropping Sam's limp body to the floor and letting out one choking sob. Sam is given a soldier's death, brought about by the grim necessities of combat, but Neville's overt pathos suggests the family connection he feels with her across species lines. This makes his refusal to grant any humanness to the Dark Seekers, technically members of his own species, all the more contradictory. In addition, this scene demonstrates Neville's inner struggle between disciplined soldier and traumatized basket case. It is a contradiction to be negotiated by all soldiers, who must learn to control their emotional responses and fear by channeling them into a productive aggression they can use on the battlefield. *I Am Legend* documents Neville's devolution from a trained officer who knows how to channel properly his aggressive impulses to a post-traumatic suicide case who cannot restrain his bestial rage.

While one could argue that Sam's death re-centers the narrative around Neville, privileging his emotional state over her suffering, it is also true that violence against a "real" non/human animal like Sam would risk disturbing viewers too much and rupturing the fictional narrative completely. As Burt argues,

> The idea that animals represent the insertion of the real or the natural into film is crucial to the question of violence. . . . The commonplace that people are

more sensitized to, or disturbed by, film violence involving animals than they
are to that involving humans is difficult to assess or quantify. . . . However,
when such sentiments are expressed by people protesting against instances of
screen violence, it does suggest that the suspension of belief that is normally in
play with regard to humans on screen does not work in the same way for
animals. (2002, 136–7)

Indeed, Sam is almost the only "real" non/human actor used in the film, with
one exception: the uninfected rats kept in Neville's lab.

Rats and mice are the most numerous research animals used today. Veterinarian and sociologist Larry Carbone estimates that mice, rats, and birds
"account for some 90% of research animals in America" (2004, 70). Yet they
are rarely seen in animal rights literature or advertising, where more emotionally relatable species like cats, dogs, and primates are the norm (Carbone
2004, 77; 79). This has to do with the images of these species as perceived
and received by humans: rats in particular "have been reviled" due to "their
beady, expressionless eyes" and "their long naked tails" (Carbone 2004, 73).
Neville disregards his rodent research subjects while showing deep love for
his dog, adhering to the status quo in his relationships with these non/human
animals. While both are played onscreen by live animals, the rats are dispos-
able lives, to be experimented upon and euthanized, while Sam is a valued
life Neville dignifies, loves, and protects.

By contrast, the lions, the deer, the infected rats, and the Dark Seekers are
all created using computer-generated imagery (CGI). As Michael Allen
writes, "The success or failure of any digital image lies in the degree to
which it persuades its spectator that it is not digital, but *is* photographic"
(2002, 110). Audience acceptance of digital creatures depends on both the
excellence of the CGI work and the duration of time they spend onscreen.
The digital lions' brief screen time abets our acceptance of them as "real" yet
compromises deep identification with them (Allen 2002, 110–11). While
CGI "works" for the lions, deer, and infected rats, whose screen time is brief,
it is less effective at creating real-seeming Dark Seekers, who are more
prominently featured and look more obviously digital. The choice to render
the Dark Seekers via CGI discourages audience empathy for them due to
CGI's difficulty crossing the "uncanny valley" to effectively capture specifically human-like faces and movements. This assures that the viewer sees
them as monstrous even before their actual "performance" comes into play.
Yet this choice is ideologically reassuring because it shows that Neville and
the viewer will have no problem spotting out Dark Seekers, who are terrorist
monsters who definitely do not look like "us."

The uncanniness of the Dark Seekers is enhanced by *I Am Legend*'s
notoriously non-photorealistic CGI creature effects. Prevalent geek culture
website io9 disparages the Dark Seekers' unconvincing appearance, stating

that "I Am Legend would have been a lot better with practical monsters" (Woerner 2011). *Entertainment Weekly*'s Owen Gleiberman, while praising the film, nevertheless calls *Legend* a "fake-demon CGI movie" (2007, 57). I mention these comments not as a value judgment about the film's aesthetics but simply to emphasize that these choices make Sam, the one prevalently featured live non/human animal on set, stand out and resonate more deeply with both Neville and the viewer. Those creatures rendered digitally may fail to rupture the semiotic field in the same affective way as do live images of non/humans. That said, in cases where the character is created entirely from CGI, as with the lions and Dark Seekers, "the digital character exists on a separate plane, but it exists wholly on that plane, rather than being one kind of being attempting to be another" (Wolf 2003, 57).That is, there are no live lions on set to which the digital ones may be directly compared and evaluated. The digital lions never even share the frame with Sam. Techniques like this may help lend *I Am Legend*'s all-digital beings a sense of perceptual reality, if not deep relatability (Prince 1996, 28).

Broadly speaking, Neville's various non/human animal encounters, especially his complex interactions with Sam, mark the boundaries between different hierarchical subject positions: Sam and Neville are non-infected, loyal, well-disciplined subjects of the patriarchal human order that existed pre-apocalypse; the deer, lions, and other wildlife are representatives of the pastoral past into which that modern order is generally devolving; and the Dark Seekers are the already devolved, bestial, infected ex-humans who stand in for the non-citizens of the Third World, those who Žižek, following Giorgio Agamben, refers to as *homo sacer*. Agamben defines *homo sacer* as a liminal figure who occupies the boundary of the state's power over its citizens, which is a power founded upon its ability to kill its subjects at will (1998, 82–84; 88–89). Whereas the full citizen is (usually) afforded due process before having their life taken as punishment or in battle, *homo sacer* is afforded no such recognition because their life does not exist officially. "The very body of *homo sacer* is, in its capacity to be killed but not sacrificed, a living pledge to his [*sic*] subjection to a power of death" (Agamben 1998, 99). The life of *homo sacer* "may be killed by anyone without committing homicide, but never submitted to sanctioned forms of execution" (103). In short, *homo sacer* is an animalized non/human, viewed in Germanic antiquity as a literal human-animal hybrid, "neither man nor beast," a werewolf existing unofficially in the border territory between the city and the wilderness (Agamben 1998, 104–5).

After the death of Sam, and even as mounting evidence (such as the trap they set for him) suggests that the Dark Seekers may be somewhat higher-functioning than he admits, Neville goes wild. He gives in to his primal emotions by taking a nighttime suicide run at the Dark Seeker lair. He lapses from his usual military discipline into a state of grief-induced, bestial rage, echoing the moment when the alpha-male Dark Seeker leaps, incensed, into the sunlight to prevent the abduction of his mate. The Dark Seekers are of the same species as Neville, infected by the global virus that changed most human survivors into nocturnal cannibals. Neville hunts, captures, and experiments upon them, learning their habits, rituals, and physiology. At the same time he refuses ever to acknowledge their underlying humanity. Though he calls his experiments on them "human trials," he does not view the Dark Seekers as capable of emotional suffering, even when some of their behavior makes it clear that they are. Their human capacities are admittedly limited—the film primarily frames the Dark Seekers as bestial and monstrous—but both Neville and the film suggest that he has more in common with Sam or the male lion than he does with the Dark Seekers.

Neville, like so many post-apocalyptic survivor-protagonists, belongs to the tradition of the lone American wilderness hero, who occupies a liminal position between civilization and wilderness, ambivalently using the techniques and traditions of indigenous Others in the ultimate service of white civilization (Ingram 2000, 74; 75).However, unlike the frontiersman figure he emulates, Neville refuses the Dark Seekers his empathy by paternalistically viewing them as "sick" mutants in need of his medical treatment (Burt 2002, 74; 117). In short, he treats them as *homo sacer*. Though Žižek's principal subjects of discussion are contemporary terrorists, he notes that those excluded from society as *homo sacer* "are not only terrorists, but also those who are on the receiving end of the humanitarian help (Rwandans, Bosnians, Afghans) [and that] . . . today's *Homo sacer* is the privileged object of humanitarian biopolitics: the one who is deprived of his or her full humanity being taken care of in a very patronizing way" (2002, 91). This description perfectly fits the Dark Seekers, who are both monstrous nocturnal terrorists and recipients of patronizing humanitarian aid via Neville's vaccine that would turn them back into uninfected humans.

In the post-9/11 American context, the Dark Seekers most strongly represent animalized Al-Qaeda terrorists. Neville's willful refusal to acknowledge their humanity therefore takes on special weight in light of his status as a U.S. Army officer. This symbolic violence that enables real-world violence is germane not only to Euro-American colonialist framing of the underprivileged Third World but also the way mainstream culture treats many species of non/human animals. Analogously, Neville's attitude toward the inhuman Dark Seekers is foreshadowed by his treatment of the rats he experiments upon in his basement laboratory. Neville treats the rats like objects for experimentation, referring to them by the number assigned to the vaccine with which he injects each of them. In contrast with Sam, who is frequently viewed in close-up, the only two lab rats seen in close-up are a monstrous infected one and number six, the recipient of his first successful vaccine. Moreover, while number six exchanges looks with Neville, it is not a personal exchange for Neville. He makes scientific observations about the rat while shining a penlight in her eye and we never see any of the rats up close again. Nor do we see close-ups of Dark Seekers unless they are roaring or attacking.

The viewer first glimpses the Dark Seekers when Sam chases a deer into the building where they dwell. Going in to find Sam, Neville peers around pitch-dark corners with his rifle-mounted flashlight in a sequence that visually echoes the door-to-door checks and night operations conducted by U.S. troops in Baghdad and elsewhere. He shines his light into a room and sees several Dark Seekers gathered in a circle, facing inward, seemingly sleeping on their feet. This image evokes both certain types of non/human animals who sleep standing up and a terrorist "sleeper cell" awaiting nightfall to emerge and strike. The shift of setting from the Los Angeles of *Omega Man* (and Matheson's novella) to the New York City of *Legend* makes special sense in this post-9/11 "sleeper cell" context. While in subsequent appearances they will appear grayish in coloration, in this shot, in the dim light of the rust-colored building, the Dark Seekers' skin looks coppery brown. This completes their visual association with nonwhite *homo sacer* while suggesting a racial connection to Neville.

Later, once Neville traps a Dark Seeker female, brings her to his lab, and subjects her to initially unsuccessful treatment with his number six vaccine, he adjourns upstairs to record his findings on video. Demoralized by the latest failure of his vaccine, he hollowly dictates a "behavioral note," stating that: "an infected male exposed himself to sunlight today. Now it's possible that decreased brain function or growing scarcity of food is causing them to ignore their basic survival instincts. Social devolution appears complete. Typical human behavior is now entirely absent." The viewer knows from his despair-laden tone that this comment refers to himself as well as to the Dark Seekers because their lack of typical human behavior is a key parallel between them. Further, Neville's interpretation of *why* the Dark Seeker leaped into the sunlight is remarkably obtuse. It reveals a hierarchical, imperialistic, racist thinking that supersedes his ability to consider the data before him scientifically. The Dark Seeker leaps into the sunlight in an attempt to recover his mate, and his angry bellow at Neville makes clear how he feels about her and the situation. Disregard for one's own safety in efforts to protect loved ones is a quality both human and non/human animals possess. Yet Neville, the ever rigid, colonial, hierarchical thinker, omits this possibility from his "devolution" report. Neville lies about the Dark Seeker's lack of social bonds, recording his inaccurate view of them as if it were scientific fact.

Shortly after this report is made, Neville is caught in a trap set by the Dark Seekers, and as a result Sam gets infected and dies. Neville's trauma at losing Sam sends him over the edge into his own undisciplined, bestial side, just as real combat with disastrously underestimated and rhetorically animalized Somalian "skinnies" sends real-life U.S. troops into abject panic after a botched American raid into Mogadishu (Bowden 2001, 10; 250). Like the threat of infection in the film, urban combat trauma reduces humans to the status of undisciplined and bestial animals. This phenomenon partly stems from many contemporary American soldiers' tendency to vastly overestimate their own military power and to disregard the possibility that relatively impoverished opponents might be able to outmatch them (Bowden 2001, 54; 95; 250). Sometimes disastrously, the enemy defenders with whom U.S. troops engage are symbolically devalued by being likened to swarms of abject animals. In *Black Hawk Down,* various American soldiers refer to Somalis as "animals," "savage mobs," and especially "swarms," evoking uncontrolled and fast-moving groups of insects (Bowden 2001, 373, 95, 55, 123). *I Am Legend* plays upon this racist colonial rhetoric in two ways. First, it reinforces its truth through depicting the Dark Seekers as physically animalistic. Second, is shows the viewer that the Dark Seekers are actually capable of much more than Neville suspects. On the one hand, the Dark Seekers roar unintelligibly, scrabble around on all fours, and even burrow through walls and ceilings like enormous termites. On the other hand, the film establishes their technical capabilities and intelligence by having Neville walk unsuspecting into a Dark Seeker trap that leads to Sam's death.

Post-breakdown, Neville's recovery consists not of him realizing that he was wrong about the Dark Seekers, but rather of him converting to enacting a Christlike self-immolation with a hand grenade that obliterates the remaining Dark Seekers in a swift act of militarized violence. Metaphorically mirroring the U.S. response to the events of 9/11, Neville's brutal turn toward mutual annihilation shows that the appropriate lessons went unlearned. By depicting Neville's violent death as spiritual and heroic, *I Am Legend* lionizes soldiers of the ongoing War on Terror to justify the imperialist notions that underpin it. Moreover, by having a Black American soldier willingly commit the ultimate sacrifice to maintain U.S. hegemony, *Legend* depicts a comforting post-9/11 national solidarity that trumps racial loyalties and belies the racism endemic to contemporary U.S. society.

I Am Legend thus reinforces imperialist messages via the image of the domesticated American Black man who serves as a mediator between the civilized and the savage. As Adilfu Nama writes,

> It is culturally comforting in the nervous America of today for black people . . . to lead the charge to defend America from attack in a sci-fi future . . . [because black heroes] are needed to assure a nation grappling with post-9/11 paranoia that voices of racial dissent, historical or contemporary, are not a threat to domestic security and to affirm the belief that patriotic solidarity transcends racial loyalty. (2008, 41)

Will Smith is the ideal Black film star to make this reassuring conservative ideological message work. Credited by Nama as the catalyst for the post-1980s centrality of Black representation in the mainstream science-fiction genre, Will Smith "is a seminal figure in American [science-fiction] cinema. His blend of the racially nonthreatening posture of Sidney Poitier with the charismatic bravado of Eddie Murphy . . . proved quite a successful formula. As a result, Will Smith became part film trailblazer, part comic relief, and pure pop sci-fi cool" (2008, 39). Smith's coolness stems from his early career as a family-friendly rapper and comedic persona on *The Fresh Prince of Bel-Air* that he subsequently integrated into film portrayals of military heroes in sci-fi films such as *Independence Day* (1996) and *I, Robot* (2004). Smith's essential quality is his nonthreatening embodiment of family values, father-hood, and clean humor. He is white America's preeminent non-scary Black entertainer and his screen persona allows him to portray noble everyman heroes who are warm and likable (Guerrero 1993, 128; 130; 132).

Ultimately, Smith's Neville acts as a self-sacrificing buffer between *homo sacer* (Dark Seekers) and "real" humans (Anna and Ethan). Anna, played by Brazilian actress Alice Braga, in turn functions as *I Am Legend*'s mediator between the savage, post-breakdown Neville and the civilized world repre-sented by the rumored survivor colony in Vermont. She is the flexible next-generation mediator figure common to imperialist narratives, negotiating be-tween Neville's hidebound militarism and lack of faith as well as the spiritual fundamentalism that lets her "just know" there are human survivors up North (Shohat and Stam 1994, 113). A thinly developed character, she primarily exists to re-humanize Neville, reintroducing him to the idea of personal purpose founded on religious faith. After Neville's death, her voice-over bridges the gap between him and the Vermont settlement to whom she deliv-ers his vaccine. The Vermont compound at first appears ethnically diverse, guarded by Black and Latino soldiers with several nonwhite denizens appear-ing in the film's last shot. However, that same shot features a white church steeple centered in the frame and a conspicuously placed American flag. This visual coding indicates an assimilationist society in which conservative, small-town American and Christian church values dominate. Ultimately, "the emblematic placement of the church and the soldiers demonstrates what exactly the forces are that provide this community with safety and collective identity" (Hantke 2011, 167). Most important, the hand that takes the blood vial from Anna, seen only in brief close-up, is masculine and white. Vermont looks multicultural but white men are still implicitly in charge.

Significantly, Neville uses the Alpha Female Dark Seeker's blood as the successful vaccine, rather than his own (as Heston's Neville does in *Omega Man*). The alpha female, while othered as *homo sacer*, is portrayed by a fair-skinned actress (Joanna Numata) and is the palest of all the Dark Seekers seen onscreen. This is *I Am Legend*'s way of maintaining the eugenics discourse that insists upon the purity of white blood, a holdover from *Omega Man* (Nama 2008, 49; 52). In the 2007 version, the Black Neville's role is to extract the life-giving white blood, then immolate himself so that the lighter-skinned South Americans can escape northward. Thus, despite maintaining the appearance of America's post-racial pro-diversity official culture via its casting of Smith and its bold depictions of interspecies identifications, ultimately non/human animals and animality in *I Am Legend* reaffirm a racialized global economic inequality. In this way, post-9/11 hegemonic American discourses can be perpetuated without explicitly acknowledging structural racism. In *I Am Legend*, Euro-American imperialism is disguised as a highly medicalized science-fictional speciesism. Infected dogs, rats, and the ambiguously sub-human Dark Seekers help draw a distinction between good domesticated animals (Sam, Neville, even possibly the lions) versus wild, terrifying, bestial killers (the Dark Seekers). In the end, we are made to feel the emotional stakes of the suffering and deaths of the former while disregarding the subjectivity of the latter.

Ecocritic Pat Brereton, who has written on dystopian science-fiction films, argues that such narratives depict a move away from the decadent technologically dependent city environments toward "hermeneutically sealed" eco-paradises representing "ecological harmony" (2005, 169; 170; 172). Similarly, Žižek calls *I Am Legend*'s Vermont a "pure eco-paradise," a "gated community protected by a wall and security guards" situated in the North that nevertheless welcomes "newcomers from the fundamentalist South who have survived the passage through devastated New York" (2001, 64). The problem with these narratives, as Žižek's comment indicates, is that they reestablish a sense of here versus there, a division between rejuvenating natures, coded white, and devolving post-apocalyptic cityscape, coded black. Žižek writes that the U.S.'s healthiest response to the 9/11 attacks would have been to "learn humbly to accept its own vulnerability as part of the world" because "the only way to ensure that it will not happen here again is to prevent it happening anywhere else" (2002, 49). Likewise, the lesson to be taken from *I Am Legend*'s fundamentalist resolution is that Neville fatally screws up when he fails to embrace the Dark Seekers' humanity and recognize "the otherness of the other" (Hantke 2011, 181). Maddeningly, the answer is right in front of him the whole time. In short, species interdependence, as Donna Haraway puts it, "is the name of the worlding game on earth, and that game must be one of response and respect" (2008, 19). This interdependence must be grounded in an anti-oppressive and nonauthoritarian relationship, where speciesism and human supremacy are absent. If Neville could have learned to be as responsive to and respectful of the Dark Seekers as he was to Sam and the lions, he might have learned to loosen "the grip of analogies that issue in the collapse of all of man's [*sic*] others into one another" and to live, as companion species do, intersectionally (Haraway 2008, 18).

REFERENCES

Agamben, Giorgio. 1998. *Homo Sacer: Sovereign Power and Bare Life.* Translated by Daniel Heller-Roazen. Stanford, CA: Stanford University Press.

Allen, Michael. 2002. "The Impact of Digital Technologies on Film Aesthetics." In *The New Media Book,* edited by Dan Harries, 109–118. London: BFI.

Bowden, Mark. 2001. *Black Hawk Down: A Story of Modern War.* New York: Signet.

Brereton, Pat. 2005. *Hollywood Utopia: Ecology in Contemporary American Cinema.* Bristol, UK: Intellect.

Burt, Jonathan. 2002. *Animals in Film.* London: Reaktion.

Carbone, Larry. 2004. *What Animals Want: Expertise and Advocacy in Laboratory Animal Welfare Policy.* Oxford: Oxford University Press.

Gleiberman, Owen. 2007. "Solitary Man." *Entertainment Weekly*, December 21.

Guerrero, Ed. 1993. *Framing Blackness: The African American Image in Film.* Philadelphia: Temple University Press.

Hantke, Steffen. 2011. "Historicizing the Bush Years: Politics, the Horror Film, and Francis Lawrence's *I Am Legend.*" In *Horror After 9/11: World of Fear, Cinema of Terror*, edited by Aviva Briefel and Sam J. Miller, 165–185. Austin: University of Texas Press.

Haraway, Donna J. 2008. *When Species Meet.* Minneapolis: University of Minnesota Press.

I Am Legend. 2008. Directed by Francis Lawrence. Warner Home Video. DVD.

Ingram, David. 2000. *Green Screen: Environmentalism and Hollywood Cinema.* Exeter: University of Exeter Press.

Ladino, Jennifer. 2013. "Working with Animals: Regarding Companion Species in Documentary Film." *Ecocinema Theory and Practice*, edited by Stephen Rust, Salma Monani, and Sean Cubitt, 129–148. New York: Routledge.

Matheson, Richard. 1995. *I Am Legend.* New York: TOR.

Nama, Adilifu. 2008. *Black Space: Imagining Race in Science Fiction Film.* Austin: University of Texas Press.

Prince, Stephen. 1996. "True Lies: Perceptual Realism, Digital Images, and Film Theory." *Film Quarterly* 49(3): 27–37.

Shohat, Ella, and Robert Stam. 1994. *Unthinking Eurocentrism: Multiculturalism and the Media.* London: Routledge.

The Omega Man. 1971. (2007). Directed by Boris Sagal. Distributed by Warner Home Video. DVD.

Woerner, Meredith. 2011. "What *I Am Legend* Would Have Looked like with Non-CG Monsters." *io9.com.* http://io9.com/5793402/what-i-am-legend-would-have-looked-like-with-non-cg-monsters.

Wolf, Mark J. P. 2003. "The Technological Construction of Performance." *Convergence* 9(4): 48–59.

Wood, Robin. 1985. "An Introduction to the American Horror Film." *Movies and Methods: An Anthology 2*, edited by Bill Nichols, 195–220. Berkeley: University of California Press.

Žižek, Slavoj. 2011a. *Living in the End Times.* London: Verso.

———.2002b. *Welcome to the Desert of the Real!* London: Verso.

Chapter 7

Ape Anxiety: Intelligence, Human Supremacy, and *Rise* and *Dawn of the Planet of the Apes*

Sean Parson

A predominant reading of the 2011 reboot of the *Planet of the Apes* series is best epitomized by the People for the Ethical Treatment of Animals (PETA) movie review. PETA writes, "Rise of the Planet of the Apes is the first live-action film in the history of movies to star and be told from the point of view of a sentient animal—a character with humanlike qualities, who can strategize, organize, and ultimately lead a revolution, and with whom audiences will experience a real emotional bond" (PETA 2015). PETA is not alone in their review of *Rise of the Planet of the Apes* (2011). PETA and others within the animal welfare movement believe the critically acclaimed movie was successful in undermining the cultural logic of speciesism. In response to this position, critical animal studies scholar Nik Taylor claims: "The film ultimately tells us more about our own beliefs about what it is to be human than it does to promote any serious engagement with animal rights or animal emancipation" (Taylor 2011). Since the film so beautifully centers on non/human primates resisting human oppression it is easy to read as a radical animal liberationist film. However, to do so misses the deeper philosophical and political dimensions of the film, which actually promote a reactionary defense of anthropocentrism.

This chapter seeks to deconstruct the dominant interpretation of both *Rise of the Planet of the Apes* and the more recent *Dawn of the Planet of the Apes* (2014) from a critical animal studies perspective. In doing so, my analysis focuses on how each film taps into contemporary anxieties related to human supremacy. Humans are regularly confronted with non/human animal intelligence—from our day-to-day interactions with companion dogs and cats to

91

scientific articles and news stories highlighting non/human animals' lived
experiences. Despite these confrontations, in order to justify their exploitative treatment of non/humans, humans construct philosophical and cognitive
rationalizations. As Melanie Joy argues, we "have a special set of defenses
that enable humane people to support inhumane practices and not even realize what they are doing" (2011, 33). The most common defense mechanism
is to either ignore or hide the intelligence and suffering of non/human animals. However, every day—either in our companion pets's eyes or in watching a squirrel in a park—the sentience of non/human animals breaks through
our barriers. The social, philosophical, and psychological barricades we use
to justify human superiority are always under assault. Humans are inundated
with anxiety around our uniqueness or lack thereof. The current *Planet of the
Apes* films use this cultural anxiety to build tension. However, this does not
mean the films are about animal rights. Rather, the films reinforce the logic
of speciesism through definitions based on human intelligence and sentience
that actually deny agency to real existing primates. As follows, the films
reinforce the barriers that justify the special treatment of the human species
over others.

"GET YOUR HANDS OFF ME, YOU DAMNED DIRTY APE!": *PLANET OF THE APES* FROM THE 1960S TO THE PRESENT

The cult classic 1968 film version of *Planet of the* Apes tells the story of
George Taylor (Charlton Heston), an astronaut who crash-lands on an unknown and underdeveloped alien planet ruled by an advanced ape civilization. The apes' civilization is structured around a rigid caste system. The
foundation of their culture is the speciesist view that humans are inferior to
apes. In an inversion of human supremacy, the apes refuse to believe George
is sentient and worry that his existence undermines their own religious order.
After a trial in which the ape magistrates decide to vivisect and experiment
on George in the name of science, the ape psychologist Dr. Zira (Kim Hunter) liberates George and they flee from Dr. Zaus (Maurice Evans) into the
"forbidden zone." While traveling through the forbidden zone he discovers
the remains of the Statue of Liberty and realizes that they are not on a foreign
planet, but on Earth.

The original *Planet of the Apes* movie was a huge success and led to four
sequels—*Beneath the Planet of the Apes* (1970), *Escape from the Planet of
the Apes* (1971), *Conquest of the Planet of the Apes* (1972) and *Battle for the
Planet of the Apes* (1973). It also produced two short-lived television series
in 1971 and 1975 as well as a 2001 reboot by Tim Burton and the most recent
rebooted trilogy, with the third installment, *War of the Planet of the Apes*,
slated for release in 2017. The series has been ingrained into popular culture

and even people who have never seen these films know the overall plot and can quote classic lines.

The series has symbolized important tensions in American culture. As *Slant* magazine film critic Ed Gonzalez writes,

> Franklin J. Schaffner's 1968 sci-fi classic was an audaciously pulpy, uniquely Serling-esque allegory for racial relations in Civil Rights–era America in which the historical relationship between whites and blacks was reversed. That sly allegory was hatefully perverted by white supremacists, even deemed derogatory by some in the Black Power movement, but its provocation is unmistakable as one directed against the forces of institutionalized racism. (2015)

A similar analysis of the ape-human relationship as being allegorical of race relations in the United States is made by Eric Greene. He notes, "The makers of the *Apes* films also told stories about simians in order to talk about people" (Greene 1998, 5). While Greene correctly notes that the *Apes* films are often about racism in America, non/human primates were symbolically used as stand-ins for people of African descent. This long-standing American cultural practice provides a racialized narrative that suggests people of African descent are humanlike but at the same time not fully human. In this regard, while the symbolism could be viewed as an attempt to criticize white supremacy, the racial politics of the original *Planets* is actually much more complicated. According to Phil Chidester:

> On one hand, *Apes* (1968) actively reinforces contemporary audience members' fears of real-world upheaval and insurgence on the part of the racial Other. Framing its ape characters as analogical counterparts of the Black male, the world unsettles viewers by presenting a speculative future in which the world has been turned upside down in violent, terrifying fashion—a world in which the racial/hegemonic center has been pushed to the fringes and the putative Other has seized the reins of power. On the other hand, while openly promoting White viewers' fears of an impending social destruction and reorganization, *Apes* (1968) also transcends those fears by reassuring audience members that the current hegemonic strata is, in fact, the most appropriate structure for maintaining a sound and functional society. (2015, 7–8)

As Chidester argues, while attempting to engage with white anxiety about a social racial revolution, it did not produce a radical or liberatory vision. Instead the film reinforces many racialized tropes in American society, in effect soothing the audience with the expectant logic of white supremacy and naturalizing the dominant system.

Even though race is central to the *Apes* stories, it is wrong to assume that other important cultural and political topics are not symbolically represented in these films. In fact, most reviews of the 1968 film never mentioned race. Instead, audiences and reviewers interpreted the film as representing human anxiety surrounding the Cold War. These films, which take place on an Earth devastated by nuclear war, show that the violent nature of human society can and will lead to planetary destruction. This view is most clearly stated by Jonathan Kirshner, who suggests the *Apes* films provide a powerful critique of the Cold War consensus around science, military might, and human supremacy (2011, 43–44). Furthermore, the simian characters serve as a metaphor that allows audiences to ponder controversial social and political topics in a way that would not have been possible otherwise.

The newest reboot continues this tradition, as the film uses the narrative to explore a range of important contemporary issues—from war and globalization to animal rights. Rupert Wyatt, the director of the 2011 reboot, implies that the *Rise* and *Dawn* films are primarily about non/human animals rising up against oppression. He claims, "It's a Spartacus story. It's a few apes rising up against their oppressor, but after that it's an escape movie, it's them trying to find paradise" (Masters, 2011). On the surface Wyatt's claim appears true. However, this is because *Rise* and *Dawn* tell the story of Caesar (Andy Serkis), an ape that gained super intelligence after being born to a mother that was experimented on by a pharmaceutical company looking to cure Alzheimer's. Caesar uses his superior intelligence to steal the drug that was used on his mother to enhance the lives of his fellow apes. He liberates apes from their imprisonment in an animal sanctuary, medical lab, and zoo. The newly freed apes escape to the redwood forests of Northern California to build a new society, while humans are simultaneously decimated by a new disease, the simian flu that proliferated as an unintended consequence of the medical experimentation at the lab. As the ape society develops, human society is pushed to the brink of social collapse, and the two sides increasingly are pushed closer and closer to war. In the *Journal of Applied Animal Welfare Science*, John Sorenson argues that the film focuses our attention on the non/human primates, centralizing their concerns, and highlights the violence that humans have done to them (2012, 293). Sorenson contends, "Thoughtful audiences will extrapolate these concerns to other animals and will be encouraged to think about our moral responsibility to all other living beings" (2012, 293). On the surface this claim seems valid, but on closer examination, a new frame emerges that centers the story on humanity. More specifically, the story is about the anxiety liberal Westerners experience in the erosion of human supremacy in the world around them. Much like the original series, the 2011 film highlights the anxiety in the upturning of the racial order. In doing so, the remake plays on human fears of losing their place as the world hegemon. This can be seen in the way that intelligence is defined throughout the film and the connection that is constantly made between violence and intelligence.

A CRITICAL VIEWING OF
DAWN AND *RISE OF THE PLANET OF THE APES*

Anthropocentrism and speciesist logic have been at the core of Western philosophy since Socrates, Plato, and Aristotle, who founded the Western philosophic canon and placed the human at the center of that project. This is most clearly demonstrated by Aristotle's attempt to distinguish humans from other animals by defining them as "political animals." In doing so, Aristotle reserved rationality, reason, language, and politics as inherently human enterprises. This also created a hierarchy that justified human domination over non/human animals, male patriarchal rule, and the Greek slave system. Furthermore, it is the philosophical foundation for European colonialism and the White Man's burden.

This human-centered approach to philosophy and ethics gained momentum throughout the Middle Ages when theologians justified human superiority by arguing that man, not non/human animals, was created in the image of God. Expanding on the medieval "great chain of being," Renaissance thinkers such as Francis Bacon and René Descartes assumed that non/humans lacked souls. As such, they viewed them as instinctual machines that felt no pain, had no emotions, and lacked sentience. The liberal thinker John Locke continued this human-centered understanding in his *Second Treatise*, where he defines animals as property. He states,

> Thus the grass my horse has bit; the turfs my servant has cut; and the ore I have digged in any place, where I have a right to them in common with others, become my property, without the assignation or consent of any body. The labour that was mine, removing them out of that common state they were in, hath fixed my property in them. (1690, ss. 28)

Accordingly, he makes non/humans a form of property and therefore a tool humans can use to expand their dominion over nature. It's therefore unsurprising that these same justifications were used to prop up slavery (Spiegel 1998). Even Karl Marx does everything he can to center the human in his theoretical analysis. In *The German Ideology* and *Capital, Vol. 1*, Marx draws a strict distinction between human and non/human, arguing that only humans *intentionally* and *consciously* alter their environment to fit their needs (1978, 150). The centering of humans in the ethical and political world of philosophy has, of course, continued into the twentieth and twenty-first centuries.

Generally, philosophers have attempted to distinguish humans from non/human animals by asserting that humans possess certain unique traits such as rationality, reason, language, tool use, politics, emotions, self-awareness, and ethics. Over the last century philosophers, anthropologists, biologists, and others have begun chipping away at the supposed wall of human supremacy. At this point, there is no scientific evidence that suggests the existence of any traits that are uniquely human. According to theorists as wide ranging as Donna Haraway and Chad Lavin, the decentering of the human in philosophy and science has led to a cultural anxiety around human superiority (1990; 2013). In this case the films, while centering the story on non/humans, still reinforce speciesism by erasing the lived experience and suffering of real, existing non/human primates.

Intelligence is defined in multiple ways within the two movies but in every instance intelligence is valued according to how closely the apes' behaviors mirror human practices. In the first film, this is clearly shown by the fact that Caesar, until the end, wears human clothes. The wearing of clothes symbolically separates Caesar from other primates so as to demonstrate his resemblance to humans. During Caesar's first day at the primate sanctuary, his shirt is ripped off his back by an angry ape. This action symbolically tears Caesar down and serves as a reminder that he is an ape, not a human. To resist this dehumanizing act, Caesar clutches the scraps of the shirt and uses them as blankets and pillows. Only after he infuses the other apes with the AZ-113 enhancing serum does he let go of the shirt; since all the apes are "becoming human," clothes no longer symbolize his uniqueness from the others.

Even more than the wearing of clothes, the use of language as a measure of intelligence highlights the strong speciesist logic undergirding the films. Caesar's use of sign language as a means of communicating with Dr. Will Rodham (James Franco) in *Rise* parallels the real-world teaching of sign language to non/human primates, which shows their complex intelligence. Communicating his wants and concerns via sign language allows Caesar to have a powerful relationship with Dr. Rodham. In one particular scene, Caesar asks if he is a pet after seeing a dog on a leash. His ability to communicate represents the separation between Caesar and the dog, defining the former as intelligent and the latter as not. The only other ape in *Rise* that uses sign language is an orangutan named Maurice (Karin Konoval), who learned the language when he was previously held captive in a circus. Interestingly, sign language bonds Caesar and Maurice together, as Caesar seems to rejoice in meeting another simian that shares a similar (human) intelligence.

Moreover, the scene in *Rise* between Maurice and Caesar using sign language to communicate foreshadows the acceptance of English sign language as the primary means of communicating between Apes in *Dawn*. In this film, the apes rely on English sign language to communicate among each other even though they already have a complex language. Instead of expanding on their own language, the apes embrace human grammatical structures in an obvious nod to the supremacy of human language. Sign language use makes ape society more human-like, and demonstrates the advanced nature of this new ape society, even though borrowing English sign language is not necessary due to the preexistence of ape language (Plooij, 1978).

The clearest example of measuring intelligence through the use of human language occurs when Caesar forces himself to speak broken English. Caesar first speaks in *Rise* when confronted by an abusive animal sanctuary worker and fights to free his people. In the ensuing fight, while being tased, Caesar stand up fully erect and yells "NO!" Human and ape appear shocked at Caesar's ability to speak, symbolizing how he has surpassed his ape status. In the process of "becoming human," Caesar is empowered to overtake his human oppressors. As the films progress, Caesar speaks more often to where, near the end of *Dawn,* Caesar regularly speaks to Marshall and his human allies. In these scenes, his ability to work with, and be an ally to, human society is predicated on his ability to speak their language. Caesar is proud of his ability to speak and it is one of the reasons that the other apes follow him. Certainly, his ability to speak English is evidence of his superior intelligence over his political rival Koba (Christopher Gordon in *Rise* and Toby Kebbel in *Dawn)*. The use of language as a marker for the apes' supposed intelligence reinforces the earlier philosophical defenses of human supremacy via superior intelligence. Hence, the films do not challenge the hegemony of speciesism, but rather actually reinforce it.

The film also naturalizes destructive human behaviors by showing them as logical outgrowths of "advanced" intelligence. There are three primary ways that this occurs within the films. First, in the final battle scenes in both *Rise* and *Dawn*, the apes ride horses into battle. Thus, using domesticated horses in battle is an example of their newfound intelligence; domestication is a sign of higher-order thinking. This representation serves to justify current human practices of factory farming, medical experimentation, and using non/human animals for war. Once again we find that those non/humans with lesser intelligence become property regardless of whether the species is depicted as dominating or enslaved.

Second, as the apes' intelligence is shown to increase, so does their desire and ability to wage war. In *Dawn*, the apes learn how to use human firearms and explosives, with Koba in particular devising a plan to eradicate the human threat. While Jane Goodall and other primatologists have described instances of real primates going to "war," these wars are more accurately described as fights or skirmishes (Barras 2015). While this does show that humans are not the only species that murders its own, it is a far cry from the genocidal war planned by Koba in *Dawn*. The connection made between war, genocide, and intelligence in the film seems to naturalize human violence to the point of implying that genocide is a byproduct of human intelligence, rather than a socially and politically constructed act.

Finally, the ends of *Rise* and *Dawn* tap into the audience's fear of being colonized by a violent other. The simian flu that devastated 90 percent of the human population between *Rise* and *Dawn* echoes the catastrophic impact of disease that devastated indigenous populations shortly after European contact. *Dawn* connects to the historical narrative of genocide in the Americas and uses this to frame the audience's anxiety related to the ape population. This anxiety compounds when we add into this mix the popular science-fiction trope that intelligent life wants to colonize and conquer. A certain level of guilt concerning settler violence is projected onto the ape population in order to naturalize these anxieties as inherent. This assuages the collective guilt by naturalizing colonization as an inevitable outgrowth of intelligence. In a way, the founding violence and continued colonization of native peoples become depoliticized as European colonizers are no longer held collectively responsible for the act. Instead, colonization becomes a part of not only "human nature," but also, "animal nature" in its entirety.

By naturalizing domestication, war, and colonial genocide, the newest *Apes* films define Western civilization as the apex of human evolution, no matter how negative and destructive that evolution is. Consistently, the films are not about the non/human but about Western society projecting its own anxiety onto the ape protagonists. Ultimately, they are not stories about non/humans overcoming their human oppressors and creating a new world in the forests of the human world. *Dawn* and *Rise* are primarily an expression of Western society's anxiety over the breakdown of human superiority. By assuming that the violence of our current culture is tied to advanced intelligence, the film argues that any species able to challenge human superiority would inevitably attempt to oppress humans in their climb to the top.

The sad outcome of such a violent narrative is that it erases the actual intelligence and sentience that exists throughout this entire planet. The violence that accompanies captivity and experimentation in the film is only represented as horrible because of Caesar's resemblance to an intelligent human. However, one does not need to wear clothes, use sign language, or be able to solve complex puzzles to suffer under human control. Furthermore, the way that intelligence is connected to Western colonization, militarism, and domestication justifies Western superiority over hunter-gather and indigenous cultures. By defining intelligence and superiority in terms of technology, war, and colonial violence, the claim that Western civilization is more "advanced" and evolved then these "primitive" counterparts is further reinforced.

Overall, a real *Planet of the Apes*, in which human society is decentered from the ethical, political, and social measure of the world, would not be one in which apes simply replace humans as the hegemonic oppressor. Instead, what animal liberationists need to do is develop a world in which there is no hegemonic oppressor and in which species can exist in a reciprocal relationship with each other. This world can only be seen as a dystopian future if one sees human supremacy as foundational to one's identity.

REFERENCES

Barras, Colin. 2014. "Only Known Chimp War Reveals How Societies Splinter." *New Scientist* 222(2968): 12. https://www.newscientist.com/article/mg22229682.600-only-known-chimp-war-reveals-how-societies-splinter.

Battle for the Planet of the Apes. 1973. Directed by J. Lee Thompson. Twentieth Century Fox. DVD.

Beneath the Planet of the Apes. 1970. Directed by Ted Post. Twentieth Century Fox. DVD.

Chidester, Phil. 2015. "The Simian That Screamed "No!": Rise of the Planet of the Apes and the Speculative as Public Memory." *Visual Communication Quarterly* 22(1): 3–14.

Conquest for the Planet of the Apes. 1972. Directed by J. Lee Thompson. Twentieth Century Fox. DVD.

Dawn of the Planet of the Apes. 2014. Directed by Matt Reeves. Twentieth Century Fox. DVD.

Escape from the Planet of the Apes. 1971. Directed by Don Taylor. Twentieth Century Fox. DVD.

Gonzalez, Ed. 2015. "Rise of the Planet of the Apes." *Slant Magazine*, August 27. http://www.slantmagazine.com/film/review/rise-of-the-planet-of-the-apes.

Greene, Eric, and Richard Slotkin. 1998. *Planet of the Apes as American Myth: Race, Politics, and Popular Culture.* Hanover, NH: Wesleyan University Press.

Haraway, Donna Jeanne. 1989. *Primate Visions: Gender, Race, and Nature in the World of Modern Science.* New York: Routledge.

Joy, Melanie. 2011. *Why We Love Dogs, Eat Pigs, and Wear Cows: An Introduction to Carnism.* Newburyport, MA: Conari Press.

Kirshner, Jonathan. 2011. "Subverting the Cold War in the 1960s: *Dr. Strangelove, The Manchurian Candidate,* and *The Planet of the Apes.*" *Film & History: An Interdisciplinary Journal of Film and Television Studies* 31(2): 40–44.

Lavin, Chad. 2013. *Eating Anxiety: The Perils of Food Politics.* Minneapolis: University of Minnesota Press.

Locke, John, and C. B. Macpherson. 1690. (1980). *Second Treatise of Government.* Indianapolis: Hackett. http://public.eblib.com/choice/publicfullrecord.aspx?p=583977.

Masters, Tim. 2011. "*Rise of the Apes* Movie Holds a Mirror to Humanity." *BBC*, August 11. http://www.bbc.com/news/entertainment-arts-14480098.

People for the Ethical Treatment of Animals. n.d. "*Rise of the Planet of the Apes.*" http://www.peta.org/features/rise-planet-apes/.

Planet of the Apes. 1968. Directed by Franklin J. Shaffner. Twentieth Century Fox. DVD.

Planet of the Apes. 2001. Directed by Tim Burton. Twentieth Century Fox. DVD.

Plooij, Frans X. 1978 "Some Basic Traits of Language in Wild Chimpanzees?" in *Action, Gesture and Symbol,* edited by Andrew Lock. New York: Academic Press.

Rise of the Planet of the Apes. 2011. Directed by Rupert Wyatt. Twentieth Century Fox. DVD.

Rogin, Michael. 1988. *Ronald Reagan the Movie: And Other Episodes in Political Demonology.* Berkeley: University of California Press.

Sorenson, John. 2012. "Two Films: A Review of *Rise* of *the Planet of the Apes* and *Project Nim.*" *Journal of Applied Animal Welfare Science* 15(3): 289–293.

Spiegel, Marjorie. 1997. *The Dreaded Comparison: Human and Animal Slavery.* Stamford, CT: Mirror Books.

Taylor, Nik. 2011. "Rise of the Planet of the Apes—'Human, All Too Human.'" *The Guardian*, Friday 19. http://www.theguardian.com/science/blog/2011/aug/19/rise-planet-apes-animal-rights.

Tucker, Robert C., Karl Marx, and Friedrich Engels. 1978. *The Marx-Engels Reader.* New York: Norton.

Chapter 8

The Vicious Cycle of Disnification and Audience Demands: Representations of the Non/Human in Martin Rosen's *Watership Down* (1978) and *The Plague Dogs* (1982)

Anja Höing and Harald Husemann

In 1982, the director Martin Rosen dared an extraordinary experiment: he created a non-anthropocentric animated animal picture. This movie, an adaptation of Richard Adams's novel *The Plague Dogs*, continuously subverts stereotypical portrayals of non/humans. Consequently, it successfully presents a passionate outcry against human indifference toward non/human animals. Unfortunately, it was an outcry doomed to fade away unheard. Despite excellent reviews, the picture was a failure at the box office and today is nearly forgotten (Wise 1985, 54). In contrast, Rosen's 1978 *Watership Down* presents a rather conventional animated animal picture. Deemed one of the most successful British pictures of its time, *Watership Down* was also adapted into a television series (Beckett 2009, 108). This chapter will explore differences between the two animated pictures regarding the setting, character representation, and the journey pattern to highlight how *The Plague Dogs* undermines traditional modes of representation in animated pictures. Insights gathered from differing public responses to the two films aid in highlighting the preconceptions of non/human animals present in Rosen's work. While viewer preference for what Steve Baker terms "disnification" reinforces an anthropocentric ideology in *Watership Down*, the anti-speciesist cinematic model used to create the virtually forgotten *The Plague Dogs* could be inspiring to filmmakers (Baker 2001, 174). This is true for those interested in ecological justice studies, cultural animal studies, or non/human advocacy and activism. Moreover, for modern viewers, the message of the film demonstrates how an animated non/human animal picture can challenge anthropocentric bias and ideologies that are still prevalent in society today.

Many visual representations of non/humans follow a code that continuously models how people preconceive non/humans (Baker 2001, 174–176). In *Picturing the Beast*, Steve Baker states, "the animal is the sign of all that is taken not-very-seriously in contemporary culture" (174). The term he coins to describe the phenomenon is "the *disnification* of the animal" (174). Baker states, "the basic procedure of disnification is to render [the animal] stupid by rendering it visual" (174). Therefore, disnification is also "common sense's construction of the visual reality of the animal" (177). This includes processes such as "neotenization" (174), or, extending the term beyond non/humans, an oversimplification of nature into an edenic idyll as happens in Disney's *Bambi* (Whitley 2008, 63). Baker, however, draws a clear line between the deliberate presentation of non/humans in Disney movies, "Disneyfication," and disnification, stating that the latter refers to "the connotations of trivialization and belittlement which are a central and intentional part of the everyday adjectival use of terms like 'Disney'" (2001, 174). As a result of continuous exposure to "disnification" audiences tend to prefer animated pictures that adhere to such codes. Subsequently, it becomes economically disadvantageous to depict human-induced non/human suffering in animated pictures.

Rosen's two films are both adaptations of novels by the British author Richard Adams and similar in many respects; they portray talking non/human characters searching for new homes. *Watership Down* is the story of a herd of rabbits forced into an exodus-like journey to establish a new colony after the destruction of their home by humans. *The Plague Dogs* tells the story of two dogs, the terrier Snitter and the black mongrel Rowf, who escape from a vivisection lab and aimlessly wander the Lake District, incapable of surviving in nature, but equally unable to return to humans, because the media (incorrectly) claim that they are infected with bubonic plague. As I will argue, *Watership Down* follows the standards of disnification more closely than *The Plague Dogs*. However, this is not to imply that *Watership Down* is a thoroughly disnified run-of-the-mill picture. Both of Rosen's films share a unique style, including many unconventional elements such as the graphic portrayal of violence that Schwebel, discussing animated pictures for adults, rightly claims broke a taboo (2010, 58). According to literary critic Sandra Beckett, the violent scenes disturbed many audience members (2009, 108).

Yet the first impression a moviegoer might get of *Watership Down* is not one of violence. Quite the contrary: *Watership Down* takes place in a peaceful agricultural landscape with smooth transitions and fading, non-aggressive colors, frequently accentuated by minutely drawn wildflowers. Additionally, other non/humans present in the film such as bumblebees, butterflies, flocks of birds, and cows grazing in the meadow represent a rural paradise. The rabbits travel to their new home on the Downs, moving through this beautiful scenery. Both the rabbits on screen and the audience members watching are likely taking this tranquility for granted. Peter Hunt states that in the book *Watership Down* "virtually the whole of human 'civilization' disappears" (1987, 13). This is even truer in Rosen's film. There appear to be no villages, no motorways, and no industry. The place is a rural Arcadia reminiscent of the pastoral nostalgia of Kenneth Grahame's *The Wind in the Willows*. The pastoral is a "trope . . . deeply entrenched in Western culture" (Garrard 2012, 36). It is even more so in English fantasy where one can place *Watership Down* (Hunt 1987, 12). The pastoral impression is enhanced by the partly fantastic weather that, true to Gothic tradition, reflects the ups and downs of the rabbits' journey. Mostly the weather is fine, and the blue-white sky is almost always underlined by a yellowish-pink glow across the horizon. In its reduction of "'land' into 'landscape,'" the pastoral is both necessarily anthropocentric and "deeply problematic for environmentalism" (Gifford 2002, 55, 58; Garrard 2012, 36). In the surreal land-turned-landscape, the natural world turns into an image of the Golden Age firmly situated in the realm of fantasy and, therefore, unthreatened. In this setting, the non/human becomes a trope, but in gaining metaphorical value it loses its non/human "animal" identity and value. Both non/human characters and setting melt into a single metaphor for perseverance and hope. This further shifts importance away from the non/human as "animal" to the non/human representing the human plight of finding one's place in the world. Reduced to this metaphorical dimension, the non/humans slip from the range the concept of non/human animal advocacy can touch. Only a real non/human can have a claim to rights, a metaphor cannot.

    The Plague Dogs in contrast is "a world apart from Disney's bright-colored, sentimental fables" (Wise 1985, 53). The background of the film is in "the dark earth-tones of wet turf, rain clouds, and fast muddy streams" (53). Scenes are frequently set at night and disturbingly dark. In day scenes, bleak moors blend into dreary mountains that melt into a gray-white sky, and drifts of fog blur the borders in between. The two fugitive dogs visually get lost in this landscape. The human audience literally loses sight of the non/ humans. Snitter and Rowf move between the sharp lines of cracks and rock promontories, not between soft hills and hedges. The dogs cannot find safety, let alone comfort in these "untamed landscapes" of wilderness (Garrard 2012, 67). As domesticated creatures, they are as estranged from nature as the humans they run from. *The Plague Dogs* graphically shows this in the contrast between the colors of the setting and the bicolored fur of the terrier, Snitter. While the brown rabbits of *Watership Down* melt into the pastoral landscape of the Downs, Snitter's almost garish whiteness disrupts the shad-

owy Lake District. It is clear that Snitter does not belong there and cannot possibly survive in the long term. This technique of deliberately breaking the unity between setting and character challenges "common sense" and achieves an effect almost opposed to disnification (Baker 2001, 177). Alienating the non/human protagonist from the setting highlights the importance of the former, and forces the audience to take the animated non/human seriously. *The Plague Dogs* intensifies this technique in the representation of other non/humans as well. Sheep wandering the moors are not picturesque scenery; rather they are prey soon to be turned into grim carcasses circled by bluebottles, not butterflies. Flocks of birds are either shooting targets for human characters or scatter once the heroes enter the scene. The exceptions to this rule are birds of prey or scavengers that observe the starving protagonists from a distance. This is the grim predatory nature of the animal kingdom, neither idealized nor belittled.

Another technique that deliberately breaks the unity between setting and character is using non/humans sarcastically. One such sarcastic scene involves a ballet-like choreography of jumping frogs that effortlessly escape Snitter's hunting attempts. Audiences familiar with Disney films may find themselves laughing during this scene. That is, until they realize that what appears to be comic relief is actually a starving dog unable to catch an easy prey. In this scene, *The Plague Dogs* deliberately employs modes of disnification to challenge what Baker describes as the "common view that almost anything to do with animals is somehow funny" (2001, 23).

The pattern sketched above repeats itself in the presentation of characters. The rabbit heroes of *Watership Down* contain many elements typical of animated non/humans. Although the characters hop and run, many of their gestures are anthropomorphized, and their bodily appearance is drawn in rounded lines. As Disney animators Thomas and Johnston state, characters in *Bambi* were drawn according to "what people imagine a deer looks like" (1981, 332). Animators deliberately created idealized non/humans to make them credible as characters with personality (332). Rosen's animators seem to apply the same technique, using oversized heads and ears, the latter overly rounded and neotenized. Equally striking is the characters' eyes-to-face ratio. To portray emotions Rosen uses far huger than natural rabbit eyes ("*Watership Down*—A Conversation with the Film Makers"). Yet this happens at the cost of verisimilitude. Verisimilitude in general is a problem with using rabbit characters in an animated picture: When one draws wild rabbits naturalistically, it is difficult to tell them apart. Rosen addresses this issue when he asks, "The question I had was . . . do I make each character the equivalent of putting a funny hat on so you could tell the difference between them?" ("*Watership Down*—A Conversation with the Film Makers"). The animators of *Watership Down* solve this conundrum by placing "natural" hats on some characters. One rabbit wears a cap of fur; another wears black on its entire head. This gives the characters a sense of individuality, but also de-naturalizes them. This is not to imply that authenticity is necessary to avoid disnification. Rather, what triggers disnification in *Watership Down* is not that the rabbits do not look like real rabbits, but that the rabbits look like cuddly toys. Again, this prompts the viewer to perceive the non/human as exclusively a metaphor. Baker discusses a comparable case of a teddy-bear-looking character, Rupert the Bear, to suggest that across the range of critical literature there is a sad tendency to presuppose "in such stories the . . . pictorial image of the animal does not signify 'animal' at all" (2001, 136).

The Plague Dogs, on the other hand, is characterized by a different drawing style. Reviewer Naomi Wise aptly states, "The canine heroes have testicles, anuses" and "are drawn with such painstaking naturalism that their flesh wrinkles when they lift their legs" (1985, 53; 54). Their illustrative forms are jagged lines, and when the dogs are starving, the viewer can see their protruding ribs. Cuteness is the one feature these characters are visibly lacking, making it difficult to apply conventional categories of making sense, or, using Baker's terminology, "making-nonsense" of them (2001, 175).

Another noteworthy difference between the films is the way wounds are drawn and the length of time injuries stay visible on the screen. Both films do not shy away from showing blood; however, wounds heal faster in *Watership Down*. Where wounds are not essential to the plot, they soon disappear. Healing is dealt with differently in *The Plague Dogs*. For instance, the scientists in the laboratory perform experimental brain surgery on Snitter. At first Snitter wears a cap, but once his cap comes loose, a huge and ugly scar from the vivisection is glaringly visible, a constant reminder of his torture in the lab. Rowf's wounds are psychological rather than physical. In the opening scene of the film, Rowf is forced to endure a conditioning experiment in which the scientists repeatedly put him into a deep water tank and wait for him to sink out of exhaustion to re-animate him and repeat the experiment. In consequence, Rowf is emotionally disturbed and mentally damaged: he is mortally afraid of humans and water. These wounds, too, never heal. Hence, the protagonists neither look heroic nor do they always behave heroically— but they neither look nor behave in stereotypical ways. Without the presence of stereotypical images, the audience is likely to rely on the ones most familiar. The only way to make sense of these characters is to accept them as images of real non/humans.

Regarding the presentation of villains, even greater differences between the films emerge upon closer analysis. In *Watership Down*, the villain Woundwort is visually coded as dark, huge and disfigured. Unusual coloring around his eyes makes him seem unnatural, even disturbing. His henchrabbits are less imposing, skinny copies of himself with scraggly fur and ripped ears, always clawing and showing teeth. When the rabbits fall victim to a nightly attack by rats, they too are drawn as all teeth and claws and so black they blend with the background. Despite being different, these villainous characters share two common denominators; they are easy to identify as villains and reside inside the characters' black-and-white world. Animators, especially from Disney, and filmmakers like Rosen, often use color symbolism to describe a simple binary of good and evil, where light colors translate as "good" and "pure" and blackness is "associated with night and death" (Whitley 2008, 20-21). In such a Disney fairy tale world, good is always victorious (Zipes 1997, 5). The image of the cute non/human operates as a metaphorical placeholder for "the good" and "the natural" (Whitley 2008, 20). Thus, non/humans become abstract concepts the audience can identify with, but not related to, "real" non/humans.

Rosen uses many of these techniques in his second film, *The Plague Dogs*. However, instead of applying them to villains as in *Watership Down*, they apply to the hero, Snitter's companion, Rowf. Rowf is a black dog, a color Disney films frequently relate to corruption, alienation, and decay, according to Whitley's classification (2008, 21). Additionally, as a black dog in a nocturnal setting, Rowf is so dark it is sometimes difficult to see him. Thomas and Johnston state that "a black dog . . . [is] almost impossible" to realize in an animated film, because he/she can easily "[go] too dark to see any detail or facial expression" (1981, 268). This is precisely what happens to Rowf. His expression often remains hidden, which renders him somewhat detached and difficult to connect with. Sometimes, however, it is possible to observe Rowf's facial expressions, most notably his eyes that openly show negative emotions such as aversion and hatred. Such negative emotions easily relate to the symbolism of Rowf's black fur, but not to his status as a hero.

From the very beginning of the film, viewers are conditioned to be wary of Rowf through a scene using extremely short clips that shift between Rowf, Snitter, and a nightmare-like apparition of wolf-like monsters. Snitter cowers on the ground in a panic, while Rowf, whose imagination conjured up the vision, walks toward the camera with his teeth bared. In each lightning-short shot, Rowf gets closer, until there is a close-up of his face; his eyes bloodshot and sparkling mad. In this scene, Rowf enacts all the negative aspects commonly associated with blackness in a Disney movie and consequently looks more evil and menacing than Woundwort in *Watership Down* ever could (Whitley 2008, 21). The shot is visible for no more than a second, and the only way to *look* at it is by watching the film in slow motion. Nonetheless, it is precisely the extreme shortness of the shot that might cement uneasiness in the audience, because the experience happens on an almost subliminal level. The shot is comparable to a single-frame advertisement in which an image flashes on screen for only the duration of a single picture frame, so that the audience is not consciously aware that they saw it.

Evil in *Watership Down* is easy to identify and thus easy to analyze; simply put, it is the fairy tale evil of a black-and-white fantasy world. In contrast, despite having a ubiquitous presence, evil in *The Plague Dogs* is nearly impossible to pinpoint. The two half-starved, ambiguous protagonists struggle through the darkness and cold of a world in which they do not belong. Unknown forces hunt them, and without the wit of the *Watership Down* rabbits, the dogs are incapable of understanding what is happening to them. The main evil in *The Plague Dogs* does not come from inside the characters' world, but from outside. The dogs never stand a chance of survival. Responsibility for their hardship cannot be easily cast on a single "bad" character. Rather, blame rests with the all-to-real unwritten codes of Western society and its non-caring attitude toward non/human suffering; a mind-set viewers are likely to recognize in themselves. The film deviates from the codes of disnification and in doing so frees the non/human protagonist from its stereotypical metaphoric dimension.

To illustrate that some characters possess noble qualities, Disney animators such as Thomas and Johnston follow a set of rules for drawing non/human characters. They claim, "the 'good guys' have to be small, ineffectual, cute and associated with nonviolence. It doesn't matter if the real animal is that way or not. You are playing off images in the viewers' subconscious" (1981, 344). Rosen's hero Rowf breaks all these rules. As a result, he operates on the subconscious level of the viewer in an even more efficient manner. It is easy to pity Rowf's predicament, but he is neither cute nor is he associated with non-violence. Quite the contrary: viewers are confronted with a large, shaggy and violent black dog, who snarls and bites; a character who, according to non/human animal animation standards, is coded as a traditional villain. However, Rowf is shaggy because he is starving, and he snarls and bites because his prior experience in the lab taught him that humans only intend to do him harm. Instead of appearing as a black-or-white fairy tale creature, Rowf gains credibility as a unique individual. Individuality of each living being is a central belief informing a biocentric worldview that demands general acceptance of all organisms as "unique individual[s] pursuing [their] own good in [their] own way" (Taylor 2001, 100). Pursuing his own good in his own way is precisely what Rowf is doing.

Building on this foundation, biocentrism urges humans to recognize the "inherent worth" of all beings and to acknowledge them as "worthy of respect" no matter if the non/humans are moral agents by themselves (71–72). The same claim also lies at the heart of animal rights advocacy, like that of Peter Singer's *Animal Liberation* and its focus on the suffering of each non/human being. Respect for the individuality of each being, human or non/human, is an indispensable step that necessarily needs to precede any possible change in human behavior toward the non/human world (Singer 1975, 172). Building Rowf as an individual character, not altogether likable, but with inherent worth, *The Plague Dogs* urges for a biocentric rethinking of human relationships to non/humans, and especially to those non/humans who are our companions.

Another interesting component for analysis is exploring how human characters are presented in both films. In *Watership Down,* human interference is mainly rendered through voices and machines so that it appears metaphoric. When humans shoot the hero Hazel, they appear as farm hands in Wellington boots, talking in rural English dialect. These humans are not "bad"; they are just doing their jobs of frightening off the marauding rabbits. Moreover, although they hurt the hero, he easily recovers and even gains crucial wisdom from the experience. In *The Plague Dogs*, on the other hand, humans are often presented using techniques that provoke uneasiness. They appear demonic, faceless, or as shadows on the wall. The eyes of the scientists experimenting on Rowf hide behind their reflecting glasses, leaving the discomforting impression that there are no souls behind the empty mirrors. Phone calls and news reports are often blended in as voice-overs while the camera follows the journey of the dogs. In Adams's book *The Plague Dogs,* humans are complex characters whose struggle to minimize personal damage and maximize personal gain leads them to fight out their intra-human battle on the dogs' backs (Höing 2015, 72–73). In Rosen's adaptation, however, humans turn into an unfathomable mass. While Rosen individualizes the non/humans, he de-individualizes the humans.

Thus, humans appear as forces superimposed on the world while the non/humans struggling through the forbidding landscape are oblivious to the greater evil building up around them. No human is singled out as an adversary, rather each human character adds a little egoism or indifference, spurring a chain reaction that culminates in the complete destruction of the non/human heroes. Herein, *The Plague Dogs* is allegorical of the current environmental crisis. Humans often do not realize the remote damage they cause through small acts such as throwing plastic litter into nature, where it might enter the food chain and potentially choke birds. They only notice the little personal gain of not having to carry their litter with them until they find a litter bin. The culmination of such small acts of indifference committed by millions of people leads to devastating ecological consequences that are often too vast and remote for individuals to feel responsible for (e.g., global warming). Precisely the same chain of events happens in *The Plague Dogs.* Yet, the picture focuses on the devastating consequences that collective indifference has on the individual as well, and in doing so renders them visible.

Rosen constructs a human-non/human companion relationship similar to Donna Haraway's making-sense of the domesticated dog in *The Companion Species Manifesto* (2003). Haraway reads the dog-human relationship as "cohabitation," "co-evolution," and "cross-species sociality" and accordingly urges humans to recognize the mutual evolutionary and cultural bonds tying together dogs and themselves (4). Rosen's *The Plague Dogs* presents these points from a unidirectional perspective. The dogs are instinctively aware of the multiple evolutionary bonds that connect the species and drive them to continuously search for social companionship with humans. The humans, in contrast, do not acknowledge their part of the bond, although they could act to remedy the disturbed relationship.

Perhaps the most effective way *The Plague Dogs* ruptures the stereotypes and metaphors is through the heroes' journey. Again, it is worth analyzing *Watership Down* first, because it retains conventional patterns that may serve to highlight dissimilarities. Several scholars such as Celia Anderson and Gillian Adams discuss the resemblances between the book *Watership Down* and classical epics. While Anderson focuses on *Watership Down* as a retelling of the *Aeneid*, Adams discusses its parallels to the *Odyssey* and the *Iliad* (1983, 12; 1986, 108). Equally self-evident are references to the biblical Exodus. The epic patterns and direct references to Joseph Campbell's *The Hero with a Thousand Faces*, in Gillian Adams's words, "invite the reader to apply a specific reading" to the rabbits' journeys (108). *Watership Down* is, in fact, a metaphorical myth that claims to be nothing more than this. The film, which reads very close to the book, likewise follows the stages of Campbell's monomyth. Campbell claims that whichever tale we follow, "it will be always the one, shape-shifting yet marvellously constant story" of a hero on an archetypal quest (1971, 3). In this universal journey the hero receives "a call to adventure," passes "threshold[s]" into unknown realms, has to suffer "trials," and finally emerges as "master of the two worlds" he has traversed (51, 77, 97, 229). The archetypal heroic quest is a pattern so well established in children's movies that it is most likely very familiar to audiences. It may also be a category that viewers can access by "common sense," and is now trivial from overuse (Baker 2001, 177). As a result, viewers may be inclined to read the images according to pre-established categories. As Anderson states, the rabbits in Adams's book take on "both epic and allegorical proportions," however, at least in this regard, these are not non/human proportions (1983, 12).

The Plague Dogs likewise contains some elements of Campbell's monomyth. However, the film also builds on a second, far less accessible theme. As Collado Rodriguez points out, Adams's novel is deeply influenced by Carl Gustav Jung's theory of the collective unconscious (1988, 52). Interestingly, Rosen uses the collective unconscious as his trope to guide the entire plot of the film. Wise notes that "a single metaphor . . . is developed throughout the length of the movie: the opening shot is of a laboratory tank, the dogs travel through the streaming wetlands of the Lake Country, and the journey concludes at the North Sea" (1985, 54). Water represents an additional dimension as the element Jung singles out as central to enabling one's return to the collective unconscious. In his words, water is not merely metaphorical, but "a living symbol of the dark psyche" (1981, 17). In the final scene of the movie, Rowf and Snitter swim into the ocean to escape humans hunting them, en route to the unreachable island of safe religious dogma Jung characterizes as taming or even subduing the immediate experience of the collective unconscious. Not only do they turn away from the shore, but they also face themselves for the first time. By this time, the viewers have been forced to let go of all categories in which they "ordinarily make sense of" animated non/humans (Baker 2001, 177). They find themselves in the same position as the dogs: they have to face themselves. They have to confront their pre-conceptions of animated non/humans and their shared responsibility for the mistreatment—and finally, the death—of non/humans. The film ends almost exactly as it began: with the sound of splashing water; however, the viewers now witness two dogs drowning, instead of one as in the opening scene.

In the archetypal journey of the hero sketched in Campbell's monomyth, and likewise in *Watership Down*, a continuous progression occurs. The hero returns home more powerful, wiser, and better equipped to handle formerly insurmountable problems. In contrast, the non/human heroes of *The Plague Dogs* end up not only physically defeated, but mentally broken as well. Even Snitter, whose hopeful motivation after escape is to find a "master" to care for him, by the end gives up any illusions of human kindness. The message embodied in this film suggests that a domesticated dog is not "(hu)man's best friend," but rather at a human's mercy. In the world of *The Plague Dogs*, human compassion does not exist. Thus, one might even go so far as to call the ending a *re*gression. The defeat of the dogs forcefully reinforces that real non/humans cannot cope like the non/human characters of most other animated pictures can.

Watership Down, on the other hand, retains the conventional happy ending. All enemies are defeated, and the hero Hazel dies of old age and enters a new life in rabbit heaven. The supernatural entity leading him into rabbit heaven even assures him that he does not need to fear for his descendants. Hazel, therefore, knows that a "static" world of pastoral nostalgia will continue (Gifford 2002, 58). Despite some cruel passages, *Watership Down* is a "feel-good movie" that follows typical conventions of fairy tales. It is set in a beautiful secondary world, frozen in time, where everything turns out well in the end. A romantic representation such as this suggests that non/human animals either live in a closed reality that humans cannot enter, or assumes humans do not *need* to enter because the non/humans can cope. It implies that the viewer can be passive, and not take responsibility for harms humans inflict. Assumedly, this Nature-turned-into-Arcadia world can regenerate eternal stability and balance and will solve its problems on its own. Such a worldview is invitingly simple, and, therefore, comforting to the audience—but it is also dangerous. This construction of human-non/human relationships is detrimental to both ecological and non/human concerns, as it idealizes a metaphor of what humans *want* the non/human to be, rather than what it *is*.

Baker, adopting Lyotard's postmodern stance, warns that "no creative reevaluation of human or animal identity is likely to emerge from representations that present the animal primarily as matter for human 'solace and pleasure'" (2001, xxi). One could even go a step further and state that as long as non/human identity is represented as metaphor, non/humans will never be understood as "real"—and one might argue, a metaphor does not need advocacy or activism.

Regarding *Watership Down*, one could even widen this claim to representations of nature. Nature, as a form of pastoral, tamed landscape represents the same idea of "solace and pleasure" as the non/human animal characters (Baker 2001, xxi). This parallel forms a convenient dualistic opposition to an equally arbitrary category of "culture." Such an understanding of the human-nature relationship cements what Colleen Clements terms the "fairy tale ideal of an ecosystem of achieved and unchanging harmony" (quoted in Garrard 2012, 64). In this ideal conception, nature is opposed to human cultural space and erroneously perceived as a *perpetuum mobile*, which will continue forever without any input of energy (or human effort) necessary to keep it going. Such a stark separation between nature/non-humans and culture/humans reinforces anthropocentric ideology, as it negates both the animal identity of humans and human cultures' inseparable interdependence with natural systems (Plumwood 1993, 6). Meanwhile, the biocentric worldview posits humans and all cultural practices as an integral part of nature and therefore as operating inside its system—in both destructive and supportive ways (Taylor 2011, 99–100).

Richard Adams's novel *The Plague Dogs* ends happily just as *Watership Down* does. Rowf and Snitter are saved in the very last second (R. Adams 1978, 444). Wise comments that in the tragic ending of the film adaptation "Martin Rosen . . . substitut[es] the touching conclusion demanded by the logic of the story" (1985, 54). This is certainly justified, yet her previous claim that Adams's original ending is "spurious" is in need of differentiation (54). Adams's book already makes the miraculous rescue of the dogs appear as a deliberate, cynical critique of the genre rather than an intentional ending. The sudden happy ending seems superimposed on the novel, as if first to present readers with the logical conclusion of the non/human plight—death—and then to throw in their face the illogical happy ending they demand. However, in the book, readers are free to choose. They can take the "drowning" ending for real, as Collado Rodriguez does, or the second one, as Wise apparently did in her harsh criticism of Adams's original ending (1988, 52–53). There is no such choice in Rosen's movie. In what Wise terms an "inexorable tragedy," the story follows the dogs' plight from its cruel beginning to its inevitable ending (1985, 54). The non/human animal does not stand the slightest chance to survive in a non-disnified world.

The Plague Dogs is a movie likely to haunt its audience long after a viewing simply because the atypical tragic ending leaves the story unresolved and open for the audience to contend with. The film defies all standard motifs that disnify animated non/humans in its portrayal of two starving canine protagonists struggling through a dreary world that is reminiscent of the Jungian collective unconscious. While the metaphoric creatures of *Watership Down* are able to cope with just about anything life throws in their path, the dogs in *The Plague Dogs* need assistance. Moreover, while *Watership Down* is clearly characterized as a fairy tale, *The Plague Dogs*, just as clearly, is not. What is more, human indifference to non/human suffering turns into a danger far greater than the single villain in *Watership Down*. Such an evil is, indeed, ungraspable, and therefore, invisible for the characters who do not possess a single spark of fairy-tale-animal wittiness. Instead of witnessing what they expected, they are confronted with the devastating effects of anthropocentric ideology on a domesticated species entirely dependent upon human consideration and protection. Viewers may expect to experience an animated picture that adheres to the codes of disnification and thus reaffirms their anthropocentric worldview, but instead are challenged to consider the inherent injustice and urged to adopt a biocentric alternative.

The final chapter of Baker's *Picturing the Beast* discusses possible strategies of visualizing the non/human that could be useful to those interested in drawing attention to the sufferings of non/human animals. One such strategy he suggests is appropriating Disney images (230). *The Plague Dogs* ingeniously infuses the "naturally" innocent animated animal picture with situations that real non/humans are likely to encounter. In fact, the very first scene the audience is confronted with is one of Rowf fighting for his life in a filthy water tank, while scientists impassively stop the time he can keep his head above water. When Snitter and Rowf run through the lab during their escape, the film also shows other animals suffering, such as a monkey clasped in contraptions and seemingly bodiless rabbit heads sticking out of boxes. Witnessing an animated non/human in this predicament may be more disturbing because viewers may not expect nor want to see real-life scenarios depicted in animation. In a daring experiment, *The Plague Dogs* depicts non/human experiences hardly explored in this genre and repeatedly challenges long-established patterns that render the non/human invisible and insignificant.

In opposition to this, *The Plague Dogs* forces its audience into a new mode of interpreting non/human characters. Instead of "making nonsense," the audience has to make sense of them (Baker 2001, 175). Unlike the metaphorical rabbits in *Watership Down*, Snitter and Rowf appear all too real, and symbolic only of the non/human itself. This enforces a rethinking of the categories that typically apply to non/human protagonists in animated pictures and other cultural productions. The standard approach portrays the non/human as a metaphor for the human, it anthropocentrizes whatever context the non/human appears in, or in Baker's words, "den[ies] the animal" (2001, 136). Making sense of the non/human might be extremely uncomfortable for the audience, yet, is necessary from a non/human animal advocacy and ecological justice perspective. Any re-contextualization of stereotypes—which is necessary to change the contemporary Western ideology regarding the non/human environment—can only begin once people dare to question what they previously took for granted, which requires stepping outside of their comfort zone.

Underlying this is a problematic essentialist notion. In our culture, people tend to define the world in dualisms such as nature versus culture, non/human versus human, and metaphor versus real. Such dualist notions "naturalise gender, class race and nature oppressions" (Plumwood 43). In the latter case, the dualisms separate humans from the rest of the natural world in a binary opposition and thus form a basis for anthropocentric thought. Such dualisms are often grouped into equally anthropocentric standard networks of interconnection: "culture" and "human" are presented as "real," or as a tenor of a cultural production, while "nature" and "non/human" are read as metaphoric mediums. In short: whenever "nature" and "non/human" appear in a cultural production such as an animated picture, the standard (anthropocentric) way to read them would be to understand both nature and the non/human as metaphors for a human condition, not as a tenor in themselves. This would, for example, be a convenient reading for *Watership Down*. As I discussed above, the rabbits' journey can easily be understood as a metaphor for the general quest for finding one's place in the world. *The Plague Dogs*, in contrast, *cannot* be read in this way. This picture tries to break the dualist bias by dissolving both the essentialist notions themselves and their traditional relation to one another. In Rosen's picture, nature and culture cannot be clearly separated but merge in the concept of the culturally-formed non/human domesticated animal. This nature/culture chimera becomes real, or, if metaphoric, then metaphoric of the struggle not of humans, but of non/humans. In consequence, it is impossible for the viewers to go the easy way and read the non/human as a metaphor for the human. It is the non/humans who are real.

These observations offer an additional and, unfortunately, discouraging pattern to explain the widely differing success of the movies. Audiences may not want to witness images of realistic, suffering non/human animals aimlessly wandering in a bleak world in desperate need of human aid that will never come. Viewers may anticipate beautiful landscapes lit by eternal sunrise, where cute, witty creatures hop toward eternal harmony. They demand evil to be easy to recognize and adequately defeated. Most important, viewers never want evil to touch or influence their own world. In short, they demand their ideological foundations be affirmed, not attacked. Studios, dependent upon consumerist culture for their financial success, supply the pictures that audiences demand. In the words of Disney's animators: "It was the audiences who selected the cute, round, anthropomorphic animals with rich personalities as the type of characters they liked best" (Thomas and Johnston 1981, 509). Accordingly, these are the non/human characters that Disney and many other animation studios produced and continue to produce.

When *The Plague Dogs* failed at the box office, Wise was quick to assert that the "Disney Syndrome" was likely the reason (1985, 54). Rosen's ambitious project to disrupt disnified representation of animated non/humans would have likely succeeded if viewers were open to new perspectives—but, unfortunately, viewers seemed unable or unwilling to adopt such perspectives. Such a close relation between audience demands and the production of animated pictures is the starting point of a vicious cycle. By providing a single image only, this image becomes cemented in the audience's imagination. This pre-conceptualization of Baker's "disnified" animal and disnified nature is repeatedly reinforced to the point where audiences reject any unfamiliar images such as the non-disnified heroes of Rosen's second animated picture. Critical reviews praised *The Plague Dogs*—but the cinemas were empty (Wise 1985, 54).

For many directors, visualizing human-induced non/human suffering in animated pictures therefore becomes impossible. This is especially true for suffering that is not retraceable to single characters branded as villains, but to anthropocentric structures deeply embedded in Western Euro–US centric culture—structures the viewers themselves are likely to find realized in their own life. The absence of far-reaching cinematic dialogues that challenge speciesism perpetuates human supremacy, through confirmation of pre-existing systems of oppression that foster social structures that aid in the domination of nonhuman animals. A film such as *The Plague Dogs* that dares to break this vicious cycle does not reach general audiences, and for the lack of financial success such a project is, unfortunately, unlikely to be repeated. Non/human and ecological justice advocates thus lose a large platform to reach vast audiences. Instead, these platforms, dependent upon the consumer-oriented system governing the mass media, continue to propagate anthropocentric ideologies.

REFERENCES

Adams, Gillian. 1986. *"Watership Down* as a Double Journey." *Children's Literature Association Quarterly. 1986 Proceedings*: 106–111.
Adams, Richard. 1978. *The Plague Dogs*. Harmondsworth, UK: Penguin.
Anderson, Celia Catlett. 1983. "Troy, Carthage, and Watership Down." *Children's Literature Association Quarterly* 8(1): 12–13.
Baker, Steve. 2001. *Picturing the Beast: Animals, Identity, and Representation*. Urbana, Chicago: University of Illinois Press.

Beckett, Sandra L. 2009. *Crossover Fiction: Global and Historical Perspectives.* New York: Routledge.

Campbell, Joseph. 1971. *The Hero with a Thousand Faces.* Princeton, NJ: Princeton University Press.

Collado Rodriguez, Francisco. 1988. "Beyond Satire: Richard Adams's *The Plague Dogs.*" *International Fiction Review* 15(1): 51–53.

Garrard, Greg. 2012. *Ecocriticism.* London: Routledge.

Gifford, Terry. 2002. "Towards a Post-Pastoral View of British Poetry." In *The Environmental Tradition in English Literature,* edited by John Parham, 51–63. Aldershot, UK: Ashgate.

Haraway, Donna. 2003. *The Companion Species Manifesto.* Chicago: Prickly Paradigm Press.

Höing, Anja. 2015. "Snit's a Good Dog. Dogs' Innate Duty in Richard Adams's *The Plague Dogs.*" In *Who's Talking Now. Multispecies Relations from Human and Animals' Point of View,* edited by Chiara Blanco and Bel Deering, 69–76. Oxford: Interdisciplinary Press.

Hunt, Peter. 1987. "Landscapes and Journeys, Metaphors and Maps: The Distinctive Feature of English Fantasy." *Children's Literature Association Quarterly* 12(1): 11–14.

Jung, Carl Gustav. 1981. *The Archetypes and the Collective Unconscious.* Princeton, NJ: Princeton University Press.

Plumwood, Val, 1993. *Feminism and the Mastery of Nature.* London, New York: Routledge.

Rosen, Martin. 1978a. (2005). *Watership Down.* Warner Home Video. DVD.

———. 2005b. "*Watership Down*—Conversation with the Film Makers on *Watership Down.*" DVD.

Schwebel, Florian. 2010. *Von Fritz the Cat bis Waltz with Bashir: Der Animationsfilm für Erwachsene und seine Verwandten.* Marburg: Schüren.

Singer, Peter. 1975. *Animal Liberation.* New York: Random House.

Taylor, Paul. 2011. *Respect for Nature: A Theory of Environmental Ethics. 25th Anniversary Edition.* Princeton, NJ: Princeton University Press.

The Plague Dogs. 1982. (2007). Directed by Martin Rosen. Optimum Home Entertainment. DVD.

Thomas, Frank, and Ollie Johnston. 1981. *Disney Animation—The Illusion of Life.* New York: Abbeville Press.

Wise, Naomi. 1985. "Review: *The Plague Dogs.*" *Film Quarterly* 38(3): 53–54.

Whitley, David. 2008. *The Idea of Nature in Disney Animation.* Aldershot, UK: Ashgate.

Zipes, Jack. 1997. *Happily Ever After. Fairy Tales, Children, and the Culture Industry.* New York, London: Routledge.

Chapter 9

The "Nature-Run-Amok" Cinema of the 1970s: Representation of Non/ Human Animals in *Frogs* and *Orca*

Fernando Gabriel Pagnoni Berns and
César Alfonso Marino

During the sixties and seventies, countercultural movements drew attention to social issues such as sexual freedom, anti-capitalism, and alternative religions. Among the topics in this new paradigm was ecological matters (McFarlane 2007, 199). The green politics of countercultural movements began to spread beyond the hippie sphere into the purview of the American public. This was thanks in part to the first Earth Day, held in April 1970. "Earth day was one of the first major efforts in the United States to bring the environmental problem to the forefront of the national agenda" and, soon enough, ecological issues infused popular culture (Maniaque-Benton 2011, 19). This analysis will use popular culture as the principal mechanism by which hegemonic forces operate in the transmission of ideology (Danser 2005, 31). Popular culture then becomes a distinct space that we make "available a historically variable, complex and contradictory range of ideological discourses and counter-discourses to be activated in particular conditions of reading" (Storey 2010, 56). Thus, it is through the reading of two cinematic case studies that we make explicit the complex, sometimes contradictory, issues of the threatening non/human animal representation in popular culture.

The first case study, *Frogs*, launched an entire new subgenre: the "nature-run-amok" film. This subgenre focuses on individual and groups of non/ human animals, larger or more aggressive than normal, attacking humans. These assaults are triggered for different reasons, such as revenge against human pollution and non/human animal experimentation. Although films with non/human animals attacking humans existed before 1970, this particular subgenre was consolidated and named around this time period (Brass 2005, 280). Sometimes, this subgenre is called "eco-horror," but this label is misleading because the majority of the films do not focus on ecological issues (Murphy 2013, 181). However, *Frogs* allows the viewer to witness the rise of indiscriminate exploitation of natural resources and non/humans within popular culture. The increasing visibility in popular culture, the linkages and incongruences in the subgenre, are all explored in this chapter.

Despite *Frogs'* pioneering approach to addressing ecological concerns, not all films within this subgenre continued down this path, unfortunately. This was especially true after the success of *Jaws* (Steven Spielberg, 1975). *Jaws* may seem like it belongs in the subgenre of "nature-run-amok," however, it cannot be classified as "eco-horror," we think, because ecological concerns are nonessential to the narrative, occupied as it is with the theme of "masculinity coming under fire" (Clarke 2004, 30). After *Jaws*, a series of imitative films flooded the subgenre, including one such film that serves as the second case study, *Orca* (Michael Anderson, 1977). In this movie, a killer whale hunts and avenges those who murdered its family. *Orca* is an overlooked film, which, beneath a narrative that tries to capitalize on Spielberg's success, presents interesting contradictions about subjectivity versus objectivity and its relationship to granting human civility to non/humans.

It is somewhat inaccurate to claim that films with murderous non/human animals were only produced in the 1960s and '70s. Killer non/human animals have appeared in films such as *The Sea Fiend* (Edwin Graham, 1936), in which a manta-ray attacks a mariner, Barry Norton. Conversely, the killer non/human in these productions played the minor role of threatening Other that must be conquered to make the human heroic. Arguably, one of the most famous films about killer non/humans, which debuted in 1963, is Alfred Hitchcock's *The Birds*. The principal menace in this film are different types of birds, though the plot doesn't focus centrally on the attack of the birds, rather it's the female paranoia embodied in the killer non/human animals that sets the stage for horror. The threat of female sexuality that Melanie Daniels (Tippi Hedren) brings to the sleepy town of Bodega Bay is subjugated through her victimhood (Halberstam 2000, 127). In fact, the film never mentions any topic related to ecology or the animal kingdom.

Non/human animals also assault humankind in popular science fiction films of the fifties, such as in *Tarantula* (Jack Arnold, 1955), *The Black Scorpion* (Edward Ludwig, 1957), and *The Giant Claw* (Fred Sears, 1957). Nevertheless, two issues separate the science fiction of the fifties from that of the seventies. First, the non/humans in these films are giant creatures and as such, more conceptualized as monstrous giants than as non/humans. Second, these monsters are produced out of Cold War fears of atomism rather than derived from ecological concerns (Hendershot 1999, 75). In spite of this, the production of horror films with non/human monsters increased greatly in the next decade (Justice 2015, 216).

In broad terms, animals as the main monsters in horror films were not a common issue before the 1970s. At this point, and taking into consideration that within the "nature-run-amok" cycle of the seventies the monster is always a non/human animal, we consider it necessary to briefly explain how monstrousness works within horror cinema (the genre to which this cycle belongs).

One of the most influential scholars in horror cinema, Robin Wood, writes in his essay "An Introduction to the American Horror Film" that dominant ideology (bourgeois capitalism) cancels any potential opposition to the hegemonic power through the repression of alternatives to that power (Wood 2004, 108). If repression fails, then oppression takes its place. Thus, the subject that does not repress itself gets harassed, sometimes to the point of imprisonment. Anyone who fails to fit in this hegemonic sphere classifies as a disruptive Other (109, 111). Alternatively, a monster comes to perturb the "natural" (i.e., the ideology of bourgeois patriarchal capitalism) order of things. "Natural" bourgeois capitalism is linked to the prevalent, mostly western, white, Judeo-Christian, heterosexual, man. Those who fall outside of this "universal" model are minorities who embody otherness, despite so few being able to fit within this universal. Women, non-Christians, people of color, and LGBTQ individuals, among other embodiments, are Others. Otherness, in this scenario, is an instrument to maintain a hegemonic sociopolitical order (Peleg 2007, 77).

The horror film is a subversive text because it portrays the Other in a monstrous form that does not fit the hegemonic discourse. The Other operates according to its repression and oppression. Furthermore, the horror genre is "the struggle for recognition of all that our civilization represses or oppresses, its reemergence dramatized, as in our nightmares, as an object of horror, a matter for terror, and the happy ending (when it exists) typically signifying the restoration of repression" (Wood 2004, 113). Thus, the horror film can be read as regressive, whereby the repressed/oppressed figures strive to return to repression as monsters, which ultimately threatens their natural essence.

Non/human animals, however, are unnamed conduits of Otherness in Wood's text. Although originally written in the seventies, non/human animals do not present as a threat, nor as a metaphor for the Other. Perhaps this is because until the sixties and seventies, the concern for ecology and non/human animals was anthropocentric in focus (Esbjörn-Hargens and Zimmerman 2009, 593). Nature was a passive sphere upon which power and dominion was exerted, and economic and social improvement required ruthless exploitation of natural resources. Grave concern for animal extinction only entered American consciousness in the seventies, when relevant legislation such as the 1973 Endangered Species Act was passed, together with theories of moral standing that addressed the treatment of animals and the environment (de Klemm 1993, 63; Rachels 2004, 164). The hope was to make moral progress by establishing moral status for, among other beings, non/human animals. "Moral standing means that, from a moral point of view, you have claims that must be heard—that your interests constitute morally good reasons why you may, or may not, be treated in this or that way" (Rachels 2004, 164). Up until these changes, if nature was transformed and pillaged or entire species of non/humans exterminated, it was only "a small price to pay for human progress" (Sonneborn 2008, 19).

During this time, Green political parties start to bloom, raising concerns within popular culture about the exploitation of the country's natural resources (Phillips and Mighall 2013, 331). Environmentalism became a theme adopted by musicians as diverse as Neil Young and Marvin Gaye and writers like James Dickey (Gair 2007, 165). Thus, the nature-run-amok films arise, focusing on the onslaught of non/human animals embodying terrifying forms. Thus, innocent bunnies get murderous in *Night of the Lepus* (William Claxton, 1972). Swarms of vicious bees kill humans (*The Swarm*, Irwin Allen, 1978). Ants terrorize Joan Collins (*Empire of the Ants*, Bert I. Gordon, 1977) and spiders invade William Shatner (*Kingdom of the Spiders*, John Cardos, 1977). Furthermore, domestic dogs are possessed by the devil (*Devil Dog: The Hound of Hell*, Curtis Harrington, 1978) and piranhas eat the flesh of unsuspecting human swimmers (*Piranha*, Joe Dante, 1978). It is not coincidental that horror cinema gave birth to the film *Frogs* around the same time these films entered the cinema during the first years of this decade (George McCowan, 1972).

Frogs, which tells the story of a human family living in a Southern mansion surrounded by swamps where non/human animals live and eventually revolt, foreshadows the subgenre to come. Snakes, spiders, lizards and, of course, frogs conspire to exterminate humanity. They start by killing this family because the family represents an old-fashioned form of capitalism that was quickly going out of style in a rapidly changing America. It is capitalism built upon the hyper-exploitation of the non/human world (Barry 2005, 69). Just as during the rise of seventies counterculture, the non/human animals in *Frogs* rise to seek revenge and to reinstate their lost equilibrium.

The film opens with Pickett Smith (Sam Elliott), a Louisiana local reporter taking pictures of the non/humans that inhabit the swamps. The cinematography shows several close shots of Smith's photographs, but soon enough, the scene changes to reveal a different scenario. The images are not of living non/human animals, but dead ones, and the waste byproducts of humans, such as plastic bags, discarded broken dolls, cans, and bottles, along with chemical water pollution, replace shots of living nature. The juxtaposition between the two scenarios, one lush with life and one decayed, symbolizes that humans are polluting the planet and exhausting the ecosystem. In 1972, a film warning against pollution and the destruction of greenery was a novelty, especially within the minor genre of horror. Furthermore, the first years of the 1970s were when "concern for pollution took its place alongside the earlier-arisen interest in natural-environment areas" (Hays 1993, 55). Thus, a correlation can be drawn between the social anxieties surrounding the environment and the starkness of cinematic shots within the beginning frames of *Frogs*.

The juxtaposition of scenes continues as Smith quietly rows his canoe, (with the sounds of nature as background noise) and the noisy presence of Clint (Adam Roarke) and Karen Crockett (Joan Van Ark), two wealthy youths driving a motorboat. The wealth of the bourgeoisie contributing to the destruction of the natural habitat is a strong trope in the film. Since Clint is drinking a beer, the viewer perceives this rich, spoiled youth as unconnected with the severe pollution witnessed only minutes ago. Moments later, the teens run over Smith's canoe by accident. The connection between the affluent youth running over nature the same way that Clint and Karen run over Smith is apparent. Since Smith, a freelancer photographer, is there to take snapshots of pollution, he comes to represent nature and the proletariat, in opposition to the Crocketts's ruthless capitalism.

Director George McCowan strives to portray the rich people in the film as more than just clichés. Even Jason Crockett (Ray Milland), the conservative patriarch who dominates the land and his family with a firm hand, is not entirely evil. The prevailing welfarist position of the time posited humanity's peaceful dominion over an everlasting ecosystem, and suggests it's acceptable to use non/human animals for human purposes, provided unnecessary suffering is avoided (Delaney 2003, 227). This approach was challenged on the practical ground that legislation was not helping non/human animal interests. The new emerging position "requires that animal exploitation must be abolished rather than regulated" (Berkoff 2010, 38). Thus, ethics of non/human animal treatment became a politically sensitive issue, one that the Crockett family, representing the America of old, of a country stuck in time, fails to accept the paradigmatic changes. Perhaps the Crocketts's unconcern about the ecosystem and the non/human animals that live nearby was, initially, more a matter of ignorance than evil.

The first encounter between humans and non/humans occurs when the family sends a man to spray poison on the bullfrogs living around the area. The family wants them exterminated because their constant croaking "turns them crazy." Moreover, Uncle Stuart (George Skaff) suggests pouring oil in the water to choke them. Meanwhile, Clint's wife, Jenny (Lynn Borden) and Karen's cousin, Michael (David Gilliam) angrily complain about their disgusting presence on their property. They simply cannot stand to share their world with animals they perceive as a nuisance. The prevailing attitude suggests non/human animals, along with their habitat, are the property of humans and as such can be exterminated at leisure because they lack the natural right to live.

The rich Crocketts's represent the old capitalism that had spoiled nature "in a reckless manner" (Kula 2013, 196) as a means to economic gain without future consequence. If Jason only views the animal kingdom as a property to play with, the old matriarch, Iris (Holly Irving) perceives the non/humans as elements of decoration. She uses the landscape to practice her hobby of chasing and capturing butterflies to transform into objects of adornment. Turning living creatures into ornaments is just another form of treating non/humans as property. In this sense, the film mirrors the 1970s philosophical issues about the status of non/human animals as legal objects of legal subjects (humans), devoid of any rights (O'Sullivan 2011, 19).

The outdated capitalism of old is also represented by the presence of the black butler Charles (Lance Taylor Sr.), his wife, Maybelle (Mae Mercer), and Bella (Judy Pace), a black model, invited (to Jason's dismay) to the family's Fourth of July celebration. Racial status and non/human animal status are shared because people of color and non/human animals are viewed as mere property. Both conceptions resist dying in this patriarchal, capitalist Southern mansion despite the prevailing civil rights movements in America (Morgan 1991, 47). Non/human animals are not the property of humans any more than people of color are the property for whites or women for men. Thus, people of color, non/human animals, and women, among other oppressed groups, can be understood as "brothers" or "sisters" in their link against institutionalized "speciesism" that frames them as objects, rather than subjects (Kemmerer 2011, 17). In this regard, Bella seems just as comfortable sharing her time with the white people at a party as she does with her servitude. The old capitalism embodied in Jason and the black servitude (a clear reference to the proslavery South) intermingles with modern sentiment allowing a black girl to share space and time with rich white people. A scene featuring a critical dialogue showcases the clash between the South of old and the changing time:

> Jenny (slightly sarcastic): That is an unusual dress, Bella. Did you make it?
> Bella: No. I didn't make it. I designed it.

Jenny tries to frame Bella within the (low-class) condition of a dressmaker, while Bella proclaims her intellectual skills as a fashion designer. In this uneasy division, Jason is incapable of admitting two things: first, that Bella's presence as a guest angers him and second, that an era of capitalism based on exploiting others (people of color, non/human animals, women) is coming to an end. Meanwhile, Stuart complains about not being able to depend on servants these days, "not unless they've been with you from the very beginning," that is, slaves. In this respect, it is worth mentioning that "similarly as today with regard to animals and to nature in general, the defenders of slavery appealed in the first place to alleged property rights" (Kohák 2000, 31). In this context, minorities made claims for rights as never before, and within these oppressed groups, we can place the non/human animal kingdom.

Although the film is titled *Frogs*, there are many other non/human animals that attack the Crockett family. The frogs are the ones that launch the initial attack by attempting to drive away the wealthy family with their loud croaking. The first murder takes place off-screen, and results in the death of the man sent to poison the frogs. Soon enough, the whole family is under attack. First, serpents and frogs invade the mansion; then others arrive and murder members of the Crockett family in different situations. Michael (David Gilliam) is killed by spider bites, Kenneth (Nicholas Cortland) is locked in a greenhouse where lizards knock bottles containing dangerous fumes off ledges. Meanwhile, Iris is bitten to death by snakes, while Stuart is devoured by an alligator and Jenny is mauled by giant turtles and crabs. In the climax, the remaining inhabitants of the mansion leave; however, Jason, the old patriarch who refuses to see his world die, remains. There he will be killed by the menacing frogs, an action that symbolizes nature, minorities, and counterculture that devour the old capitalist values.

The counterculture encourages the non/humans to run amok, thus the filmmaker's choice to portray a conservative Southern family exterminated by animals such as reptiles, batrachians, and snakes were not made by chance. In the seventies, with the Vietnam War still raging, youths were organizing in protest, and materialism had fallen out of favor. A new way of being was a necessary next step in the paradigm change. The emphasis was on creating a new world order that ends dominance and, instead, encourages community (Shasta 2010, 44). Popular culture, inextricably intertwined with social context, mirrored and reinforced this growing sense of ecological interdependence. The interconnectivity between non/human animal and environmental oppression with social oppression within *Frogs* constitutes a wake-up call to those willing to acknowledge the damage and abuse caused by progress, science, and economy. *Frogs* is a rarity among the films of nature-run-amok. After the opening of *Jaws*, ecological issues were tossed aside to favor different approaches to animality, and nearly all are based on non/human animals as monsters whose defeat would restore the status quo.

Jaws is one of Spielberg's "closed universes within which the forces of civilization defeat those of chaos," a recurrent plot in horror cinema (Friedman 2006, 125). In *Jaws*, the main white shark symbolizes many different things; chief among them are the human instincts for revenge and greed. Furthermore, the shark is so polyvalent that some film critics state this creature symbolizes a vulva and for others, a penis (Caputi 1987, 147; Hoberman 2004, 212). Exact opposites embodied in the same non/human animal. In fact, the only thing that the shark does not represent is the non/human world. At no point during the film do any ecological matters of importance transpire.

Jaws' success spawned a gigantic global chain of imitations that followed the same sequence of events of Spielberg's film. In the American *Grizzly* (William Girdler, 1976), the Mexican *Tintorera* (René Cardona Jr., 1977), or the Italian *Tentacoli* (Ovidio Assonitis, 1977), a non/human animal threat (a shark, a bear, piranhas, dogs, and bees, among others) suddenly appears in a small town to kill and eat the people. Generally, the plot follows the same script; there is a morally virtuous character that understands what is happening and alerts the town to take cover, which goes against the wishes of the mayor, who is a greedy, unconcerned unethical character. This same plot is repeatedly recycled, espousing the central theme of human greed and obstinacy. Sharks attacking people on beaches became so formulaic that it produced its own subgenre. It is what I. Q. Hunter calls, "sharkploitation" and "jawsploitation" (Hunter 2009, 14). In this long chain of *Jaws* imitations, non/human animals ceased to represent matters related to ecology except in a passing way. The non/humans are monsters that come to replace the horror genre creatures of old, such as vampires, mummies, and werewolves. *Frogs* had ecology at its core while films within the nature-run-amok subgenre after *Jaws* are more like adventures where non/human animals attack for reasons not related to the ecosystem. It is not that ecological matters had suddenly become unimportant, rather filmmakers were trying to replicate Spielberg's formula to capitalize on his success. This shift relegated non/humans to monsters unrelated to ecology, thus privy to being killed without concern, and maintaining the status quo.

This is not to say that the subgenre of nature-run-amok that follows *Jaws* is obsolete. On the contrary, as cultural artifacts, these films are interesting to examine. However, what they have lost is the representation of non/human animals as an oppressed Other, which represents nature and animality itself. The white shark, as already mentioned, is a psychoanalytic representation of a penis or a vagina, and not necessarily a non/human animal. Still, there are exceptions that offer a more compelling and complex representation of the non/human, as found in the film *Orca*. At first, the film seems to match the plot of *Jaws* closely; however, upon closer reading, Michael Anderson's film is more than just an imitation. *Orca* is a film that contradicts itself and its intentions constantly. Part "sharkploitation," part meditation upon civilization and what makes us human, the film struggles to blend commercial intent with philosophical inquiry. This contrast provides fertile ground to analyze the intentionally blurred lines between human and non/human to foreground a dialogue concerning non/human rights.

Orca tells the story of Captain Nolan (Richard Harris), a fisherman trying to rehabilitate himself by capturing and selling a great white shark to an aquarium. When two divers become involved, the situation nears tragedy because the white shark nearly kills one of the divers. However, an orca intervenes, killing the shark and sparking the curiosity of Captain Nolan. Enlisting the reluctant aid of Rachel Bedford (Charlotte Rampling), a marine biologist, Nolan decides to change course and pursue the capture and sale of a killer whale that is a complete failure. In the process, a male Orca is wounded, its mate is killed, and the female's unborn calf is gruesomely miscarried on the deck of Nolan's ship. After all of this tragedy, the male orca pursues Nolan to exact its revenge.

In *Orca*, the relationship between humans and non/humans occurs through a distorted mirror. Humans perceive in the non/human animals a virtue that humanity is rapidly losing: integrity. Furthermore, the orca is monogamous, exhibits altruistic behavior, and lives in peace with the rest of the underwater ecosystem (Grille 2005, 7). In turn, through Captain Nolan, the cracks in civilization are visible. The film continually reminds us what the social order is no longer able to sustain: the rites of civilization, while exposing human order as truly responsible for the chaos.

Unlike *Jaws* and *Frogs*, the non/human animals in *Orca* are living non-threatening beings. The menacing "from-under-the-water" point of view made famous in *Jaws* is replaced with beautifully photographed scenes of orcas swimming, almost dancing, under the sea. The magnificent, non-threatening music (with religious overtones) that accompanies the scene sustains the glory of the non/human animals. The titular non/humans are not hidden in shadows. Instead they appear after the initial credits in all their glory. Anderson refuses to showcase the orcas as monsters, preferring to portray them as peaceful beings full of wonder (at least, until humans attack them).

The first dreadful scene takes place with the appearance of a white shark while divers are investigating the sea floor. Sadly, the sharks embodied the cliché of dangerous monster, a necessary stunt to capitalize on Spielberg's success. In the opening minutes of *Orca*, the central conflict between menacing and peaceful humans is established, the former embodied in Nolan and his companions who hunt white sharks to sell, and the latter in the biologists led by Rachel Bedford, who work to keep marine life safe from humans.

The plot frames the orcas within constant contradictions, just as it seeks to capitalize on the horror genre while defending the interests of the undersea world. One such example is when the white shark attacks a swimmer, then an orca kills the shark, thus saving the diver. With this scene, the orca is construed as a potential menace and at the same time, a friend. Even the humans stand by watching in confusion, as evidenced by Nolan's expression of amazement, and Rachel's proud proclamation that only orcas are capable of winning such a battle. The orca presents as a mighty being, friend or foe; all depends on what humans do with it.

There is one crucial scene in which the viewer can finally understand the complex nature of how humans perceive orcas. When Rachel gives a speech to her class about killer whales, she insinuates that orcas can be dangerous yet peaceful, magnificent but also monstrous, interconnected with humanity and, at the same time, superior to humans. Rachel insists orcas possess civilized traits, especially when she states:

> Rachel (showing slides): Here's a killer whale in familiar guise: tamed, on exhibition. If treated with kindness, there is no greater friend to man. But if not . . . the orca has 48 teeth set in two impressive rows. Killer whales are better parents than most human beings. And like human beings, they have an instinct for vengeance. But the most amazing thing is neither gentleness nor violence, but their brains. . . . We know little about its intelligence except that it is powerful, and in some respects may even be superior to man.

Following Rachel's monologue, a staff member shows the audience how comparable an orca fetus is to that of a human's, noting in detail the many similarities. The speech ends as she explains the highly sophisticated system of communication that orcas use to communicate with each other. This scene makes clear the fluctuating representation of the orca that blurs the line between what is considered human and non/human. This one scene demonstrates how the non/human animal gets raised to the level of humanity, and humanity is lowered in comparison to animality since the orca, in some aspects, is superior. This jostling for position reoccurs throughout the film, making the orca both the monster and the victim. Likewise, similarly to the orca, Captain Nolan is framed as a monstrosity (his obsession with killing the beast) and victim (the orca hunts him, which threatens many of his friends).

Orca disrupts the formula inaugurated by *Jaws*, because in creating a subsidiary subgenre, horror is not embodied in the creature that tramples the human order, but in the human sphere that tramples the natural order of the creature. Even within "sharkploitation," *Orca* channels a nonexistent reflection in the source (*Jaws*): the damage caused by man over the non/human animal sphere. At this point, *Orca* continues the path forged by *Frogs*: socially critiquing the exploitation that humans exercise on non/human animals. In *Orca*, just as in *Frogs*, the non/human is not configured as truly monstrous. Rather, the source of horror is bestowed upon the man whose aberrant acts committed in pursuit of ambition ignites the tale of revenge. If the non/human in *Jaws* comes to the beach without any apparent purpose, yet still triggers a horror story, the non/human animal in *Orca* attacks only when provoked by humans. Thus, the horror in *Orca* is embodied in the victim, not the perpetrator.

Despite making ecological headway, *Orca* is still defined as "sharkploitation" since, in the end, the creature creates havoc by sinking boats, coastal houses, and, in one of the most famous scenes, tearing apart Nolan's friend

Annie (Bo Derek). That a creature of the sea could do this much damage slightly debunks its descriptor as a film completely centered on human destruction. Accordingly, *Orca* creates an undeniable affiliation: the creature becomes a fierce follow-up of the monster that precedes it (the white shark of Spielberg's film), leaving behind a homologous trail of destruction. However, it would be unjust to ignore how *Orca* problematizes the relationship between both orders, the human and the non/human. The movie continually stages damage provoked in a sphere by the other, highlighting the problematics of such a relationship.

In *Orca*, the creatures re-create the covenant of civilization: they are communicative and live peacefully in their community. Meanwhile, Nolan becomes increasingly estranged from the commonwealth because of the havoc that encircles him. Wherever he goes, the male orca follows him, leaving behind destruction and death. As a result, humans are incapable of sustaining the rites of civilization. Meanwhile, among the rough waters of the sea that has not yet been pierced by the imprint of humans, the orcas echo the same rites of civilization: mating, singing, mourning, and seeking justice from the human characters who, with few exceptions, refuse to acknowledge these rites. One such example is when Nolan is expelled from his community, humans choose to abandon him with his problems rather than help him cope. With the human community in crisis, it is paradoxical that the orcas chase Nolan because a sense of revenge was born from killing his companion. The feeling of community of the non/human animals seems stronger and more enduring that that of humans.

The acquired human traits give civility to the beasts, and thus, it grants them rights. Rachel, after enumerating the orcas's human-like qualities to Captain Nolan, states that the orcas "have rights." This is both a progressive and regressive statement because on the one hand, it blurs the idea of human and non/human as mutually exclusive spheres. However, it also suggests non/humans have proper rights provided they are framed under a specific idea of humanity. In this sense, when Nolan questions whether it's possible to sin against a non/human animal, the idea of soul in animality is surfaced. This surfacing foregrounds the subquestion of whether non/human animals are objects or subjects, with rights. If one were to consider non/humans as beings with rights similar to those of humans, this might negate the representation of animals as property (Garner 2005, 44). However, the film leaves us with a few questions such as, do orcas only have rights because they share issues with humans? If not, then which non/humans have rights? Only those who share characteristics conceptualized as human? If one adopts the stance that non/human animals with rights are those akin to humans, then rats and mosquitoes, for example, are devoid of protection (Sunstein 2004, 12). Non/humans that can fit, in some aspects, into human characteristics and civilized human ways are granted rights in this film. However, paradoxically, human beings cease behaving in civil ways near the end of the film, and the premise of the film rests on this contradiction.

Orca advocates for the rights of non/human animals and peaceful ecological cohabitation. To achieve this end, orcas are neither framed as utterly monstrous, nor is the captain represented as truly evil. After the incident with the male whale, Nolan tries to avoid further confrontation with the orca, however it is the orca's human capacity for revenge that prompts Nolan to take a stand against the non/human animal. Despite this contemptuous relationship, the filmmakers succeed in presenting both non/human animals and humans as not entirely malevolent. Nevertheless, to promote the rights of non/humans to live without suffering, the human qualities of the orca are over emphasized to legitimize this claim. In this sense, only those who possess human-like features are spared. Michael Anderson chose to emphasize the human-like characteristics of the orca, thus foregrounding an ethical commitment to non/human animal rights. The shark in the beginning, however, was killed rightfully because it inflicted harm on a human. Rights and legal protections against harm are then inextricably tied to notions of humanity, even when Anderson's purpose was to shed light on the problematic representation of non/human animal as monster that was so prevalent in the "nature-run-amok" genre of the 1970s.

One of the most significant ways in which ecological issues were addressed in the 1970s was through the cinematic subgenre of "nature-run-amok." Within the subgenre one can find complexities and diversity with how filmmakers address non/human animal rights and ecology. *Frogs* was the first film within this subgenre, and is still one of its best offerings because ecological matters take center stage and the non/human animals, if framed as menacing, were embodiments of then-current state of nature. Interestingly, *Frogs* ends with a negative forecast about the future of humanity. The viewer is led to believe that non/human animals have taken by assault the entire world, and the credits give the greatest clues. The credits roll with only the ominous sound of frogs croaking in the background. The film denies a restoration of the status quo: While man continues to pollute nature, only a bleak future awaits humans. The films following *Jaws* restore (as Spielberg's film did) the status quo once the non/human animal threat is destroyed. An exception is *Orca*, a film that blends animal philosophy and exploitation while capitalizing on *Jaws'* influence (McBride 2010, 257). Like *Frogs*, the non/human menace, the male killer whale, ends the film still alive, while Captain Nolan floats dead in icy waters. In both *Frogs* and *Orca*, the non/human animals are not defeated in the end. Still, in Anderson's film the status quo is restored when the main menace, Capitan Nolan, is killed. It was he, and not the titular non/human animal, who disturbed the natural order. In this sense, the bleakness of *Frogs'* end still haunts the big screen: only with the death of humans can peace be achieved.

Both films are sophisticated in their representation of non/human animals: *Frogs* presents non/humans as menacing creatures; however, they are not displayed as supernatural or mutations, which would constitute truly monstrous representation. They are simply non/human animals, living their lives, embodying their essences, and ultimately striking back. *Orca* also avoids, to some extent, the trap created by *Jaws* of non/humans as monstrous. In Anderson's film, there are no real monsters, only humans and non/human animals incapable of peacefully cohabiting. The orcas are showcased favorably, but are only magnificent creatures precisely because of their co-opting of humanity. "Sharksploitation" is used in *Orca* to propose a new form of representation that is questionable in its intent to "civilize." It is questionable because civilization is only achieved by bridging non/humans with human spheres based on "humanizing" pillars such as being "nurturing" and "mourning." These complex contradictions remain highly dubious, and this is what makes these films still interesting to the general noncritical public audience that does not take into consideration the oppressive frameworks constructed in these films that aid in the stigmatization of humans and nonhumans. As critical scholar-activists we must inform the public about the simplistic and stigmatized representation of humans and nonhumans. In conclusion, we must begin to publicly challenge, critique, and not allow these false images in film to continue to re-create oppressive relationships between humans and nonhumans.

REFERENCES

Barry, John. 2005. *Environment and Social Theory*. New York: Routledge.

Bekoff, Marc. 2010. *Encyclopedia of Animal Rights and Animal Welfare*. Santa Barbara, CA: Greenwood.

Brass, Tom. 2005. *Peasants, Populism and Postmodernism: The Return of the Agrarian Myth*. New York: Frank Cass Publishers.

Caputi, Jane. 1987. *The Age of Sex Crime*. Bowling Green, OH: Bowling Green University Popular Press.

Clarke, James. *Steven Spielberg: The Pocket Essential Guide*. North Pomfret, VT: Trafalgar Square Publishing, 2004.

Danser, Simon. 2005. *The Myths of Reality*. Loughborough: Alternative Albion.

De Klemm, Cyrille. 1993. *Biological Diversity Conservation and the Law: Legal Mechanisms for Conserving Species and Ecosystems*. Cambridge: IUCN.

Delaney, David. 2003. *Law and Nature*. New York: Cambridge University Press.

Esbjörn-Hargens, Sean, and Michael Zimmerman. 2009. *Integral Ecology: Uniting Multiple Perspectives on the Natural World*. Boston: Shambhala Publications.

Friedman, Lester. 2006. *Citizen Spielberg*. Champaign, IL: University of Illinois Press.

Gair, Christopher. 2007. *The American Counterculture*. Edinburgh: Edinburgh University Press.

Garner, Robert. 2005. *The Political Theory of Animal Rights*. New York: Manchester University Press.

Grille, Robin. 2005. *Parenting for a Peaceful World*. New South Wales: Longueville Media. http://site.ebrary.com/id/10397454.

Halberstam, Judith. 2000. *Skin Shows: Gothic Horror and the Technology of Monsters*. Durham, NC: Duke University Press.

Hays, Samuel. 1993. *Beauty, Health, and Permanence: Environmental Politics in the United States, 1955–1985*. New York: Cambridge University Press.

Hendershot, Cynthia. 1999. *Paranoia, the Bomb, and 1950s Science Fiction Films*. Bowling Green, OH: Bowling Green State University Popular Press.

Hoberman, J. 2004. "*Nashville* contra *Jaws*, or the Imagination of Disaster." In *The Last Great American Picture Show: New Hollywood Cinema in the 1970s*, edited by Alexander Horwath, Thomas Elsaesser, and Noel King, 195–222. Amsterdam: Amsterdam University Press.

Hunter, I. Q. "Exploitation as Adaptation," in *Cultural Borrowings: Appropriation, Reworking, Transformation*, edited by Iain Robert Smith, 8–33. Ebook published by Scope: An Online Journal of Film and Television Studies, 2009. http://clublum.com/images/Scope-Cultural_ Borrowings_Final%20clublum.pdf#page=20.

Justice, Christopher. 2015. "Cooling the Geopolitical to Warm the Ecological: How Human-Induced Warming Phenomena Transformed Modern Horror." In *Eco-Trauma Cinema*, edited by Anil Narine, 207–230. New York: Routledge.

Kemmerer, Lisa. 2011. "Introduction." In *Sister Species: Women, Animals, and Social Justice*, edited by Lisa Kemmerer, 1–44. Champaign: University of Illinois Press.

Kohák, Erazim. 2000. *The Green Halo: A Bird's-Eye View of Ecological Ethics*. Peru, IL: Carus.

Kula, Erhun. 2013. *History of Environmental Economic Thought*. New York: Routledge.

Maniaque-Benton, Caroline. 2011. *French Encounters with the American Counterculture, 1960–1980*. Burlington, VT: Ashgate Publishing.

McBride, Joseph. 2010. *Steven Spielberg: A Biography*. Jackson: University Press of Mississippi.

McFarlane, Scott. 2007. *The Hippie Narrative: A Literary Perspective on the Counterculture*. Wilmington, NC: McFarland.

Morgan, Edward. 1991. *The Sixties Experience: Hard Lessons about Modern America*. Philadelphia: Temple University Press.

Murphy, Bernice. 2013. *The Rural Gothic in American Popular Culture: Backwoods Horror and Terror in the Wilderness*. New York: Palgrave Macmillan.

Nordhaus, Ted, and Michael Shellenberger. 2007. *Break Through: From the Death of Environmentalism to the Politics of Possibility*. New York: Houghton Mifflin.

O'Sullivan, Siobhan. 2011. *Animals, Equality and Democracy*. New York: Palgrave Macmillan.

Peleg, Ilan. 2007. *Democratizing the Hegemonic State: Political Transformation in the Age of Identity*. Cambridge: Cambridge University Press.

Phillips, Martin, and Tim Mighall. 2013. *Society and Exploitation through Nature*. New York: Routledge.

Rachels, James. 2004. "Drawing Lines." In *Animal Rights: Current Debates and New Directions*, edited by Cass Sunstein and Martha Nussbaum, 162–174. New York: Oxford University Press.

Shasta, Peter. 2010. *Adventures of a Western Mystic: Apprentice to the Masters*. Bloomington, IN: AuthorHouse.

Sonneborn, Liz. 2008. *The Environmental Movement: Protecting Our Natural Resources*. New York: Infobase.

Storey, John. 2010. *Cultural Studies and the Study of Popular Culture*, 3rd edition. Edinburgh: Edinburgh University Press.

Sunstein, Cass. 2004. "Introduction: What Are Animal Rights?" In *Animal Rights: Current Debates and New Directions*, edited by Cass Sunstein and Martha Nussbaum, 3–18. New York: Oxford University Press.

Wood, Robin. 2004. "An Introduction to the American Horror Film." In *Planks of Reason: Essays on the Horror Film*, edited by Barry Keith Grant and Christopher Sharrett, 107–141. Lanham, MD: Scarecrow Press.

III

Advertising Representations of Reality

Chapter 10

Cyberbeasts: Substitution and Trivialization of the Non/Human Animal in Home Movies, Memes, and Video Games

Joseph Anderton

In John Berger's chapter "Why Look at Animals?" from his 1980 book *About Looking*, he claims: "Zoos, realistic animal toys, and the widespread commercial diffusion of animal imagery all began as animals started to be withdrawn from daily life. One could suppose that such innovations were compensatory. In reality, the innovations themselves belonged to the same remorseless movement as was dispersing the animals" (2007, 260). Berger describes the strange disappearance of non/humans from human experience since the industrial age, even as representations of them proliferate. They are mutated and marginalized as objects of knowledge, leisure activities, utile tools, and allegorical vehicles, rather than perceived and treated as kindred neighbors sharing in the experience of being. In turn, imagery of non/humans attempts to palliate the absence but exacerbates it. Instead it raises an obfuscating veil of mimesis, caricature, and fabrication despite the intention to restore a level of non/human presence in human culture. The prevailing implication is that real non/human animals, which were once acquainted more intimately with humans, according to Berger, are reduced to a priori negatives by the influx of animal images. That is, the process of re-presenting only preserves the concept of the original non/human animal as an implicit but invisible counterpart. Ultimately, the images exist as a sign of the absence of the real thing.

Berger's contemporary, Jean Baudrillard, revises the conception of human severance from nature and non/human animals in *Simulacra and Simu-*

lation. He explains that notions of reality have become untenable because humans construct "hyperrealities," where the distinction between reality and illusion breaks down. Baudrillard writes, "The impossibility of rediscovering an absolute level of the real is of the same order as the impossibility of staging illusion. Illusion is no longer possible, because the real is no longer possible" (1994, 19). For Baudrillard, the notion of an absolute level of reality is a chimera that people continue to posit through its contradistinction to illusion because "we require a visible past, a visible continuum, a visible myth of origin, which reassures us about our end" (1994, 10). If non/human images are simulacra that discredit the real, people must subscribe to the possibility of knowing non/human animals to maintain that reality exists beyond humanity's constructed orders. Although Baudrillard acknowledges that representations of non/human animals reassure us they survive as pure beings, beyond the contamination of human thought, he maintains there is no unassailable distinction between illusory and real creatures.

In this chapter I will continue to trace the trajectory that Berger observes and that Baudrillard complicates, following the non/human animal's disappearance to its twenty-first-century apotheosis in the rise of cyberculture. This phenomenon, particularly home movies and memes posted on the Internet, as well as the advent of video games, has paved the way for an increase in lieutenant non/human animals: reproductions that replace the real and therefore call into question the possibility of the real. My argument in this chapter is that images of non/human animals in cyberculture, besides being anthropomorphic and anthropocentric, frequently fall into two dominant and related themes: substitution and trivialization. Substitution ultimately conveys cyberculture's role in re-devising animality through the genealogy of non/human imagery, whereby each subsequent generation of re-presentation refers to the last before transfiguring and overlaying it. Trivialization describes the cursory re-evaluation of non/human animals and alludes to the general transmutability of non/human animal conceptions in modernity when predominantly accessed through the accreted layers of virtual substitutes. I contend that the filter of superficial twenty-first-century animal imagery refracts our perception, consciousness, and treatment of the living non/human animals we do encounter. The casualness and ubiquity of cyberculture, in particular, contribute to the indiscriminateness regarding real living beings and desultory constructed impressions. This hyperreality, or indeterminacy between the actual and the image, risks muddling ethical conduct. Interactions with doctored, narrativized, and fictitious imagery contour the status of non/human animals profoundly and legitimize carelessness, which can increase mistreatment, cruelty, and suffering.

NON/HUMAN ANIMAL ENCOUNTERS NOW: BERGER, BAUDRILLARD, AND CYBERCULTURE

Berger speculates that the first metaphor was the animal (2007, 253). For Berger, non/human creatures have been perceived as other than themselves for many millennia. He recognizes that images of non/human animals abound more than any other type in the form of zoological gardens, mimetic objects, and comparable portraits (Berger 2007, 259). Since the late 1970s, when Berger was writing his essay, the rise of cyberculture has intensified the representation of non/human animals. Private life has become virtually social, owing to easy access to digital video recorders and cameras in mobile devices, and the expansive capacity of the Internet as a means of dissemination. Websites like Facebook and Twitter encourage remote, edited, and fragmentary social interactions that effectively diminish the boundaries between private reality and communal broadcast. Instant wireless media transfers through dedicated applications close the gap between the living and sharing of thoughts and experiences. A 2010 survey found that 73 percent of wired teenagers and 47 percent of online adults use social media sites, with a growth of 600 percent in adults between 2005 and 2009 (Lenhart et al. 2010). As people increasingly project their lives through global computer networks, non/human images have developed a pervasive presence in cyberculture by proxy.

However, Berger's and Baudrillard's prescient works strike notes of caution about accepting the images of non/human animals as a sign of greater intimacy, conscious treatment, and real knowledge. Certainly, the widespread presence and reproduction of non/human imagery on the web appears to answer Berger's question, "Is there not one way in which animals, instead of disappearing, continue to multiply" (Berger 2007, 256)? The multiplication of non/human animal representations in the form of bite-size videos, viral memes, and amusing video games has consequences for the way people receive non/human animals wholesale. Cyberculture enacts the culmination of Berger's view of non/human animals as "co-opted into the family and into the spectacle" (2007, 257). Displaced from an original sphere of existence "with man at the centre of his world," non/human animals emerge as figures of alterity, represented in ways that fall short of the real lives of non/human animals (Berger 2007, 252). This is the disappearance of which Berger speaks: "The zoo to which people go to meet animals, to observe them, to see them, is, in fact, a monument to the impossibility of such encounters" (2007, 258). Cyberculture has further effectuated this absence as non/human animals now appear as a spectacle through the pixels of the screen.

Internet users can observe the cute, funny, shocking, or most exciting parts of non/human lives as brief fragments that bypass their otherwise ordinary existences. Non/human animals are thus altered. As Berger insists, the "reproduction of animals in images—as their biological reproduction in birth becomes a rarer and rarer sight—was competitively forced to make animals ever more exotic and remote" (2007, 261). The radical extension of Berger's angle on the contrived differences and distance of non/human animals— which Baudrillard proposes—is that nature, as it is now understood, is tainted by human intervention and consequently not strictly natural at all. In Berger's observations, non/human images indicate a vicious cycle of loss and inadequate replacement that continues to pursue and preclude the re-acquaintance with real non/human animals. Jonathan Burt rightly asserts "this is the fiction of the direct encounter. Standard animal imagery will inevitably be considered palliative (substitutive), empty (spectral), and excessive (mass-produced)" when measured against this (2002, 26).

However, for Baudrillard, the dependency on imagery exposes the fallibility of grounding non/human animals in the reality of nature, as opposed to culture. Nature has never existed except through immanence that is oblivious to nature as part of any dichotomy and that could not recognize nature without transcending and denaturalizing. As Laurence Simmons explains,

> "Nature" is a simulacrum: it exists because it is completely artificial. Both in the sense of a "reality" shaped over many thousands of years by human activity, and as an empty signifier whose referent is constituted by its relationship to other freefloating signs. There is no "original" nature, it is not an "other" to culture, and, as Baudrillard declares elsewhere, "You cannot trust nature." (2010, 136)

Baudrillard's theories suggest that non/human animals have no relation to the real. The real non/human animal is not only absent, it is effectively nonexistent because they are unable to be figured without reference to what they are not. The image is, therefore, constitutive. It constructs as much as reflects the non/human animal.

Baudrillard exposes non/human animals and nature as predicated on what he describes as a grotesque sideshow. In *Simulacra and Simulation*, in a chapter dedicated to non/human animals entitled "The Animals: Territory and Metamorphoses," Baudrillard identifies "a spectacular monstrosity: that of King Kong wrenched from his jungle and transformed into a music-hall star" (1994, 135). In this reference to the monumental ape-like character, Baudrillard pinpoints the shift from immersion in nature to performance of the wild. Kong is riven from his place of belonging and becomes the representative of nature for audiences so they can apprehend him outside of that environment. As with the zoo, the move from habitat to stage estranges the non/human animal, marking an incipient phase in the visual commodification of the non/human animal. They are not apprehended as pets, beasts of burden, or farmed foodstuff, but as the focus of media consumption. If non/ human animals function as a reminder of truth in a world of replicas, the irony is that as people increasingly engage with semblances, the more they descend into a hyperreality and cannot distinguish the difference between reality and representation. As images prevail over the things they portray, their bearing on reality becomes perilously tenuous.

Home movies, memes, and video games indicate a movement away from images as compensatory referents in place of veritable, authentic, or original beings toward disconnected, shallow, and self-sustaining inventions. Baudrillard's arguments look past the loss of direct contact with the non/human to infer that our encounters and treatments of them must abide by the logic of our imagery. Thus, visual media is partly responsible for shaping perceptions that ensure meaningful and moral interactions with live non/humans. Video, viral, and virtual images are not gestures of reverence for real creatures to somehow maintain their aura. Rather, they are an instrumental factor in forming conceptions of animality that influence people's conduct toward non/human animals.

HOME MOVIES: VIEWING NON/HUMAN ANIMALS

The spread of mobile technology and the invention of video-sharing have changed how humans experience non/human animals. Humans have gone from visiting physical spaces dedicated to housing non/human animals, to browsing online zoos from home. They also film non/human animals in and around the home, and then upload the videos for the Wi-Fi ready world to view. Inspired by television shows such as *Planet's Funniest Animals* (USA) and *Animals Do the Funniest Things* (UK), YouTube serves as the main portal for these videos. It archives a glut of home movies starring predominantly domesticated non/human animals exhibiting "cute," "funny," or "stupid" behavior. On one hand, the popularity of these videos attests to the fact that they are pleasurable for both the posters and viewers, and it can be noted that there is a great deal of benignity evident in home movies featuring non/human animals. For some users, there is a tendency to emphasize this appreciation by labeling the videos "Animals Are Awesome," despite invariably containing the same material as those labeled "Funny Animals," "Cute Animals," or even "Animal Fails." As with Randy Malamud's early assertion on virtual zoos, however, the clips "play for a few seconds without providing any momentous insights" (1998, 263). Non/human animals appear to be central subjects because the technology is within easy reach and their chance antics interrupt the monotony of human domestic activities, not because their lives are deemed inherently significant and worth documenting. Furthermore, the brevity and superficiality of home movies are inimical to the serious acts of attention required to do justice to non/human life.

A video compilation entitled "Animals can be Jerks" has over 50 million views and includes various creatures, predominantly domestic pets, exhibiting behavior potentially misconstrued as purposefully provocative or spiteful. The clips advertise human kinship with non/human animals through the shared behavior of the species. However, by framing the non/human animals' motivations, actions, and reactions in a humanizing way, it resorts to a specious anthropomorphic explanation. Cats are often featured in such videos thanks to the projection of human traits onto them since they "seem more serious than other animals, so it is funny when the camera catches them doing something stupid" (DeMello 2012, 338). When "serious" non/human animals are described doing "stupid" things, and are "caught" doing so, it suggests that the veil of performance has slipped. This is only possible through the human framework imposed on the lives of non/humans. As a result, this particular type of home movie has an anthropocentric gravitation inasmuch as it comprehends non/human behavior through the lens of the human. They have a discernible specular quality, which redirects attention away from the non/human animal qua non/human animal to the non/human animal as a reflection of the human.

Besides acting as a mirror for a homogeneous conception of the human, the non/human animal also reflects the individual keepers and numerous viewers more acutely. Social networking sites are potent personal marketing spaces on which to project an ideal self, or at least an identity one is willing to endorse. "Participants in visual culture can take on new roles. They can change sex or age or occupation and interact electronically with an altered identity" (Croteau and Hoynes 2003, 150). Pets are not exempt from being appropriated as part of these carefully constructed personas. Encoded in personal home videos are values that can be attached to the poster to forge an impression of personality and lifestyle. The companion animal and their actions offer indications about the poster, even while, for the most part, the person hides behind the camera. Despite being safely invisible, the camera-person is nevertheless implicit in the video as an attendant and, therefore, the non/human animal appears in their stead. This association with non/human animals can signify an enriched life, a compassionate and attentive person, and the benignity I suggested earlier. The representative function of animal home videos is more compelling on sites where accounts are frequently personalized, such as Facebook or Twitter. Yet, even on more anonymous media sharing sites like YouTube, where the content is not anchored to an individual as securely, the aspirational connotation of non/human animal antics associated with a colorful life remains present.

However, the non/human animal's role in communicating the keeper's endorsed identity to other people is secondary to the role pets, and subsequently home videos, play more generally in developing the self-knowledge of the poster or viewer. Berger proposes in his essay that a pet is an objectifying and revelatory presence for the keeper. "The pet completes him [*sic*], offering responses to aspects of his [*sic*] character, which would otherwise remain unconfirmed" (Berger 2007, 256). Non/human animals can realize or reaffirm parts of the self that require a form of validation and thus allow people to know themselves better. In this light, home movies featuring non/human animals support Burt's challenge to "the assumptions that most human-animal relations in modernity are in various ways wrongful—either sentimental or hollow, or a disconcerting combination of the two" (2002, 25). The problem with home videos, however, is that the validation for the viewer does not occur in a live situation but vicariously through remote observations. This means the physical non/human animal is marginalized or at least competes with his or her highlights reel. Moreover, employing the non/human animal to delineate the human self could perpetuate the polarity that casts pets as utile others and betrays ignorance toward companion species as beings in their own right. This hierarchical use of adjacent lives borders on a rather narcissistic and tyrannical attitude toward the non/human world. This approach exposes sentient creatures to further discrimination and exploitation based solely on the assumption of species entitlement, which is grossly appropriating, devoid of compassion, and morally reprehensible.

A prevalent subgenre of animal home movie is "Cute Animals," which has engendered the curious offshoot "Babies and Animals." These types of video clips promote a sense of affection for our most familiar pets as people share the endearing qualities and adorable moments of their lives. Yet the videos are also responsible for reinforcing a superficial impression of non/human animals and contributing to their popularity as an aesthetic accessory. They place emphasis on the appreciation of appearance as well as emotional responses to feebleness and guilelessness. Such home videos exemplify the sentimentality toward non/human animals that Baudrillard finds disdainful.

> In particular, our sentimentality toward animals is a sure sign of the disdain in which we hold them. It is proportional to this disdain. It is in proportion to being relegated to irresponsibility, to the inhuman, that the animal becomes worthy of the human ritual of affection and protection, just as the child does in direct proportion to being relegated to a status of innocence and childishness. (Baudrillard 1994, 134)

Sentimentality demotes non/human animals to an undignified subordination. They are no longer held up as worthy of sacrifice and symbolic resonance, but adopted and cosseted as vulnerable objects. It is telling that Baudrillard refers to children as non/human animals since it applies directly to the irresistible partnership with equally lovable human infants in the "Babies and Animals" home videos. The interactions between species in these clips inspire a heady mixture of light amusement and interest. They are successful because they satisfy a deep-seated fascination with the primitive and indulge in the similarities and differences between non/human animals and undeveloped humans. Akin to Baudrillard's assertion, the human and non/human animal double serves to expose the human propensity to court dependency and, by implication, assume a kind of power.

While the predilection for pets does evidence tenderness toward living creatures and disdain, according to Baudrillard, these recorded images also underline a growing dissemination of the reproduced digital animal. In the aforementioned video genres and in those with wild animals such as "Animal Attacks," "Animals Fight Back," and "Wild Animal Fights," the subjects are captured in a brief video and viewed repeatedly at a whim. This repetition causes a vapid reanimation of the non/human, displacing context to produce an uncanny creature confined to the clip. When discussing virtual zoos, Malamud recognizes that "wild animals are infinitely decontextualized, to the point where spectators enjoy complete access to what is physically absent. Viewers retain cultural/cognitive mastery over animals, without the smell of shit" (1998, 258). The tangible experience of wildlife falls foul to visual media's accessible and convenient modes of receipt through sanctioned narratives that reconfigure non/human animals. The home movie betrays its debt to the entertainment industry here and, like television, "transforms real nature into *our* nature, distanced and distinct from the original" (Malamud 1998, 256–257). Domestic pets endure this process twofold: first domesticated to become our non/human animals and then recorded to become our representations of our non/human animals. Because of this cumulative adaptation, human intervention is more than ever a fixture in the exposure to and appreciation of other creatures.

MEMES: VIRAL NON/HUMAN ANIMALS

Many home movie clips on the Internet featuring non/human animals have achieved "meme" status. According to Limor Shifman's tripartite definition in *Memes in Digital Culture*, memes are "(a) a *group of digital items sharing common characteristics* of content, form, and/or stance; (b) that were created *with awareness of each other*; and (c) were circulated, imitated, and/or transformed *via the Internet by many users*" (2013, 8). Humanization and humor are the shared common characteristics of home video memes. For example, the "Keyboard Cat" clip shows a tabby cat playing ditties on an electronic keyboard with the help of a pair of false feline limbs. With over 40 million views, the protagonist achieves a remarkable level of fame and set opportunistic marketing machines whirring to produce advertisements, television appearances, supplementary websites, and lucrative merchandise (Dredge 2014). The success of such memes may actually revise and deprecate celebrity culture because the public nominates and controls fame. As Will Braden, creator of YouTube sensation Henri le Chat Noir, remarks, "You don't have to listen to Warner Brothers anymore. 'I'm into this cat, so suck it!' It's almost like sticking it to The Man. 'I'm going to buy a cat shirt'" (Dredge 2014). By enthusing over naïve non/human animal stars, online audiences help to insinuate the inordinate preoccupation with human celebrity icons and the imperious authority of mega media companies. However, for this to be a meaningful criticism, the memes must appear fatuous. Furthermore, the positive spin on the critical impact of video memes is self-defeating in that the videos are unable to diminish the vitality of celebrity culture. On the contrary, they necessarily add further beams of limelight, albeit toward less likely objects of mass interest.

A more frequent type of meme is the image macro, which is "a general form of pictures with overlaid text" (Shifman 2013, 111). Examples of animal memes in this form include: Lolcat, Grumpy Cat, Surprised Kitty, Bad Advice Dog, Socially-Awkward Penguin, Lame Pun Coon, Paranoid Parrot, Bachelor Frog, and Courage Wolf. As this list shows, memes apply single characteristics to pictured non/human animals, often completely different from the typical associations of the featured non/human animal, and usually aiming for comic effect. The original Lolcat meme, for instance, is a photograph of a cat with a look of wonder and the words "I Can Has Cheezburger?" The expressive image, awkward phrasing, and peculiar hankering amount to a quirky juxtaposition of human and non/human animal elements. Similarly, Socially-Awkward Penguin represents many difficult situations for socially inept people, although it is unclear why a penguin was the elected non/human animal unless its reserved "suited" appearance connotes an aloof personality. Nevertheless, both of these creatures are used as blank canvases, for their simplicity, accessibility, and universality, not their specificity. The difference between these two types of memes is that Lolcat plays on incongruity, which recognizes the implausibility of the cat's caption, whereas the Socially-Awkward Penguin disappears behind human sentiments. Both memes present a superficial connection, barely related to the lives of non/human animals in the world. This fosters a general dissociation from, disregard for, and loss of pragmatic engagement with, the real individual beings.

Image macro memes appropriate the appearance of non/human animals and give them a human voice, thus making memes an exception to DeMello's assessment that "animals on the Internet rarely act as symbols. Instead, they act as themselves" (2012, 338). Crucially, the silence of the non/human image is denied by the accompanying words in memes, which superimpose human thoughts and expressions onto the non/human animal. Such memes primarily address humans, and ostensibly engage with non/human animals. DeMello notes, "We can relate to the sentiments expressed in Lolcat captions, because they are, after all, our sentiments" (DeMello 2012, 340). Yet the thinly veiled comments on humans in memes also betoken the enigma of non/human animals that humans confront. Baudrillard believes speaking non/human animals are a soundboard for commentary on human culture. Owing to the indecipherability of non/human animals "nowhere do they really speak, because they only furnish the responses one asks for. It is their way of sending the Human back to his [*sic*] circular codes, behind which their silence analyzes us" (Baudrillard 1994, 138). The token presence of non/human animals accompanied by human ventriloquist voices in memes rehearses the reflective surface of the non/human's poker face. They appear as insubstantial exteriors because of their tenebrous depths.

Although the non/human animals in memes are hollow facades onto which people can project human ideas, the memes are not without complexity for human culture. In Shifman's book, she refers to Kate Miltner's research on Lolcats to expand on the significance of memes in cyberculture. Shifman writes that, whereas "Lolcats are often dismissed as emblems of a silly and whimsical culture, Miltner shows that they actually fulfill diverse and complex social roles" (2013, 111–112). Memes help to order and assess the diversity of identities. They are simultaneously symptomatic and formative of social and cultural circles, reflecting and revising the behavior, language, and interests of the Internet generation. They also indicate localized structures of knowledge, partaking in the shared codes and meanings of social constructivism. Indeed, memes can diffuse "the sweet scent of an inside joke, understood by those who are immersed in the digital cultural landscape" (Shifman 2013, 111). The musings of the slovenly, adolescent Bachelor Frog, for example, will not be understood by or appealing to everyone. Their punch lines ("Spill drink on the floor/Time will clean it up") portray a loafing character whose main interests include masturbation, gaming, and avoiding domestic chores. Its puerile observational humor is reliant upon recognizing such a personality type. The variability and sheer multitude of memes mean they can be adapted to meet individuals' needs and spread exponentially according to the voraciousness of the like-minded audience. It is not that the meme as a form is insignificant, but that its ability to pervade privy groups cements non/human animals in facetious material and renders them vacuous figureheads subsidiary to human meanings.

Besides reflecting particular social types, memes can also transcend their initial audience to attract a second-wave audience, which may be ignorant of inside jokes and latent social critique. These audiences seem willing to accept the phenomenon at face value. Memes circulate for mass consumption by definition, and although smaller enthusiastic groups can achieve a disproportionate presence on the Internet, other more relatable animal memes have a mass appeal. Grumpy Cat is a financially successful meme enterprise. The frowning dwarf cat Tardar Sauce has secured various commercial deals, including a brand of coffee called "Grumppuccino." She has generated profit from book contracts and appearances on prime-time television shows such as

American Idol (Withnall 2014). The meme itself draws on a misanthropic characterization, with the cat negating all things optimistic and happy in a similar tone to countercultures that reflect dissatisfaction with the unassuming acceptance of the status quo. It has a great reach among anonymous online audiences more prone to an excoriating or dismissive reaction to culture. Yet, considering that the Grumpy Cat meme has been adapted for a television movie called *Grumpy Cat's Worst Christmas Ever*, it is patent that this medium is spawning spinoffs that promote a kind of self-sustaining image of animality. In drawing on a meme for source material, the film is twice removed from the domestic cat. This move introduces an external standard independent of the exemplary lives of non/human animals and produces a doubly autonomous approach to animal imagery.

The "Sneezing Baby Panda" meme, which boasts over 215 million views on YouTube, is another example of a funny and cute clip giving rise to a feature film. The tongue-in-cheek film is devised by Australian documentary-makers Lesley Hammond and Jenny Walsh to fight piracy of their original viral clip. It follows a plan to save a struggling zoo by adding a star attraction, the sneezing panda Chi-Chi. The film employs a voiceover for the panda, includes mockumentary techniques to invent a bizarre biography, and copies both the cross-species attraction and Empire State Building iconography from *King Kong*. The movie industry, therefore, repeats the superficial non/human caricatures from memes to feed an interminable hunger for the constructed narratives of non/human animals over attempts to appreciate their realities. Film critics refer to the original web clip as indigenous and superior, rather than critique the film's corruption of non/human animals: "sneezing pandas are best seen in their natural habitat. On YouTube" (Wilson 2014). As a result, Berger's implied original non/human animal is buried under the accretion of humanized and humorous images that depart from the benefits of vigilance, passivity, and modesty. As trivial depictions gain prevalence, and non/human animals continue to be fodder in videos and memes, it will be difficult to perceive non/human animals without the insidious influences of cyberculture.

VIDEO GAMES: VIRTUAL NON/HUMAN ANIMALS

Video games have grown exponentially as a medium since the 1980s in terms of popularity, technical achievement, and narrative sophistication. In the United States in 2011, the Supreme Court awarded video games the rights of the First Amendment, effectively granting the medium the same status as visual arts, film, and music. For Seth Schiesel of the *New York Times*, "this decision reflects society in that video games have already become the most vibrant new form of media entertainment in decades" (2011). In 2014, British developers encouraged Parliament to label video games "cultural products," as opposed to the European Union's "software" description (Blake 2014). They did this to benefit from tax breaks and highlight the influence of video games in contemporary society. Indeed, the magnitude and diversity of the global gaming audience means video games have a pervasive cultural cachet that deserves critical attention.

Since the introduction of home entertainment consoles to the mass market, non/human animals have featured heavily in video games. Admittedly, the representation of non/human animals is varied, and the first major non/human animal character in Nintendo's Donkey Kong shows how they have versatility as both antagonists and protagonists. Mario's barrel-throwing ape nemesis from the 1981 original is the hero of the 1990s *Donkey Kong Country* series. Sega's *Sonic the Hedgehog* also features a non/human animal protagonist, although Sonic is nearly unrecognizable as a hedgehog because he moves rapidly, and balls up into an electric blue creature. Given that a common complaint about video games is their encouragement of an indoor hermetic lifestyle, Nintendo and Sega both appear to move away from non/human animals as antagonists toward playable non/human animal characters (Kutner 2008, 6). This can be interpreted as an attempt to preempt criticism about video games distracting from real-world issues and contributing to insensitivity toward ecology. It is telling, for example, that in the first incarnation of *Sonic*, the hero releases forest animals captured by his archenemy Doctor Robotnik. As his name and appearance as a madcap scientist in a flying machine suggest, Doctor Robotnik is emblematic of machines and technology as opposed to wildlife and nature.

However, the games' development histories and gameplay psychologies do not give credence to the idea that non/human animals feature as a consolation for the medium's supposed insularity. Playing as a non/human animal character has an ambivalent quality because it suggests the human gamer cares for the non/human depicted while the gamer's sense of agency promotes a self-centered mind-set that disregards the non/human. The playable non/human animal can, therefore, oscillate between the human "I," human-animal kinship, and the non/human character as a discrete other. Indeed, the non/human animal, its experiences and environment are seldom the determining subjects of games. A conversation between Sega's Tom Kalinske and Al Nilsen during the development of *Sonic* reveals that the specific non/human animal used was unimportant to them. "Seriously, though, don't worry about it . . . yet," Nilsen reassured Kalinske. "We haven't even seen any game play. And in this business, it could look like a duck and talk like a duck, but in the end nobody cares if it's a duck, or even a neon-green wolverine, as long as it makes for a fun gaming experience" (Harris 2014, 120). The interactivity in video games ensures that the means of interaction with the game take precedence over the ideology of its representations. Gamers will essentially empathize with anything that represents their presence in the game world.

Some video games take advantage of the human desire to care for dependents. Pet simulation games, such as *Nintendogs* in 2005 and *Nintendogs + Cats* in 2011, redirect care to virtual copies of domestic non/human animals. Continuing the trend for pet simulation formats spawned by the Tamagotchi phenomenon of the 1990s, Nintendo gave greater realism to the pet-keeper relationship through the increased tactility of touch screen gestures and interactivity of voice commands. Regardless of the increasing sophistication of the technology, however, the version of the non/human animal the gamer receives remains programmed and inorganic. It is two-dimensional in several respects, offering a prescribed model of care with relatively fixed criteria for success. As a screened replacement for a live dog the game provides only some of the stimulation and comfort of companionship without the bodily reality of non/human animals, or what Malamud refers to as "shit" to capture the unsavory parts of non/human animal life. Such games erase the live non/human animal from Baudrillard's observation that "pets are indeed an intermediate category between human beings and objects" (Baudrillard 2005, 95). Instead, long-term intimate human-animal relationships are fetishized as the simulated pet objectifies creatures to satisfy the demand for non/human animal engagements. Gamers ignore the production of animal images as a capitalist commodity, which obscures the possibility of more meaningful relationships. Virtual pets occlude domestic pets that betray the human nostalgia for the non/human animal's immersion in nature. The human fascination with non/human animals leads to interactions with the semblances of animals, which, even while they reference live creatures, conjure a greater disregard for the meaning of non/human animals beyond human conception.

The realistic simulation of non/human animals in virtual pet games also gives rise to its farcical opposite. In the darkly humorous indie title *Goat Simulator*, the non/human animal is deployed to conjure incongruous laughter and lowbrow levity. By the developer's admission, "*Goat Simulator* is a small, broken and stupid game" (Coffee Stain 2014). The player takes control of a calamity goat from a third-person perspective in a suburban setting and must cause damage to both non/human animals and the environment in as many hilarious ways as possible. The game employs "rag-doll" physics that animate the movement of the torso and limbs, usually in explosion, falling, or death sequences. Although its frivolity partially nullifies the impact of the depicted violence toward the goat, *Goat Simulator* reinforces the flippant use of non/human animals in exaggerated scenarios for cheap laughs. The radical danger of the game is not in inspiring extreme acts of copycat violence toward non/human animals as much as its contribution to the obtuse palimpsest of represented non/human animals that deepen cultural ignorance. It adds to a diffuse human chauvinism and fosters a callous self-

regard as a more widespread normative position, which entrenches desensiti-
zation to other sentient beings. Such hegemonic speciesism condones discrimination and exploitation tacitly at an underlying ideological level. This
oppression must be resisted, not only through written and visual forms of
representation, but through activism and education in schools and in the
community.

However, embedded in *Goat Simulator* is a critique of the principles of
simulation games generally, which aim to re-create reality at large, besides
the specific subjects or environments they replicate. In fact, the prevailing
joke of *Goat Simulator* is that it is not strictly a simulation game at all. While
the developers jest, "You no longer have to fantasize about being a goat, your
dreams have finally come true," the game does not simulate the experiences
or activities of a goat (Coffee Stain 2014). It lets a goat protagonist loose in
the virtual playground of an open world sandbox game. Using the word
"simulation" therefore offers a wry reaffirmation of the futility of simulation
if parity to reality remains the aim. When non/human animals "have been
drawn within succeeding orders of simulacra, and lose whatever reality they
may once have had," one simulation is as beyond truth and falsity as the next
(Hegarty 2009, 136). The game's ironic title feigns the idea that the game can
repeat the life of a goat, and, therefore, its purposefully outlandish portrayal
defers to the inscrutability of the non/human animal. The game developers
candidly state that "it would be best if you'd spend your $10 on a hula hoop,
a pile of bricks, or maybe a real-life goat" (Coffee Stain 2014). These sug-
gestions reveal that the virtual is in competition with reality as time, effort,
and money is spent on a self-professed "stupid" game as opposed to the
phenomena of the real world. In effect, *Goat Simulator* delivers a mixed
message that appears to acknowledge its potential damage to engagements
with reality, particularly real-life non/human animals, albeit through a dangerously trivial image of animality.

COUNTERPOISING CYBERBEASTS

The themes of substitution and trivialization in home movies, memes, and
video games seemingly reinforce Berger's emphasis on disappearance. They
evoke the non/human animal as a thing being replaced and devalued, which
maintains in principle the notion of an original place and value. In contrast,
Baudrillard's theories evince cyberculture's profound influence on visual
representation, and its intertextuality accentuates the divide between human
abstractions of non/human animals and the material lives of non/human animals. Home movies, memes, and video games reveal the necessity of reor-
ienting considerations of non/human animals from conceptions of the real or
knowable to a consciousness of the live and physical. The imperative for

non/human animal representations including visual, viral, and virtual forms is to sidestep the profound epistemological problems concerned with knowing the real non/human animal again. There is a need for a pragmatic ethos that will make humans more cognizant of how conceptualization shapes non/human animal simulacra. It must also encourage the ethical treatment of sentient, mortal beings in the world. Although home movies, memes, and video games clearly construct cyberbeasts—humanized, objectified vehicles of transient entertainment and humor—these forms can administer a counterpoising cultural education. This would produce images that stimulate meaningful, deferential, and wholesome coexistences with non/human animals, even if creaturely neighbors remain unfathomable in essence.

REFERENCES

Baudrillard, Jean. 1994a. *Simulacra and Simulation*. Translated by Sheila Faria Glaser. Ann Arbor: University of Michigan Press.
———.2005b. *The System of Objects*. Translated by James Benedict. London: Verso.
Berger, John. 2007. *Why Look at Animals?* In *The Animals Reader*, edited by Linda Kalof and Amy Fitzgerald, 251–261. New York: Berg.
Blake, Jonathan. 2014. "Video Games Need Same 'Cultural' Status as TV and Film." *BBC Newsbeat*, December 12. http://ww.bbc.co.uk/newsbeat/30439126.
Burt, Jonathan. 2002. *Animals in Film*. London: Reaktion.
Coffee Stain Studios. 2014. "Goat Simulator." http://www.goat-simulator.com.
Croteau, David, and William Hoynes. 2003. *Media and Society: Industries, Images and Audience*. Thousand Oaks, CA: Pine Forge Press.
DeMello, Margo. 2012. *Animals and Society: An Introduction to Human-Animal Studies*. New York: Columbia University Press.
Dredge, Stuart. 2014. "What's New, Pussycat? The Growing Economy of Internet Cat Videos." *Guardian*, March 9.
Harris, Blake J. 2014. *Console Wars: Sega, Nintendo, and the Battle That Defined a Generation*. London: Atlantic Books.
Hegarty, Paul. 2009. "Fate of the Animal." In *Jean Baudrillard: Fatal Theories*, edited by David B. Clarke, Marcus Doel, William Merrin, and Richard G. Smith, 136–146. Oxford: Routledge.
Kutner, Lawrence, and Cheryl Olsen. 2008. *Grand Theft Childhood: The Surprising Truth about Violent Video Games and What Parents Can Do*. New York: Simon and Schuster.
Lenhart, Amanda, Kristen Purcell, Aaron Smith, Kathryn Zickuhr. 2010. "Social Media and Mobile Internet Usage among Teens and Young Adults." http://pewinterent.org/Report/2010/Social-Media-and-Young-Adults.aspx.
Malamud, Randy. 1998. *Reading Zoos: Representations of Animals and Captivity*. Basingstoke: Palgrave Macmillan.
Schiesel, Seth. 2011. "Supreme Court Has Ruled; Now Games Have a Duty." *New York Times*, June 28.
Shifman, Limor. 2013. *Memes in Digital Culture*. Cambridge, MA: MIT Press.
Simmons, Laurence. 2010. "Nature and Animal." In *The Baudrillard Dictionary*, edited by Richard Smith, Edinburgh: Edinburgh University Press.
Wilson, Jake. 2014. "Sneezing Baby Panda: Review." *Sydney Morning Herald*, May 1.
Withnall, Adam. 2014. "Grumpy Cat: How a Reddit and YouTube Star Earned Its Owners $100m in Two Years." *Independent*, December 8.

Chapter 11

Pet-Animals in the Concrete Jungle: Tales of Abandonment, Failures, and Sentimentality in *San Hua* and *Twelve Nights*

Fiona Yuk-wa Law

While pet-keeping in the urban space is becoming a fashionable sign of economic prosperity, stories about such human-non/human relationships have illuminated the dialectics of alienation and intimacy of city dwellers. There have been popular cinematic narratives about alienated humans finding emotional anchorage in the non/humans in the urban context, like *Hachikō* (1987), *Cala My Dog* (2003), and *Marley and Me* (2008), to name a few. Among these tales, dispossession or abandonment is a shared theme that constructs the sentimental narrative world of encouragement, rehabilitation, trust, and affinity across species. Donna Haraway's notion of "entanglement" would accurately address this mutuality and affective constructiveness in multispecies relationships by suggesting that there are multiple ways in comprehending the communicative subject-making beyond linguistics (2008). However, instead of marveling at the transmission of affect among humans and non/human animals, it is more urgent to examine the situation when affectivity fails to connect. In light of the growing urban landscape of the concrete jungle, the ethics of caring also needs to be rethought when questions of affection and cruelty toward pet-animals are foregrounded. As a result, the non/human has emerged from the disappeared to the epitomized in the cosmopolitan everyday life. Non/human animals like pet-animals have triggered both the compassionate facet of the lonely urban humans as well as deterred the way these humans comprehend the limitations of affect. This is especially the case when the emotional connection is challenged, affection is unequal, and non/human animals are abandoned.

With the increasing concern over animal abuse and animal welfare by the media, there have been a number of films and microfilms on this issue in Chinese societies such as Hong Kong, Taiwan, and the People's Republic of China (PRC) in recent years. The Society for the Prevention of Cruelty to Animals (SPCA) in Hong Kong collaborated with Tencent (a China-based corporation that owns one of the biggest social media platforms in the PRC) to initiate the "Care for Life" microfilm series. Apart from institutions such as SPCA, independent filmmakers also work on this issue. Dissident artist Ai Weiwei produced *San Hua* (2010), a documentary that crudely traces the circulation of cat meat and fur industries throughout China. Popular Taiwanese writer Giddens Ko produced *Twelve Nights* (2014), a documentary that sentimentally chronicles the final days of homeless dogs in a shelter before they are euthanized or adopted. Through a comparative study of these two independent film projects, this chapter attempts to map out the topography of an affective sphere mediated by the visual narratives between the non/human animal-other and the human-self. It is found that narratives of abandonment and sentimentality about these hapless non/human animals have often been used as tools to attract public awareness of animal rights under a didactic discourse. It is questionable whether compassionate and sympathetic attitudes emitted from these on-screen representations would transmit or impede enlightenment. This chapter aims at provoking contemplation on the impact of speedy urban development on the wavering yet intimate relationship between human and non/human animals by focusing on the sentimental representations about pet-animals and examining the potential susceptibility of such representations.

FAILURES TO CONNECT: ABANDONMENT AS THE LIMBO OF THE COMPANION NON/HUMAN

Abandonment is often seen as an unsolicited act to the other when the reciprocity of affect fails to happen between subjects. This condition of being deserted also happens to non/human animals who fail to establish a sustainable affective relationship with their human companions. In many popular melodramatic narratives ranging from television dramas to popular song lyrics in the Chinese-language societies, abandonment in romantic and familial relationships is a common plot where the cold-hearted lover is blamed for their act of irresponsibly leaving their beloved ones. However, humans are often excused for their act of abandonment in most narratives about human-non/human relationships because such abandonment is often related to the constraints of urbanization and economic difficulties. These difficulties may include the prohibition of dog-keeping in housing estates, home moving, human pregnancy, and unaffordable medical treatment. Despite the fact that animal abandonment has been regarded as a "cruel and degrading act" since the Universal Declaration of the Rights of Animals in 1978, the unequal affective circuit between humans and other species has never been addressed. It is ironic that although the word "pet" etymologically refers to the status of being loved and pampered, such a beloved status is not sustainable. Haraway states that "The status of pet puts a dog at special risk . . . when human affection wanes, when people's conveniences takes precedence, or when the dog fails to deliver on the fantasy of unconditional love" (2003, 38). Such a fault line between fantasy and reality exposes the vulnerable boundary that defines and defies human-non/human relationships. Although using the term "companion" would alternatively suggest a less objectified notion by its association to partnership and comradeship of equal status, the emotional investment embedded in the cross-species relationship felt from the anthro-pocentric perspective has been largely influential to the extent that its vulner-ability could easily be overlooked (Adams 1994, 145).

Such fragility in the cross-species relation is often intensified and made problematic as the city expands its geographic boundary. On one hand, the expanding urban space has gradually reduced the natural environment for non/humans to live. On the other hand, the population of domesticated com-panion animals has been increasing. In Hong Kong, around 10.6 percent of all domestic households include dogs or cats, and there has been an increase in the overall pet population (HKSAR government 2011). In the PRC, there had been more than 1 million registered pet dogs in Beijing by 2012 (Larson 2014). While these figures only indicate the situation of "owned" pets, those non/human animals who are in the limbo of dispossession are often left outside this promising picture of expansion. According to the SPCA in Hong Kong, a total of 18,268 abandoned and stray animals were received and handled by the SPCA and the government in 2011–2012, with more than half of them euthanized (SPCA 2014). In Taiwan, more than 70 percent of the dogs held in public animal shelters have been euthanized from 1999 to 2009 (Tung et al. 2010, 180). In the face of this fracturable human-animal relation-ship in the urban context, I argue that this is a result of the gap between popular representations and the actual experience of pet-keeping. Such an interpretive gap in abstaining emotional attachment to the non/humans can be explained by the following reasons: 1) the cute factor or cute-response; 2) sentimental narratives; and 3) the avoidance of unease in looking at images of suffering.

One of the foremost barriers to sustaining cross-species affection is the cute factor or cute-response. In addition to Konrad Lorenz's early study of humans's immediate loving and nurturing response to the infantile visual features, Angier extends this psychological response to the human reaction to other species. She states that "cute cues are those that indicate extreme youth, vulnerability, harmlessness and need. . . . As a species whose youngest members are so pathetically helpless they can't lift their heads to suckle without adult supervision, human beings must be wired to respond quickly and gamely to any and all signs of infantile desire" (Angier 2006). Human beings develop a caring attitude to other species, in particular domesticated ones, by attending to this positive emotion expressed in non/human animal representations in popular culture, from Snoopy to Hello Kitty. This suggests that the representation of cuteness should encourage cross-species affectivity. However, the cuteness of non/human animals is often a self-deception imposed by the human believers in absolute innocence, purity, obedience, and infancy possessed by non/human others. As Sherman and Haidt argue, cuteness is a mechanism that causes social engagement and care only in an indirect sense (2011). The caring attitude generated from the cute-response is often unwarranted and deteriorates over time because this cuteness-induced caring sentiment is based on a fantasy of infancy. Dispossession and abandonment seems to be an inevitable and rational decision when these non/human companions "fail" the human. For example, when they no longer obey human commands; when their beastly qualities surprise humans due to the lack of trustworthy linguistic communication; when the human living environment can no longer tolerate these non/human residents because of incoherent habits; or when they grow old and get sick.

Second, in most popular representations, the cuteness of non/human animals is often narrated in a sentimental manner. Although sentimentality as a form of emotion generally carries "negative connotations of shallowness, insincerity, and inappropriateness" or even "culpable naivety" since the mid-eighteenth century (Winston 1992, 118–119; Jefferson 1983, 520), it is often used as a pedagogic device in animal advocacy and invites audience identification to the non/human animals in question. This aesthetics of sentimentality is often highlighted in cinematic texts, such as *San Hua* and *Twelve Nights*, to awaken moral awareness, sympathy, and empathy. This strategic way of representing and narrating stories of non/human animals often successfully advances a sense of responsibility to the species on the screen. This is because "emotion is a product of belief" and what humans feel is what they think they should act for (Jefferson 1983, 526). The "warm, sympathetic (including to oneself) love-sorrow spectrum of feelings . . . lead people to quite drastic actions" because most people are easily motivated by their sentimental responses to "spectacularly violent courses of behavior" such as animal abuse and abandonment (Tanner 1976, 130–131). Although feeling sentimental to what is represented may induce action, it is often merely temporary. The sentimental attachment produced by the emphasis upon "the sweetness, dearness, littleness, blamelessness, and vulnerability of the emotions' objects" is largely a result of a "gross simplification of the nature" of these animals (Jefferson 1983, 526–527). Mary Midgley explains that sentimentality is a rather "ill-formed notion" because being sentimental is a "self-deception" by "misrepresenting the world in order to indulge our feelings" that makes people "unable to deal with the real world" (1979, 385–386). Stephen Clark argues that "sentimentality is our enemy: the inability to see the real, suffering animal for a haze of aestheticism, misplaced piety and emotional projections" (1977, 9). Such a constructed fantasy about the triggered sentimentality through simplified or distorted representation of the world is one of the reasons why some people cannot sustain their emotional connection to the non/human animals in the everyday context. Worse still, sentimentality is shallow and not helpful to advocate radical social changes because it "reduced intensity and duration of emotional experience," and all powerful feelings are "diluted to a safe strength" (Winston 1992, 120). Therefore, sentimentality could be instigating mediocrity.

While charges of cute-response and sentimentality are related to that of anthropomorphism, the visual representations of these two features also produce a sugarcoated emotional bumper that allows the audience to shy away from the discomfort of seeing the unfamiliar side of other species. The mildness of cute images easily diverts the negative emotion that results from tragic situations. While cuteness and sentimentality help people awaken from their ignorance in order to compel action, their selectiveness in representing non/human animals hinders a deeper contemplation of the root of the problem because the spectator is encouraged to feel good about such representations. In *Regarding the Pain of Others*, Sontag makes a stern critique of the spectator's habitual response to images of atrocity, cruelty, and other representations of suffering. She argues there is merely provocation instead of a moral charge attached to representations of cruelties so that the spectator simply gets "satisfaction of being able to look at the images without flinching" (2003, 41). Similar to the pleasure of self-indulged sentimentality resulting from mild representations of suffering, the pleasure of flinching in the face of suffering accustoms the spectator to stop at "simply the bemused awareness" (Sontag 2003, 13). One will be "continually restocked" by the visual information that terrible or tragic things happen, and being turned into a "moral monster" if he or she does not feel pain and strive to abolish the cause of the represented havoc (Sontag 2003, 8–13). This easy consumption of pleasant and cruel images without thinking and acting is often fortified by popular representations, consumerist habits, and the circulation of new social media campaigns. The result encourages an ungrounded affective connection between humans and other species, as if abandonment of companion animals does not need to be justified in this fast-food visual culture.

Although *San Hua* and *Twelve Nights* are non-commercial productions, their representational strategy follows the popular discourse of cuteness or sentimentality. In light of the "void" of animal welfare laws in China and minimal ones in Taiwan, the problems of animal abandonment and abuse are even more severe due to the vague status of some non/human species in the cultural context of Chinese societies (Li 2006, 117–118). Despite the increasing attention to animal rights in recent years, it is still not a surprise to find that dogs and cats are regarded as meat and fur resources in addition to companion animals. The special cuisine of dog and cat meat is often found in restaurants in suburban areas and secondary cities of these Chinese regions. As shown in *San Hua*, stray dogs and cats are the major sources of these dishes and fur products. It seems there is no guarantee to human affection to the non/human companions, or that such human affection to non/human animals is confined within speciesism. The companionship of cats and dogs is no different from their usefulness as meat and fur because they are of inferior status to human beings; instead of offering their meat and fur, companion cats and dogs create a stress-releasing comfort zone to their humans. However, the speciesist root is exposed and this comfort zone is rendered ineffective when the non/human companions get old, sick, and disobedient. This further reveals the ambiguous status of dogs and cats, or the absent boundary between companion species and eating animals (McHugh 2004, 31–37). In addition, the popularity of anthropomorphized non/human representations forecloses the possibility of understanding non/human species in an everyday context, and the increasing pet-keeping population leads to more abandonment, maltreatment, and factory breeding.

In the Chinese cultural context, *San Hua* and *Twelve Nights* show the cruel consequences to abandoned animals when there is a moral disconnect between human and non/human animals. By promoting the urgent need for animal adoption and unveiling the tragic consequence of abandonment, the two films subtly critique current policies by exposing the invisible scenes of cruelty and highlighting the problematic status of companion animals in Chinese societies. Both films imply human vulnerability through either focusing on the powerlessness of animal advocates or by evading the experiences of shelter workers in the face of animal cruelty. Through different sets of visual narratives, the two films remind the public of the need to see the precarious status of those companion animals whose human counterparts no longer accompany them. Their condition of desertion both highlights and throws into question their status as a human possession. This notion of possession does not only refer to the objectification and consumption of non/human animals by humans, but also the shaky affective possession that is often one-way and temporary, and therefore highly subject to cessation by one party.

Responding to the general urban development in Chinese cities, the two films advocate the need to understand non/human animals by redeveloping humans's "sympathetic intellectual capacities" (Donovan 2007, 177). When the urban setting causes the waning of sympathy, and economic and pragmatic thinking overrides ethical choice, it is paramount that we should regard sympathy not only as a sentiment but as a "form of knowledge" (Donovan 2007, 177). By getting rid of the one-sided, anthropocentric conception of non/human animals, the inter-subjective cross-species affective linkage could be reestablished and fortified in a sustainable fashion. As Willett states, "affects can spread like a physical contagion across thousands of miles via waves of energy transmission" (2014, 85). The visual public sphere of social media and cinematic medium might generate "an appropriately communitarian basis for moral norms" through the energy produced and mediated by images (Willett 2014, 80). Although Willett does not directly refer to the role of mass media in her discussion of multispecies ethics, she points out the possibilities technologies provide to modern humans to "relearn" the old knowledge about the felt relationships across species so that the imperceptible communicative channels across species can be recovered (2014, 98–99). I would add that through the transmission of visual images across screens and human bodies, an imagined community could be formed on a communicative-pedagogic landscape where humans are awakened by mediated affective contagion. An emancipatory social change and a multispecies social dynamic about the situation of non/human animals can be formed when "communicative awareness of ethical claims and social expectations" are activated through "affect attunement" and self-cultivation (Willett 2014, 84).

Although *San Hua* and *Twelve Nights* do not apparently provide a unified discourse about what is best for non/human animals in the city, they channel the idea of an affective attunement through the media. By exposing the different visual narratives of sentimentality about human-non/human relationships in the context of animal advocacy, this chapter elucidates some of the problematic aspects of the debates and gives credit to the problematized narratives that mobilize animal liberation. In so doing, this chapter sheds light on rethinking the current representations of non/human animals in domestic captivity and the ethics of caring in the age of global pet-culture.

SAN HUA: A DOCUMENTARY JOURNEY OF TEAR, FEAR, AND INDIFFERENCE

Produced by dissident artist-activist Ai Weiwei's studio, the circulation of *San Hua* (literally meaning "three flowers," a common description of calico cats in Chinese) is available free of charge on the Internet via YouTube and other online media platforms. This mode of circulation is similar to the SPCA's short film series as both of them rely on social media to advocate for social change. However, different from the SPCA's short films or other popular narratives that promise an imaginary intimate human-non/human animal relationship through sentimentalizing this bonding, *San Hua* is a documentary that crudely draws on various footage ranging from interviews with animal advocates and customers at restaurants to images of hidden cameras that follow cat rescue actions and retailers of the cat fur industry. These materials offer extremely diverse opinions about how Chinese people regard cats either as food or sentient beings, thereby eliciting an emphasis on the emotional charge and the indifference of its human subjects in light of non/ human suffering.

The film is structured as a journey across the country from the north— including Tianjin, Shanghai, Jiangsu, and Hebei—to the south—including Guangzhou—in order to narrate the overall doomed fate of cats as abandoned pets, stray animals, captive food source, and raw materials for the fur market. As shown in the documentary, advocates cannot rescue these cats from smuggling to the south due to the lack of legal protection of animals nation-wide as well as indifference of the local governments. This documentary not only problematizes the controversy of non/human animals as meat by the passionate animal advocates, apathetic gourmets and cooks, and unconcerned traders and officers; it also exposes the ungoverned meat and fur trade indus-try within the nation. The film exposes such hidden controversy through the journeys of animal advocates and animal traders, as both parties work cease-lessly in opposite directions to expose and bury the cruel reality about cats and dogs in the PRC. An implied commentary on the rapidly developing economy in the PRC is woven by using images of tears from the animal advocates, images of indifference from consumers and producers, and im-ages of fear from the non/human animals in question.

The documentary opens with a calico cat facing the camera in medium shot. A strong sense of individualism and agency is conveyed as she moves her head sideways in slow motion. Then it cuts to a handheld camera follow-ing a group of women stopping a truck filled with cages of captured cats on a highway at midnight. Some government officials offer to help these middle-aged women who are yelling at the truck driver. They keep the whole truck at the police station overnight for investigation. The next morning, these wom-en complain to the police for not offering food and water to the hundreds of captured cats who are still on the truck in the cold weather. They also com-plain about the impolite attitude of one police officer and the local govern-ment for permitting such trade. They do not believe the truck driver's claim that these 600 collared cats are being transported for adoption in Guangdong. The camera continues to follow these middle-aged women as it reveals that they are a group of animal advocates from Shanghai who have been tracing the trafficking of domestic and stray cats in their neighborhood. One of them has been supporting the trap-neuter-return program of stray cats solely on her pension. Another woman even rents an empty apartment in order to take care of a large number of rescued cats. She explains that all these cats are lovely, cute, and too harmless to be killed. All these women cry in front of the camera in expressing their worries about the precarious condition of the cats; they also optimistically envision that the PRC will implement animal welfare laws one day. This passionate group of female animal advocates, who emotionally attend to the suffering of cats, connotes a feminist ethic of care that draws a connection between the "attention to the individual suffering animal" and the "attention to the political and economic systems that are causing the suffering" (Donovan and Adams 2007, 3). The tear-jerking interviews with these crying women uncover a sentimental critique of the government with its lack of animal rights, which results in the suffering of the non/human animals. As Li points out, animal welfare has received increasing attention by policy-makers in the PRC since 1997, but there is an absence of actionable welfare stipulations and an absence of overarching anti-cruelty laws (2006, 117). The animal-related legislation in the PRC is problematic because it was established to regulate "reasonable use of animal resources" in order to advance the interest of humans and not how non/human animals are treated (Li 2006, 117). Also, since the existing laws mainly concern endangered species, common species such as cats, dogs, and other domestic species fall outside the protection of any laws, resulting in an unregulated continuance of these non/human animals being abused (Li 2006, 117).

However, the indifference of the general public in Chinese society to animal cruelty is apparent not only in inadequate legislation. It also reflects a problematic ideology which does not regard non/human species as sentient beings. In the documentary, interviews are conducted with customers at a local restaurant in Guangdong, and conversations are recorded on hidden camera with fur dealers and other anonymous people who are familiar with the trade of cat meat and fur. All these conversations reveal their apathy to the suffering cats. For example, a gourmet speaks honestly and cheerfully about his lack of feeling when eating cats. In contrast to the emotional animal advocates, these people exemplify the horrible result of the use of "meat" and "fur" as false mass terms (Adams 1994). In short, using terms like "meat" and "fur" reduces specific species to an object or "something that has no distinctiveness, no uniqueness, no individuality" (Adams 1994, 27–28). This encourages people to see non/humans as machines or crops instead of bodies. Hence, customers do not care about the lives of what they eat, and the fur retailers do not attend to the cries and struggle of cats who are brutally killed in the process. This deceptive use of mass terms for non/human animals is even more disturbing because the same group of cats is regarded as both companion animals and daily resources under different circumstances.

While the documentary exposes the underground trade in cat meat as being disguised as other meat sources in producing sausages, the problem is no longer only the double standard in treating cats as both pets and as meat. The treatment of cat fur also becomes an issue of pollution. This is shown by the abstract image of tumbling cat fur in a watermill at the end of the documentary. The unwarranted food industry, food safety, and pollution caused by intense industrialization in the PRC are intertwined with the brutal treatment of non/human animals. All these point to the loopholes in the ideological system the PRC upholds. This implied political commentary is revealed in the uncaring attitudes of the interviewees as well. Borrowing from Samantha Power's work on human apathy in genocide, Carol Adams suggests that "the ability to objectify feelings" is another reason people have not cared (2007, 33). In turn, people are trained to stay outside the political realm, become afraid to care, and discouraged from breaking the "normalizing ideological screen" (Adams 2007, 33). Worse still, the objectification of feelings is required as a sign of submission to authority. This apathy leads to people's desire to move away from uncomfortable feelings, resulting in an overall passivity sustained by thoughts of futility and the fear of caring attitude. The fear of discomfort and fragility of care is based on an ideologically conditioned presumption that caring causes obliteration of human power, knowledge, and experience. In the documentary, the contrast between those who care and those who do not shows two different sets of attitudes to the same authority.

The documentary also weaves a crude texture about the miserable reality of cats and dogs being slaughtered for meat and fur by revealing images of their fear and suffering. Juxtaposed with the interviews and conversations are other images that serve as supplementary background information, ironic commentary, and quiet protests from the non/human animals. For example, right after showing a stray Shih Tzu dog wandering in busy traffic in a duration shot, it cuts to a hidden camera footage of cats being slaughtered and cooked in the street with the off-screen voice of the slaughterer introducing the taste of cat meat. The next scene jumps to a TV screen showing an animation about the Enlightenment of Buddha. The juxtaposition of this didactic animation with footage of cats being killed is an ironic critique of the inexcusable fact that, while the public is encouraged to become compassionate in Buddhist teaching, they are ignoring the brutal slaughtering of non/human animals happening in the street. Furthermore, other footage is incorporated to introduce the scenario of animal welfare in China, including an online streaming of the process of a cat being suspended, killed, and stripped of skin, and news reports about the increasing number of pet-keepers, animal abuse, and the need for animal rights legislation. Although it seems to be true that the "harm done to animals is rendered invisible to most people" due to the "massive ideological screening," all these secondary visual materials prove that brutality is actually not invisible, especially in an age of social media (Donovan and Adams 2007, 3).

Taking the view that this documentary may suggest and encourage a political analysis of the ideological system in relation to animal advocacy in China, it is found that the root of the problem about the lack of animal rights legislation could be more complicated. Scholars such as Peter J. Li, Song Wei, and Paul Littlefair point out that the lack of public conscience to the conditions of non/human animals, inadequate actionable stipulations of existing laws, and the fundamental anthropocentric moral values in Chinese culture are the major problems that prevent change (Li 2006, 111–128; Wei 2006, 101–110; Littlefair 2006, 225–237). In addition, the investigation of animal cruelty in China could potentially lead to the disclosure of many other social problems related to the differences and indifference of regional governance, environmental issues related to urban development and allocation of land use, the emergence of charity groups and their political implications, food safety, and so on.

TWELVE NIGHTS: TOWARD AN AESTHETIC OF LYRICAL DOCUMENTARY ABOUT ABANDONMENT

Released in 2014, *Twelve Nights* is an independent documentary co-produced by Taiwanese popular writer-director Giddens Ko and actress-model Sonia Sui. The celebrity effect of this film grabbed public attention about this marginal topic in popular Taiwanese cinema—in addition to the hugely successful box office return that the producers donated to animal protection groups. Unlike the crude unveiling of the meat and fur industry by *San Hua*, *Twelve Nights* expresses an entirely opposite documentary texture about the equally gloomy condition of non/human animals in captivity. As its title suggests, the documentary records the stories of captured stray dogs in a shelter in Taiwan within a period of twelve nights in early 2013. These twelve nights are in fact a symbol of finitude. According to the Animal Protection Act in Taiwan, unclaimed or "properly disposed" non/human animals kept in shelters over twelve days may be euthanized. Euthanasia is still a "nearly universally accepted 'necessary evil' simply because people were not willing to deal with the causes of pet overpopulation" (Pamental 2004, 213). The documentary showcases this supposed necessary evil by showing the cruel countdown process where seemingly healthy dogs are captured, wait in limbo, and finally die from infection or diseases or get euthanized. Sadly, there is an absence of austere criticism of such treatment or the unhygienic environment through the film's diminishing of human involvement in the plot. Instead, the film is textured by an overall lyricism, or what I call the aesthetic of lyrical cruelty and radical sentimentality, in expressing an alternative way to effectuate animal advocacy.

The plot covers these twelve nights in chronological order. Among the 450 dogs in the shelter, around 41 are identified and introduced with names throughout the film. Their stories are narrated by intertitles that define the temporal development and provide additional information about the shelter and the dogs: their condition when they are captured, the origins of their names, their relationships to other inmates, the circulation of canine distemper virus and canine parvovirus infection within the shelter, the daily routine within the shelter, and the procedures of euthanasia. Although all the dogs are not identified with microchips, most of them are wearing collars: an indicator that they used to have human guardians before they were found wandering in the streets. The state of being unclaimed by the human "owners" in fact registers the non/human animals in eternal limbo. When the ex-companion animals are abandoned or unclaimed as human properties, some are captured in the street by various organizations until they are either adopted again or euthanized. This in-between status of dispossession usually falls outside of normative discussions on the ethics of captivity and care. The deferral of care is often highlighted as the shelter is usually seen as an undesirable place for dispossessed non/human animals to stay. More often, rules and regulations are imposed on the operational logic of these shelters as they often lack sustainable support to run for the long term. As a result, liminality or the status of suspension becomes cessation when the dogs are regarded as unwanted obstacles. Abandonment therefore epitomizes such ambivalent in-between-ness of non/human animals in human habitat. In turn, the cinematic images of these canine protagonists, who mostly die before the documentary ends, become the "only evidence that proves these dogs were once alive."

The stories of these 41 dogs begin at the moment when they are brought to the shelter. Being the major narrative space in the documentary, the shelter invites a rethinking of the notions of captivity and caring. As Lori Gruen suggests, most institutions of captivity such as prisons, farms, laboratories, and even domestic spaces are largely invisible and hidden from sight and the condition of imprisonment is often beyond our consciousness (2014, 1–2). On the other hand, the shelter's status of captivity is defined by an opportunity of being taken care of. As Edminster puts it,

> [D]ogs in animal shelters, especially euthanizing shelters, are in unquestionably vulnerable positions. Their quality of life, including freedom of movement and access to food, as well as their continued existence, is entirely dependent on human decisions, whether capricious, thoughtful, rationally calculated, or emotionally motivated. When dogs are adopted they are often seen as "being given a chance" to live. (2011, 132)

However, the situation of dogs in this documentary is not so positive since the shelter represents a literal death camp where nearly 90 percent of the captives cannot survive after twelve nights. There were debates about such a representation when some of the workers and veterinarians in the animal shelter felt upset after watching the documentary since it seems to suggest maltreatment (Chen, Chou, and Pan 2013). In response to such critical reception, Giddens Ko publicly expressed his gratitude to the shelter for being the only animal shelter in Taiwan that granted permission for their film-shooting. He also explained, "Animal shelters are helping to solve a difficult problem that our society has long neglected. They are not the documentary's target of criticism. . . . Our criticism is aimed at the people who have created this problem: The pet owners who abandoned these animals" (Chen, Chou, and Pan 2013). In fact, the shelter's permission for film-shooting means that the initially enclosed and invisible scene of cruelty should be changed and exposed to public surveillance because animal shelters like the one in the film lack financial, governmental, and public support to improve their environment. Exposing the daily routines of the shelter also triggers humans to become aware of the horrible aftermath of abandonment.

Various representational strategies are adopted to invite audience dwelling into this dreadful world. The intentional effacement of human presence in the documentary helps direct the audience identification to the subjectivity of the dogs instead of their human counterparts. While human faces of the shelter workers, veterinarians, visitors, and adaptors are blurred, fragmented, and out-of-frame, the individual faces of the dogs are constantly put in focus when their stories are narrated in a sentimental manner. Some of the dogs are granted elaborated narration about their social networks within the cage such as their kinship with other dogs, their changing health conditions, and even how other dogs respond to these dogs' waning conditions. One of the startling examples shows a yellow mongrel named Bodhidharma shiver and turn his head to the dead body of his friend Pikachu next to him. Editing is employed to suture the subplots of various dogs to convey a sense of coherence about their responses. A "structure of sympathy" is therefore constructed between the human spectator and non/human protagonists (Porter 2006, 409–410). The spectator does not only identify with the protagonists, he or she also cultivates the consistent alignment with the non/human protagonists.

In addition to intertitles, close-ups and point of view shots are employed extensively to convey the dogs' state of mind. As Bousé observes, close-ups are commonly used in wildlife films in order to portray non/human animals as possessing human-like thoughts and emotional responses (2003). He suggests that a "false intimacy" between the human audience and the non/human animal is expressed through close-ups. In order to initiate narratives, establish characters and point of view, indicate feelings, portray subjective experience, and create identification, the use of close-ups results in a misapprehension of images after the audience has undergone regular viewing over time (Bousé 2003, 123–132). This misapprehension may even put the human audience at risk as their expectation of personal interaction with wild animals may lead to wrong and unrealistic perceptions of animal behaviors. Although the non/human subjects in *Twelve Nights* are domesticized dogs, the use of close-ups in a sentimental and lyrical fashion should be taken seriously as to whether it can advocate human concerns with their situations.

Accompanied by melodic background music, the overall yellowish and greenish color tone and occasional bluish touch throughout the documentary highlights the depressing and surrealistic environment inside the shelter in an impressionistic manner. The camera's attention paid to the occasional gleams of sunlight may have suggested the bleak future of these dogs, as each occurrence and passing of daylight is a visual reminder that a day is gone and the deadline is approaching. While this lyricism and poetic texture is rarely found in animal documentaries about suffering and death, this documentary is exposing the cruel fate of the dogs in the shelter and aims to change the scenario through eternalizing their shortened lives in a poeticized expression. Another way of understanding the lyricism in this documentary would be through Deleuze's concept of lyrical abstraction (1986). According to Deleuze, lyrical abstraction is about the affective qualities of visual alternatives such as light and shadow, that an "alternative, a spiritual choice instead of a struggle or a fight" is emitted from the visual style (1986, 113). The spirituality of lyrical abstraction lies in the affective potentialities of the image in expressing "an alternative between the state of things itself and the possibility, the virtuality, which goes beyond it" (Deleuze 1986, 112). This means that by negating the impressionistic portrayals of the suffering dogs in the shelter, the visual abstraction of this documentary offers the aesthetics of lyrical cruelty in providing an alternative spiritual choice to the audience instead of the non/human subjects. Although the dogs are already euthanized by the time this documentary is shown to the audience, their crystallized cinematic form proposes that there is the potential to avoid repeating such cruelty. The emotional recognition of the individual subjectivity of these dogs through close-ups, naming, and narrating their social relationship is therefore a result of the lyrical exposé of cruelty, which can be a possible communicative strategy to awakening our compassion from the numbing effect of massification by "asserting the individual and maintaining our ties to the dead as individuals" (Adams 2007, 25). It is therefore crucial to address the posthumous nature of the sensory-loaded images to establish a compassionate tie.

On the other hand, this visual mode of representing non/human animals on the screen can be easily accused of anthropomorphism. With the fact that verbal communication between humans and other species is limited, it seems to most people that the adaptation of non/human animals' subjective viewpoint is actually that of human interpretation. Although Donovan argues that non/human animals' subjective standpoint needs to be articulated as a form of resistance to the institutionalized process of slaughtering, she has not explained how to articulate the non/human animals' subjectivity within the boundary of institutionalized killing (2007b, 360–362). On the other hand,

Porter argues that anthropomorphism can propose the possibility of redefining or revising what "personhood" is, which results in de-privileging humanness as a prestige (2006). By elaborating on Smith's study of spectator engagement with non/human characters, Porter proposes three forms of non/human personhood: the attribution of personhood to a non/human character performed by a non/human, the assertion of non/human personhood through a human character or narrator, and the human performance of the non/human (2006, 406). *Twelve Nights* adopts such cues by including a silent human voiceover in the form of intertitles, which functions as a "human intermediary who asserts features of nonhuman personhood" (Porter 2006, 406). In addition to providing background information, the de-humanized intertitles play a heavy role in this documentary by creating an ambivalent in-betweenness of human existence that situates itself as both omnipresent and absent, verbal and nonverbal, as well as descriptive and critical. At the same time, the viewer is invited to identify with this muted human-like narrator who is both among and detached from the non/human characters.

Although the aesthetics of lyrical cruelty reinforces the affective qualities of its visual texture, *Twelve Nights* still shies away from the eternally wretched condition in the dog shelter. Emphasizing adoption as the resolution to the current situation, the documentary does not trace back to the cause of suffering—abandonment—since most of these sad stories begin with the aftermath of dispossession. To a certain degree, the magical colors and the transient light and shadows allow this visual testimony to remain a fantasy of sentimentality. Audiences who dare not watch the crude reality as it is recorded in *San Hua* might prefer engaging in this sentimental fantasy of lyrical cruelty and respond by shedding tears. This deviation in the representational strategies of the two documentaries does not mean that *Twelve Nights* is less effective as an advocacy documentary than *San Hua*. Rather, the sentimentality of *Twelve Nights* is reinforced by an overall discourse about the frailty of the human counterparts in the shelter system.

For example, the intertitle for the ninth night states, "I can only mark a Triangle on your name." This suggests that the veterinarians ("I") can do nothing but euthanize the dogs in order to make space for the next batch of captured stray dogs. This wretchedness is further foregrounded as these veterinarians' faces are never clearly shown on screen, forbidding their expression of thoughts and feelings to the audience. The intertitles state, "There is at least one vet in every shelter. But their job is not to treat the animals," "the dogs are put down by veterinarians hired specifically for this task," and "every year more than 6,000 dogs are sent to this shelter. More than 5,000 of them failed to escape from euthanasia. This 12-day deadline dampens the spirits of the animals as well as the people who are involved." Accompanying these literal explanations are images of skinny dogs staggering in cages and vomiting after they are sedated but before receiving their injections of potassium chloride or barbiturates. They will later end up in plastic bags that are piled on top of one another, filling the screen.

The endless twelve-nights cycle looks dehumanizing and cruel, but at the same time lyrical and tear-jerking. Questions may arise as to why humans cannot do something to stop this victimizing system initiated by humans themselves. In fact, the documentary does offer an answer to this question by inserting a pedagogic message of "Adopt, not Abandon" at the beginning and ending. Only a few dogs can survive beyond the twelve deadly nights by being adopted. This seemingly didactic strategy may have proved successful. In fact, following the release of this documentary and the emerging discussion about existing legislation, 25 revisions to the Animal Protection Act were passed in Taiwan in January 2015, including a ban on euthanizing captured stray animals by 2017 (Lin 2015). The twelve nights have not ended, but hope remains, and the approach of daylight is possible.

THE PET SHOP AS SWEATSHOP: RETHINKING CAPTIVITY AND THE ETHICS OF CARING

I grew up on a street in Hong Kong filled with aquariums and pet shops located in Mongkok, one of the most densely populated districts in the city. Combined with the fact that there is no large-scale zoo in Hong Kong, this means that there is insufficient chance for urban dwellers to know what life is like to the non/human species. Without non/human companion animals, one's imaginary about other species could only be confined to screened representations, the spectacles of pet shops in the city, a brief glimpse of sparrows flying among the concrete jungle, or non/human animals exhibited in the closest zoo, in Guangzhou, Southern China. Yet, non/human animals like guinea pigs, parrots, rabbits, cats, dogs, exotic fish, tortoises, lizards, and frogs are all easily available in the shopping windows of the various pet shops. These shops are often flooded with potential consumers and curious spectators who imagine rosy futures of living harmoniously together with these cute surrogate "children." Few of these people would find this spectatorship distorted and disturbing as the visual pleasure produced in the pet shop is a matter of life and death to the displayed "objects" whose lives are "reproduced" by commercial breeding. "Cute" is a dangerous adjective. We use it in an excited tone when a fluffy, cuddly, and seemingly amiable creature enters our field of vision. Using this word in such a daily context, we are also making it even more precarious as this word both describes the lovely vulnerability of the non/human animals and our shameless foreclosure to understand who these creatures are.

The pet shop is actually a sweatshop. Behind the orderly façade of affective consumerism is the scene of blood and sweat as female dogs and cats are converted into laboring machines. Throughout their lives, they are trapped in prison-like cages in puppy and kitten mills that are mostly illegally operated in Hong Kong. We should never forget what Yi-fu Tuan stresses about the cultural history of non/human captivity in the form of domestication (1984). Human affection for non/human animals is synonymous to cruelty due to the hierarchical boundary between us and them. "Domestication means domination: the two words have the same root sense of mastery over another being—of bringing it into one's house or domain" (Yuan 1984, 99). In light of this ambivalent power relationship and incongruous emotional attachment to our non/human companion animals, how can we understand the meaning of domestication? Since we seem to have no obligation to end domestication or to stop holding domesticated non/human animals captive, perhaps one basic and beginning step toward the ethics of domestication could be that of Cochrane's suggestion "to eradicate and overhaul those institutions and practices that ensure that domesticated animals lead short lives full of suffering" (2014, 157). Putting the stories of suffering on screen, attending to what is not seen, and opening up a compassionate leeway of care is still a method for public transformation to help stop desertion from happening. The next step after the public views such oppressive stories must be to act to fight against this violence through community organizing and activism. The traits of sentimentality are perhaps unreliable in advancing human-non/human animal relationships, but humanity in its imperfection may need to develop its empathy from this defective starting point.

REFERENCES

Adams, Carol J. 1994a. *Neither Man Nor Beast: Feminism and the Defense of Animals*. New York: Continuum.
———.2007b. "The War on Compassion." In *The Feminist Tradition in Animal Ethics*, edited by Josephine Donovan and Carol J. Adams, 21–36. New York: Columbia University Press.
Bousé, Derek. 2003. "False Intimacy: Close-ups and Viewer Involvement in Wildlife Films." *Visual Studies* (18)2: 123–132.
Census and Statistics Department, Hong Kong SAR. 2011. *Thematic Household Survey Report 48*. Hong Kong: Census and Statistics Department.
Chen, Christie. 2014. "'Twelve Nights' Director Donates All Film Proceeds to Animal Groups." *Focus Taiwan News Channel*, May 20. http://m.focustaiwan.tw/news/aedu/201405200011.aspx.
Chen, Wei-tsung, Chou Nien-chu, and Jason Pan. 2013. "Documentary Gives Viewers Wrong Impression, Animal Shelter Staff Say." *Taipei Times*, December 22.
Clark, Stephen R. L. 1977. *The Moral Status of Animals*. Oxford: Clarendon Press.
Cochrane, Alasdair. 2014. "Born in Chains? The Ethics of Animal Domestication." In *The Ethics of Captivity*, edited by Lori Gruen, 156–173. New York: Oxford University Press.
Deleuze, Gilles. 1986. *Cinema 1: The Movement-Image*. Translated by Hugh Tomlinson and Barbara Habberjam. Minneapolis: University of Minnesota Press.
Donovan, Josephine. 2007a. "Attention to Suffering: Sympathy as a Basis for Ethical Treatment of Animals." In *The Feminist Tradition in Animal Ethics*, edited by Josephine Donovan and Carol J. Adams, 174–197. New York: Columbia University Press.

————.2007b. "Caring to Dialogue: Feminism and the Treatment of Animals." *The Feminist Tradition in Animal Ethics*, edited by Josephine Donovan and Carol J. Adams, 360–369. New York: Columbia University Press.

————.2007c. "Introduction." In *The Feminist Tradition in Animal Ethics*, edited by Josephine Donovan and Carol J. Adams, 2–20. New York: Columbia University Press.

Edminster, Avigdor. 2011. "Interspecies Families, Freelance Dogs, and Personhood: Saved Lives and Being One at an Assistance Dog Agency." In *Making Animal Meaning*, edited by Linda Kalof and Georgina M. Montgomery, 127–143. East Lansing: Michigan State University Press.

Gruen, Lori. 2014. "Introduction." In *The Ethics of Captivity*, edited by Lori Gruen, 1–4. New York: Oxford University Press.

Guo, Ke. 2010. *San Hua*. Online video, 1:08:24. https://youtu.be/D-M7CYhzeQs.

Haraway, Donna. 2003a. *The Companion Species Manifesto: Dogs, People, and Significant Otherness*. Chicago: Prickly Paradigm Press.

————. 2008b. *When Species Meet*. Minneapolis: University of Minnesota Press.

Jefferson, Mark. 1983. "What Is Wrong with Sentimentality?" *Mind* 92:519–529.

Larson, Christine. 2014. "China's Skyrocketing (Pet) Population." *Bloomberg Businessweek*, August 21. http://www.businessweek.com/articles/2014-08-21/chinas-skyrocketing-pet-population.

Li, Peter J. 2006. "The Evolving Animal Rights and Welfare Debate in China: Political and Social Impact Analysis." In *Animals, Ethics and Trade: The Challenge of Animal Sentience*, edited by Jacky Turner and Joyce D'Silva, 111–128. London: Earthscan.

Lin, Enru. 2015. "Legislation Orders No-kill Shelters by 2017." *China Post*, January 24. http://www.chinapost.com.tw/taiwan/national/national-news/2015/01/24/427283/Legislature-orders.htm

Littlefair, Paul. 2006. "Why China Is Waking Up to Animal Welfare." In *Animals, Ethics and Trade: The Challenge of Animal Sentience*, edited by Jacky Turner and Joyce D'Silva, 225–237. London: Earthscan.

Luke, Brian. 2007. "Justice, Caring, and Animal Liberation." *The Feminist Tradition in Animal Ethics*, edited by Josephine Donovan and Carol J. Adams, 125-152. New York: Columbia University Press.

McHugh, Susan. 2004. *Dog*. London: Reaktion Books.

Midgley, Mary. 1979a. "Brutality and Sentimentality." *Philosophy* 54:385–389.

————. 1983b. *Animals and Why They Matter*. Athens: University of Georgia Press.

Pamental, Matthew. 2004. "Pragmatism and Pets: Best Friends Animal Sanctuary, Maddie's Fund, and No More Homeless Pets in Utah." In *Animal Pragmatism: Rethinking Human-Nonhuman Relationships*, edited by Erin McKenna and Andrew Light, 210–227. Bloomington: Indiana University Press.

Porter, Pete. 2006. "Engaging the Animal in the Moving Image," *Society & Animals* 14(4): 399–416.

Sherman, Gary D., and Jonathan Haidt. 2011. "Cuteness and Disgust: The Humanizing and Dehumanizing Effects of Emotion." *Emotion Review* 3(3): 1–7.

Smith, Murray. 1995. *Engaging Characters: Fiction, Emotion, and the Cinema*. Oxford: Oxford University Press.

Song, Wei. 2006. "Animal Welfare Legislation in China: Public Understanding and Education." In *Animals, Ethics and Trade: The Challenge of Animal Sentience*, edited by Jacky Turner and Joyce D'Silva, 101–110. London: Earthscan.

Sontag, Susan. 2003. *Regarding the Pain of Others*. New York: Picador.

SPCA. 2014. "Animal Welfare in Hong Kong." http://www.spca.org.hk/en/animal-welfare/what-is-animal-welfare/animal-welfare-in-hong-kong.

Tanner, Michael. 1976-1977. "Sentimentality." *Proceedings of the Aristotelian Society* 77: 127–147.

Tuan, Yi-fu. 1984. *Dominance and Affection: The Making of Pets*. New Haven, CT: Yale University Press.

Tung, Meng-Chih, Chang-Young Fei, Jeng-Yung Chiang, Chung-Hsi Chou, Lih-Sen Yeh, Chen-yuan Liao, Yao-Chi Su, Jen-Chauch Chang, and Kwong-Chung Tung. 2010. "Surveys of Dog Populations in Taiwan from 1999 to 2009." *Journal of the Chinese Society of Animal Science* 39(3): 175–188.

Twelve Nights. 2013. Directed by Raye. Taiwan: Fashion Multi-media. DVD.

Willett, Cynthia. 2014. *Interspecies Ethics*. New York: Columbia University Press.

Winston, Andrew S. 1992. "Sweetness and Light: Psychological Aesthetics and Sentimental Art." In *Emerging Visions of the Aesthetic Process: Psychology, Semiology, and Philosophy*, edited by Gerald C. Cupchik and János László, 118–136. New York: Cambridge University Press.

Chapter 12

In Defense of Non/Humans: Mystification and Oppression in the Sports Mascoting Process

Guilherme Nothen and Michael Atkinson

A considerable share of the embodied and symbolic violence perpetrated against a broad spectrum of non/human animals in North America is both socially undertaken and culturally justified under the aegis of organized sport. The institutional breadth and depth of animal mistreatment in sport stands in sharp contrast to the paucity of scholarly work tackling similar issues. It is true that the study of traditional "sporting" practices such as hunting, for example, speaks to the very emergence of a sociological perspective on sport (Elias 2008). Only recently have scholars granted concerted attention to the precarious, vulnerable, and relatively powerless positions that non/human animals occupy within sports, exercise, and leisure zones. This emerging field of study brings to the forefront the political underpinnings of a problem mainly naturalized in the realm of sport and physical culture (Atkinson and Young 2008). Nonetheless, numerous handbooks, chapters, and journal articles are devoted to the intersections between sport, inhumanity, cruelty, suffering, and violence against non/humans that remain entirely overlooked or referred to tangentially.

Sports that pursue, wound, bait, or kill non/human animals are called "blood sports"—most of which possess deep historical roots (Dunning 1999; Young 2014). As the engagement in these gruesome sporting activities is unevenly distributed, they have experienced, particularly during the second half of the twentieth century, thoroughly different regulatory policies. The result of this process is that their present manifestation, at least in this part of the world, divides into three broad categories. First, there are activities that sanction and tolerate a certain degree of violence toward non/humans provided it is performed according to particular rules as in hunting or fishing, for example. Second, there are those activities that are illegal, and which, therefore, constitute the source of an underground economy, such as dogfighting or cockfighting. Finally, there are activities that inhabit what one could perhaps refer to as sociocultural gray areas, which may be legally prohibited in certain contexts but permissible in others. Quite frequently, sponsors and advocates of these activities formally deny allegations of animal abuse, regardless of whether they emerge as the outcome of so-called accidents (Gerber and Young 2013) or hidden in the "backstage" (Atkinson and Young 2005) of sporting arenas. This is the case, for instance, of rodeos or greyhound racing.

It is perhaps not surprising that inquiries seeking to expose all such variants of animal blood sports as neither sport nor sporting by any cultural standards have so far dominated the scholarship dealing with non/humans in sport (Franklin 1996; Evans and Forsyth 1998; Best 2003; Kalof 2014). Quite simply, the most dramatic, spectacular, and bloody instances of non/human insertion into sport are the easiest to deconstruct and protest as inhumane or speciesist in their very orientation (Atkinson 2014). A smaller, but conceptually intriguing trend in contemporary sports-animals studies includes a wave of recent work centered on sports practices that arguably entail forms of inter-species cooperation, rather than physical domination. This includes predominantly human-dog and human-horse relationships in the leisure sphere, as exemplified by activities such as dog agility (Haraway 2008; Lund 2014) and horse riding (Gilbert and Gillet 2012; Hansen 2014). And yet, this almost exclusive emphasis on non/human animal sports has left a much broader social phenomenon unexamined. Namely, the manifold ways whereby mainstream sporting cultures implicate the reproduction of animal exploitation—both in material and symbolic terms.

In contrast to blood sports, often deemed as rotting reminiscences of previous generations, other manifestations of speciesism exist at the heart of contemporary sports and constitute, in many respects, burgeoning social concerns (Atkinson and Young 2008). What follows is an examination of one of these emerging issues: the under-studied question of non/human animals used in a variety of manners as sports mascots. Furthermore, this chapter draws upon the embodied, symbolic, and metaphorical use of non/humans in four major North American professional sports leagues. They include the National Football League (NFL), the National Basketball League (NBA), the National Hockey League (NHL), and Major League Baseball (MLB). In this realm, non/humans are either: (a) depicted as stereotypically ferocious creatures in a fashion that largely mystifies their natural behaviors and positions them as the antitheses of the civilized human; (b) anthropomorphized, hybridized, and caricaturized to the extent that they barely resemble their original form; or, (c) held in captivity within the zones of the sporting field, often exposed in crowded stadiums. Thus, this analysis will inspect the struggles against both the real and representational abuse of non/human animals in the realm of professional and amateur sports.

The present chapter centers on institutionalized perspectives, anchored in official representations, pictures, logos, merchandise, and media releases made publicly available by the organizations affiliated with the leagues mentioned above. Since men's organized sports leagues are the ones that receive the most representational space, they are the focus. It must be noted, however, that there are women's leagues, such as the Women's National Basketball Association (WNBA), which endorse the use of non/human animals as mascots. Exploring this, of course, would further complicate the question. It pushes one to consider how, beginning to combat their marginalization within professional sport, those responsible for managing women's leagues may complicitly overlook the rights of other marginal actors.

A growing body of critical scholarship is beginning to interrogate the historical, political, and cultural meanings embedded in the conception and representation of sports mascots. Some studies focus on the political and commercial production of Olympic symbols, expressed among other things through the commodification of Olympic mascots and their role in promoting certain cities or national identities. The head shape of the two official mascots for the 2012 London Olympics, for example, was designed as the upper light of London's iconic black taxis (Griggs et al. 2012). The mascots of the 2000 Sydney Olympics generated millions in merchandise sales, "with their images appearing on everything from pens to bed linen" (Magdalinski 2004, 84). In North America, research on the matter has, for the most part, concentrated on the stereotyped use of Native American imagery and motifs forming sports mascots (Spindel 2000; Strong 2004; Staurowsky 2007). The discriminatory practice of appropriating Native American cultural icons for similar purposes has created extensive controversy stretching far beyond the scholarly scope, to triggering heated discussions in media and policy-making circles (King 2010). This convergence of critical perspectives has brought into scrutiny the nuanced links between sports, whiteness, and masculinity, links that have for so long helped to shape a romanticized, yet inaccurate view of Native Americans that many individuals find disrespectful (Jacobs 2014).

Efforts at constructing counter-hegemony have yet to generate a serious analysis of how non/human animals are positioned as actors with agency in the construction of sports mascots. More commonly, the forms of representation to which they are subject, coupled with broader societal trends (such as their use in food systems, clothing manufacturing, pet ownership, and scientific testing), tend to de-personalize, stultify, and disparage their sentience. There has been even less academic interest in theorizing how these two seemingly disparate struggles against domination are fundamentally entangled as struggles of and by the marginalized for respect, inclusion, and equity. Such an approach becomes more pressing knowing that the growing social discord against the (mis)representation of Native American cultures has intensified the further exploitation of non/human animals within sports. This is exemplified by several cases in which high school and college sports teams have replaced their Native American mascots/names with non/humans (Change the Mascot). The ensuing analysis—particularly in its closing section—seeks to denote, instead, greater sensitivity toward the ways in which these issues, among others, intersect.

In the NFL, 20 out of the 32 teams currently showcase animals as mascots, with 15 using a direct or indirect reference to these non/humans in their team logo. In the NBA, 21 of the 30 teams feature animal mascots, 10 of which have artistic depictions of them in their logos. In the NHL, the numbers are very similar, with 23 animal mascots (out of 30 teams) and 8 references non/humans in the logos. In the MLB, the league with the lowest number of cases, there are in total 18 teams that feature animal mascots while only 3 of them display non/humans in the logos. The figures presented here have been obtained through the analysis of the official websites of all the franchises associated with these professional leagues.

The authors of this chapter have encountered, it must be noted, several difficulties in compiling these numbers. The Toronto Raptors, for example, are named after an extinct non/human animal. The logo of the San Antonio Spurs, on the other hand, does not contain a direct reference to a non/human animal. Instead, it features a tool used to inflict pain upon them (thus, an indirect reference). A similar case is that of the horseshoe in the logo of the Indianapolis Colts. When analyzing sports teams from Buffalo, a non/human animal reference is already embedded for the city rather than the manufactured name of the franchise. Still, both the Buffalo Sabres and the Buffalo Bills display images of buffalos in their logos while the mascot of the latter is also a representation of a buffalo. The case of the Buffalo Bills itself is noteworthy for several reasons in that it plays on the name of the city and a human with profound and disturbing connections to buffalos. The Bills are of course named after American cultural icon William Frederick Cody, who earned his nickname after the American Civil War. As a reputed marksman and hunter, Cody received a limited-term contract to supply Kansas Pacific Railroad workers with buffalo meat. Cody is purported to have killed over 4,200 American bison over the course of his eighteen-month contract between 1867 and 1868. The organizations that contain direct references to non/human animals are as follows: 14 on the NFL (Buffalo Bills excluded); 9 in the NBA (San Antonio Spurs and Cleveland Cavaliers omitted); 6 in the NHL (Minnesota Wild and Buffalo Sabres excluded); and 6 in the MLB. A very intriguing case, in this respect, is that of the Green Bay Packers, which represents a clear allusion to the meatpacking industry established in the city.

The former NHL franchise the Hartford Whalers (referring, of course, to whale harvesters of the American Northeast coast) perhaps represented the most violent use of animal imagery in a team's iconography. This data was collected from July 2014 to February 2015 (during this period, the franchise Charlotte Bobcats was renamed to Charlotte Hornets).

It's hard to identify a consistent pattern for why a particular non/human animal is associated with a given team, within a particular town, or in a specific cultural context save for the obvious geographic connection (e.g., Arizona Coyotes, Denver Broncos, Miami Dolphins, Toronto Blue Jays). However, an immediate geographic connection does not always provide a cogent rationale for the team name and mascot. Many non/human mascots are not endemic to North America nor have any connection to the team or local environment (e.g., Detroit Lions, Pittsburgh Penguins, Cincinnati Bengals, Toronto Raptors). Furthermore, there seems to be a pronounced preference for large predatory creatures (tigers, bears, lions, panthers, jaguars) and birds (hawks, eagles). Here too, one can find numerous exceptions. At the representational surface is the supposed link between the creatures' predatory powers, their ferocious or stealth-like nature, and an image of tenacity to signify the team's character.

Exploring the use of non/human animal representations in the NCAA for team names reveals far more ubiquity and disconnection between the team, the sport, the institution, the geography, and respect for non/human animals. Also deeper yet, they demonstrate the primitiveness of all non/human animals. While professional sports teams often adopt stereotypical animal monikers (tigers, lions, bears, hawks, etc.), NCAA team names illustrate the broadest range of classification from human perspective and signification. Even a small selection of names—including the University of California Anteaters, University of South Carolina Gamecocks, Campbell College Thundering Herd, Texas Christian University Horned Frogs, University of Arkansas Razorbacks, University of Maryland Terrapins, Indiana Purdue University Mastodons, University of Michigan Wolverines, University of Wisconsin Badgers, University of Delaware Fighting Blue Hens, University of Florida Gators, and University of California Banana Slugs—draw on well-worn cultural stereotypes about the inherent viciousness of all non/human animals. These names illustrate a nearly complete lack of conceptual connection between the non/human animal, place, sport, and human action in the signification process.

However, if the factors influencing the adoption of non/human animal mascots have varied from sports team to team and from level to level, the same cannot be said about their representations. This is a domain where two clear-cut tendencies may be singled out. Both of these representational biases spring from a common non/human referent. For example, the bird chosen to be the mascot of the Arizona Cardinals is represented in thoroughly different ways depending on what is at stake. The logo of the franchise features what one could describe as an austere, relentless cardinal. The mascot section of website of the franchise, on the other hand, displays a fuzzy, playful bird called Big Red. This is, of course, not a unique case; such a twofold fashion of (mis)representing non/humans appears to be, instead, a trademark of North American sports. Similarly to the ancient Roman deity Janus, typically portrayed as a double-faced entity, most animal mascots featured by professional sports teams bears a double appearance, "of which one looks at the People, the other at the Lar" (Ovid 2013, 4). The one that looks at the people, to whatever is external to the team, tends to be depicted as a ferocious creature capable of inspiring fear upon the outsider. The one that looks at the Lar, to those familiar spaces populated by supporters of the team, is commonly rendered, by contrast, like a docile and charismatic figure.

FEROCIOUS CREATURES

In nearly every case analyzed in this study, teams featuring non/human animals in their logos and emblems portray them as hostile or highly essentialized creatures. Their fierce physiognomies and expert physical abilities are accentuated by brightly colored eyeballs or sharply contoured eyebrows. Not even those non/humans who are commonly represented as docile beings are spared. From bulls (Chicago Bulls) and bears (Memphis Grizzlies) to dolphins (Miami Dolphins) and penguins (Pittsburgh Penguins), all animals can seemingly be transfigured into a fearsome entity. As it stands, the only two exceptions are the friendly bird displayed in the logo of the Baltimore Orioles and the rather sober bird in the logo of the Toronto Blue Jays. Quite frequently, they are depicted in an intimidating position as if they are about to charge a rival. Not surprisingly, therefore, claws, canines, horns, and wide-open wings are among the most common elements in these drawings. For example, the non/humans in the logo of the Florida Panthers, the Nashville Predators, the Detroit Lions, the Buffalo Bills, and the Atlanta Falcons embody some of these traits. Needless to say, such an overarching attempt to attach aggressive features to non/human animals constitutes, by and large, a marketing enterprise. Moreover, it may also be framed as yet another corollary of the naturalization of symbolic—for example, structural—homophobia (Pronger 1990) and physical—for example, fighting in ice hockey (Atkinson 2010)—violence within contemporary sports.

Some scholarly work shows how team and club membership often functions as an organizing principle in the formation of collective identities (Giulianotti, Bonney, and Hepworth 1994; Armstrong and Giulianotti 1999). Such identities, as these authors have noted, are constructed both by affirming participation in a particular group as well as by antagonizing rival formations. In other words, affiliation with a given sports team or club is often defined in terms of how one behaves in relation to insiders and outsiders. Somewhat consistent with this scholarship, provided the differing attitudes toward insiders and outsiders alluded above, the brute representations of non/humans under discussion here may be said to be directed toward the latter, given that they are typically incorporated to the external façade of sports franchises. These images are embedded in the ways sports teams advertise themselves to the public in general. Depictions of fierce non/humans are often found on the uniforms they wear, within the league's website, and on all merchandise commercialized and sold on their behalf.

Moreover, this fashion of (mis)representing non/humans also influences the production of humanized sports spaces. Guarding the gates at the main entrance of the Comerica Park in Detroit and of the Bank of America Stadium in Charlotte, for example, one can find several massive sculptures of enraged tigers and menacing panthers. Both of these constitute clear allusions to the logos and names of the teams that belong to these cities. That these statues are on display in the stadium's outer perimeter, mimicking various ancient civilizations (Egypt, Rome, Greece) further proves that these fierce depictions intentionally embed the values of the organizations.

Conventional sports representations of non/humans in aggressive postures not only mystify and decontextualize their so-called natural behaviors but also reproduce the categorization that many of them already bear. Notably, they are classified as large predators with simple minds, emotions, abilities, and destructive tendencies. While referred to in the plural, they are rarely portrayed as social, sentient, rights-holding, or anything other than unreflexively brutal and passive recipients of human classification. This stigmatizing system of classification and signification is among the root causes of an ideological reversal that takes (overwhelmingly) the victims, and portrays them as the aggressors instead. One of the best examples of such a reversal is the logo of the San Jose Sharks, which features a hockey stick torn apart by a great white shark. Great whites very rarely engage with humans (let alone with hockey sticks). More typically, they are the victims of human actions, killed by the thousands annually. Conservationists are at pains to protect this species, an endeavor that has become significantly more challenging due to the negative stereotypes perpetuated by mediated representations (Neff and Hueter 2013).

CHARISMATIC FIGURES

An entirely different picture emerges when one investigates what happens inside stadiums and arenas. It is in these public spaces that the most widespread form of (mis)representing non/human animals in North American professional sports has found fertile terrain. Notably, it is the anthropomor-phized/caricaturized figures that float across the field, often performing tricks and dance numbers during intermissions, that are most problematic. Their friendly attitudes toward the team and the crowd have become synony-mous with the experience of attending live games.

If the external façade of numerous teams is to some degree characterized by untamed non/humans, an examination of the inner dynamics of sporting arenas suggests a different approach. In contrast, non/human animals are represented as domesticated and almost human child-like beings so that they may have direct contact with the fans of a given franchise. Thus in an odd role reversal, the very same non/humans once depicted as ferocious creatures morph into cheerful, charismatic characters that interact with audiences in a range of scenarios. They lead cheers and chants, pose for pictures with spec-tators, sell merchandise and other concession items, and perform dances and other athletic feats during half-time shows. This transformation is accom-plished by wearing furry costumes resembling children's stuffed/plush ani-mal versions of non/humans. These puppets are continually bestowing confi-dence and, more often than not, a large smile and a distinctive human emo-tional/social warmth on the fans.

As the marketing mythmakers of professional sports show, these animal mascots are not only friendly characters, but also the most avid consumers of sports merchandise. Hence, they are adorned with all types of sports apparel, including official jerseys and shorts, headbands, caps, gloves, and helmets. Sometimes, these items are even portrayed as the source of their prowess. A cartoon that tells the story of Swoop, the bald eagle mascot of the Philadel-phia Eagles, serves as a good example. Swoop is a "weak little bird" who, after getting an official jersey, becomes a dominant athletic figure. He has found "the strength and vision that would now match the power of his mighty heart" (Philadelphia Eagles). Such muscular representations are not uncom-mon since most non/human animal mascots are given male names. These tendencies display the profound connection between fan culture and mascu-linity that has historically thrived in North American sports (Kimmel and Messner 2007). This relationship becomes even more evident when one con-siders the gendered role typically performed by these mascots when interact-ing (often in a sexualized manner) with cheerleaders.

Furthermore, several animal mascots are featured in online profiles, where they are anthropomorphized and caricaturized in fans's fantasies. Roary, the lion who serves as mascot for the Detroit Lions, for example, claims to be "10 paws high," whereas his favorite food is "Barbequed Bear [in reference to the Chicago Bears] and Viking Venison [in reference to the Minnesota Vikings] with melted Cheeseheads [in reference to the Green Bay Packers] on top" (Detroit Lions). What is striking is how overtly they are represented in direct (symbolic) combat with human mascot representations (i.e., lions fighting bears and Vikings and animal meat packers). Often, Facebook and Twitter accounts are created for animal mascots, thus constituting an outlet whereby they can engage socially with fans. The (mis)representing non/humans for sport is often done to grab the attention of the youth or future fans. This perspective is further strengthened by the fact that these animal mascots often take part in outreach activities targeting children and adolescents.

Scholars have taken different stances on the question of anthropomorphizing non/human animals. The conventional critique advanced by some animal rights advocates suggests that all such attempts should be taken with a grain of salt because they necessarily conflate the experience of humans into that of non/humans (Regan 2004). Others argue that, in some cases, such undertaking might help humans become empathically, ontologically and epistemologically, closer to non/humans. It may even lead us to "correctly identify an attribute that different species have in common" (Harley 2014, 105). The term "critical anthropomorphism" refers to this endeavor (Karlsson 2012; Best 2014). To reconcile both these perspectives, John Simons (2002) differentiates between "trivial anthropomorphism" and "strong anthropomorphism"—although his account seems scarcely critical of the former. In any case, it is unnecessary to unpack the anthropomorphism occurring in professional sports because it's easy to grasp the subjectivities of non/humans, engendering a thoroughly mystified and commodified account of their lives instead.

RITES OF OPPRESSION

The representational fantasies fabricated about non/humans in the realm of sports represent an amalgamation of singular cases within a much broader constellation of speciesist ideologies. Such ideologies either downplay or negate the standpoints of animals as sentient creatures with complicated lives. The conceptual links between these ideas and the reproduction of animal exploitation in broader sports culture remain under-critiqued. However, there are occasions when it is possible to perceive, with astonishing clarity, how some of these sport-related fictions descend from abstraction into the flesh of non/humans.

To summarize what's been described thus far; numerous sports franchises have arbitrarily chosen different types of non/human animals to be their mascots. Many of these franchises provide two disparaging representations of the non/human; a fierce and a furry one. What occurs next in the signification process is, however, the most intriguing: the materialization of these mystifications upon actual non/humans. As Melissa Boyde remarks, non/humans are "captured in culture," as well as they are "captured in practice," and the point is often to understand how these "aspects of capture operate and interact" (2014, 3). In short, for several members of those species who have had the misfortune of being adopted as animal mascots by professional sports teams, this interaction has resulted in captivity and, quite frequently, death.

There are countless examples of non/human animals (such as jaguars, horses, ravens, and hawks) held in captivity for their role in professional sports, especially in the NFL. Even further, what makes this practice particularly distressing is that these non/humans are often (mis)represented as passionate advocates of their own misery. One the most striking cases involves the Jacksonville Jaguars partnering with a local zoo to make a newborn jaguar cub their mascot. Even further, as Tony Vecchio, the director of the zoo, puts it, "we look at this cub as more than a mascot for the Jags and for the Zoo. We'd like to think of him as the City of Jacksonville's mascot" (Jacksonville Jaguars 2013a). Thus, in an article that reproduces the superstitious tone that pervades much of the rhetoric around sports, among other things by referring to the newborn cub as "a great omen for the Team, the City and the Zoo," these unexpected partners subvert any measure of reasonableness and reassure us that this is as well the will of the cub:

> The Jacksonville Zoo and Gardens and Jacksonville Jaguars are excited to announce the birth of a new jaguar cub in time to kick off the 2013 football season. Born July 18, and coincidentally sharing a birthday with Jacksonville Jaguars owner Shad Khan, the Zoo's new cub is doing well and is looking forward to being drafted as the newest Jaguars teammate (Jacksonville Jaguars 2013b).

Another situation occurred during the 2014 Super Bowl involving the Denver Broncos and Seattle Seahawks. Both teams are famous for publicly showcasing their live animal mascots, thus they decided to ship their mascots to New Jersey, the site of the 2014 Super Bowl. Thunder, the white Arabian horse who performs for the Denver Broncos, was transported to the East Coast on a FedEx cargo plane. He was "dressed in a dark blue, padded Broncos rug," yet not before "announcing" on his Facebook page that his bags were packed and he was ready to go (Otis 2014). In New Jersey, he was placed in the company of Taima, the augur hawk "who has led [Seattle] Seahawks players out of the tunnel for every home game since 2007" (Drovetto 2014). This bird, a commentator argues, is trained "to keep his nerve as he navigates 12-foot spires of flame, screaming cheerleaders, booming fireworks and thousands of crazed fans to his trainer's gloved hand" (Otis 2014). Despite the preparation, several months later during his stadium entrance, Taima accidentally flew to the stands and landed on a fan's head. Possibly fearing sanctions from the league, the organization quickly issued an apology via Twitter, stating they waive responsibility for the incident, and cynically blamed the bird (who undersigns the note):

> I apologize to my family, fellow birds everywhere, the Seahawks organization and fans. I am embarrassed by the pregame incident and the poor judgment I showed. Please understand my actions were not consistent with the type of bird I hope to become. (Seattle Seahawks 2014)

Birds are the most common non/humans handled as live sports mascots—particularly birds of prey. The Atlanta Hawks, the Philadelphia Eagles, and the Baltimore Ravens have used live birds, which requires close collaboration between their marketing departments and local zoos. In a press release featured on the Baltimore Ravens website, written just after the team adopted two new birds, the commercial underpinning of their confinement is openly articulated. The passage indicates as well, with striking eloquence, the intellectual labor that lies at the heart of this oppression:

> Thousands of fans stood against the barricades separating the bleachers from McDaniel College's practice fields, some reaching out to slap five with Poe, the Ravens' beloved mascot. But, the excitement level was raised when the new Ravens mascot joined the giant playful bird. Poe was joined Monday by Conquer, the 13-week-old African white-nape raven that the team recently adopted. Conquer and Rise, so named from a poll on BaltimoreRavens.com, will fly out of the tunnel at M&T Bank Stadium this season, leading the team much in the same way Poe does during pregame introductions. . . . The live birds are the brainchild of team vice president of marketing Gabrielle Dow, who said that she expects at least one of the birds to take flight when the Ravens open the preseason against the Minnesota Vikings. (Duffy 2008)

These tales of captivity pale in comparison to a custom that has thrived in NHL folklore for decades. During the 1952 Stanley Cup playoffs, a fisherman threw an octopus onto the ice before a Detroit Red Wings game. This set in motion a superstition that would claim the lives of dozens of octopuses annually, most especially when the team made the playoffs. The tradition of throwing a dead octopus on the ice after a Red Wings goal in the playoffs promotes good luck. In 1995, the same year the franchise adopted an anthropomorphized octopus as its official mascot, "a record 54 octopuses hit the ice here [Joe Louis Arena, Detroit] in a single game" during the Stanley Cup finals (Bradsher, 1996). On the team's website, the Detroit Red Wings enthusiastically express their endorsement of such vicious violence by sharing the story of two brothers who managed to toss a fifty-pound octopus onto the rink. The organization contends, "although the feat received no airtime on the nationally broadcast game, the octopus was proudly displayed on the hood of the Zamboni between periods" (Detroit Red Wings). The popularity of this gruesome ritual prompted fans of other teams to adopt their own versions of it. Reportedly supporters of the San Jose Sharks and of the Anaheim Ducks, for example, throw dead sharks and ducks onto the ice (Mcaloon 2011). An incident took place during a 2010 playoff game against the Detroit Red Wings when a shark landed on the ice with an octopus stuffed into his mouth (Wyshynski 2010). It is unclear if any animal rights advocates or other organizations were involved in planning or protesting these events since no one has claimed responsibility.

SHARED STRUGGLES

The (ab)use of non/human animals as sports mascots is certainly not among the most pressing issues those campaigning for the total liberation of non/humans have to wrestle with today. However, neither it is an irrelevant phenomenon. The actions described in this chapter constitute powerful illustrations of how the lives of non/humans are trivialized and subverted for sports capital. Accumulation is the driving force behind the ferocious and the friendly countenance of animal mascots, the glue that holds these disparate representational trends together. And it is, as well, the leitmotiv for the seizure of live non/humans into captivity. As such, combating these oppressive conditions unequivocally represents a point of contention within the broader struggles against the naturalization of the exploitation of non/human animals in society at large.

This is nonetheless a point of contention in which remarkably little has been achieved. This is particularly disappointing when contrasted to the strides made by those who oppose sport-related misappropriation of Native American cultures. In many respects, the lack of mutual support seems highly illustrative of how speciesist most movements on behalf of social justice still remain. Building these alliances could translate their specific demands into a common, rights-oriented struggle. Insofar as this remains true, there will be instances when the achievements made in one domain will simultaneously represent the intensification of exploitation elsewhere.

As Steve Best maintains, however, the reluctance of certain groups to associate their interests with those of non/humans is better understood in light of deeper historical processes (2014). Because Native Americans have often been equated, in a pejorative manner, to non/humans, they have good reason to be suspicious of any efforts to reignite this connection. Yet, one task for those engaged in animal liberation is to break through such apprehension by showing that forms of oppression are interconnected and produced from the same colonial attitudes toward otherness. This chapter is a small contribution in this direction.

Further research dealing with the sports mascots will eventually have to move beyond the limited milieu of professionalism and enter the much vaster terrain covered by the educational sports system in North America. It is in this sphere that one will encounter some of the most striking cases of non/humans held in captivity because of the fancy around sports mascots, including large mammals like bears (Baylor University), lions (University of North Alabama), jaguars (Southern University), and tigers (Louisiana State University and University of Memphis)—some of whom are even taken to crowded stadiums, confined in small cages, to be displayed during games.

REFERENCES

Armstrong, Gary, and Richard Giulianotti. 1999. *Football Cultures and Identities*. Basingstoke, UK: Macmillan.

Atkinson, Michael. 2010. "It's Still Part of the Game: Violence and Masculinity in Canadian Ice Hockey." In *Sexual Sports Rhetoric: Historical and Media Contexts of Violence*, edited by Linda Fuller, 15–30. New York: Peter Lang Publishing.

Atkinson, Michael. 2014. "The Terrier [Men]." *Sociology of Sport Journal* 31(4): 420–437.

Atkinson, Michael, and Kevin Young. 2005. "Reservoir Dogs: Greyhound Racing, Mimesis and Sport-related Violence." *International Review for the Sociology of Sport* 40(3): 335–356.

Atkinson, Michael, and Kevin Young. 2008. *Deviance and Social Control in Sport*. Champaign, IL: Human Kinetics.

Best, Steve. 2003a. "Barbarism in the Afternoon: Bullfighting, Violence, and the Crisis in Human Identity." *Impact Press* 46, August–September.

———. 2014b. *The Politics of Total Liberation: Revolution for the 21st Century*. New York: Palgrave Macmillan.

Boyde, Melissa. 2014. *Captured: The Animal within Culture*. New York, NY: Palgrave Macmillan.

Bradsher, Keith. 1996. "When Octopuses Are Flying in Detroit It's . . . " *New York Times*, April 14.

Change the Mascot. n.d. "History of Progress." http://www.changethemascot.org.

Detroit Lions Official Website. n.d. "All about Roary." http://www.detroitlions.com/youth-programs/roary-mascot.html.

Detroit Red Wings Official Website. n.d. "Legend of the Octopus." http://redwings.nhl.com/club/page.htm?id=43781.

Duffy, Mike. 2008. "Conquer Arrives at Training Camp." Baltimore Ravens Official Website, July 28. http://www.baltimoreravens.com/news/article-1/Conquer-Arrives-at-Training-Camp/D20A3B01-99E2-469D-9724-B58793B25B8E.

Dunning, Eric. 1999. *Sport Matters: Sociological Studies of Sport, Violence, and Civilization*. London: Routledge.

Drovetto, Tony. 2014. "Reaction to Taima the Seahawk's Statement." Seattle Seahawks Official Website, November 11. http://www.seahawks.com/news/articles/article-1/Reaction-to-Taima-the-Seahawks- statement/6d9df132-5a2f-451a-8c8a-5921232aa39c.

Elias, Norbert. 2008. "An Essay on Sport and Violence." In *Quest for Excitement: Sport and Leisure in the Civilizing Process*, edited by Norbert Elias and Eric Dunning, 150–173. Amsterdam: University College Dublin Press.

Evans, Rhonda, and Craig Forsyth. 1998. "The Social Milieu of Dogmen and Dogfights." *Deviant Behavior: An Interdisciplinary Journal* 19: 51–71.

Franklin, Adrian. 1996. "On Fox-Hunting and Angling: Norbert Elias and the 'Sportisation' Process." *Journal of Historical Sociology* 9(4): 432–456.

Gerber, Brittany, and Kevin Young. 2013. "Horse Play in the Canadian West: The Emergence of the Calgary Stampede as Contested Terrain." *Society and Animals* 21(6): 523–545.

Gilbert, Michelle, and James Gillett. 2012. "Equine Athletes and Interspecies Sport." *International Review for the Sociology of Sport* 47(5): 632–643.

Giulianotti, Richard, Norman Bonney, and Mike Hepworth. 1994. *Football, Violence, and Social Identity*. London: Routledge.

Griggs, Gerald, Ina Freeman, Peter Knight, and Norman O'Reilly. 2012. "A Vision of London in the Twenty-first Century or Just Terrifying Monsters: A Semiotic Analysis of the Official Mascots for the London 2012 Olympic and Paralympic Games." *Leisure Studies* 31(3): 339–54.

Hansen, Natalie. 2014. "Embodied Communication: The Poetics and Politics of Riding." In *Sport, Animals, and Society*, edited by James Gillett and Michelle Gilbert, 251–267. New York: Routledge.

Haraway, Donna. 2008. *When Species Meet*. Minneapolis: University of Minnesota Press.

Harley, Alexis. 2014. "Darwin's Ants: Evolutionary Theory and the Anthropomorphic Fallacy." In *Representing the Modern Animal in Culture*, edited by Jeanne Dubino, Ziba Rashidian, and Andrew Smyth, 103–118. New York: Palgrave Macmillan.

Jacksonville Jaguars Official Website. 2013a. "Jacksonville Zoo and Gardens Announces Jaguar Cub Naming Contest," August 20. http://www.jaguars.com/news/article-PressRelease/Jacksonville-Zoo-and-Gardens-announces--Jaguar-cub-naming-contest/6905d1d0-f28d-4393-9ad8-ab6d11b08457.

———. 2013b. "Jacksonville Zoo and Gardens' Newborn Jaguar Shares Birthday with Jaguars Owner Shad Khan," August 12. http://www.jaguars.com/news/article-JaguarsNews/Jacksonville-Zoo-and-Gardens'-newborn-Jaguar-shares-birthday-with-Jaguars-Owner-Shad-Khan/4687d46e-22f1-4ba9-ad78-3fda1f7300ae.

Jacobs, Michelle. 2014. "Race, Place, and Biography at Play: Contextualizing American Indian Viewpoints on Indian Mascots." *Journal of Sport and Social Issues* 38(4): 322–345.

Kalof, Linda. 2014. "Animal Blood Sport: A Ritual Display of Masculinity and Sexual Virility." *Sociology of Sport Journal* 31(4): 438–454.

Karlsson, Fredrik. 2012. "Critical Anthropomorphism and Animal Ethics." *Journal of Agricultural and Environmental Ethics* 25(5): 707–720.

Kimmel, Michael, and Michael Messner. 2007. *Men's Lives*. Boston: Pearson Allyn and Bacon.

King, C. Richard. 2010. *The Native American Mascot Controversy: A Handbook*. Lanham, MD: Scarecrow Press.

Lund, Giuliana. 2014. "Taking Teamwork Seriously: The Sport of Dog Agility as an Ethical Model of Cross-Species Companionship." In *Sport, Animals, and Society*, edited by James Gillett and Michelle Gilbert, 101–126. New York: Routledge.

Magdalinski, Tara. 2004. "'Cute, Lovable Characters': The Place and Significance of Mascots in the Olympic Movement." *Olympika: The International Journal of Olympic Studies* 13: 75–92.

Mcaloon, T. J. 2011. "Ducks vs. Sharks: Dead Duck Thrown on Ice Will Start New Tradition." *Bleacher Report*, December 27. http://bleacherreport.com/articles/999073-ducks-vs-sharks-dead-duck-thrown-on-ice-will-start-new-tradition.

Neff, Christopher, and Robert Hueter. 2013. "Science, Policy, and the Public Discourse of Shark 'Attack': A Proposal for Reclassifying Human-Shark Interactions." *Journal of Environment Studies and Sciences* 3(1): 65–73.

Otis, Ginger Adams. 2014. "Denver Broncos' and Seattle Seahawks' Mascots Head to Town for Super Bowl." *New York Daily News*, January 30. http://www.nydailynews.com/sports/football/broncos-seahawks-mascots-head-super-bowl-article-1.1596711.

Ovid. 2013. *Fasti*. Oxford, UK: Oxford University Press.

Philadelphia Eagles Official Website. n.d. "Swoop." http://www.philadelphiaeagles.com/fanzone/swoop.html.

Pronger, Brian. 1990. *The Arena of Masculinity: Sports, Homosexuality and the Meaning of Sex*. Toronto: Summerhill Press.

Regan, Tom. 2004. *The Case for Animal Rights*. Berkeley: University of California Press.

Seattle Seahawks Official Website. 2014. "Statement from Taima de Seahawk," November 11. http://www.seahawks.com/news/articles/article-1/Statement-from-Taima-the-Seahawk/4d025255-7a1a-4378-8185-eb3e90a285d8.

Simons, John. 2002. *Animal Rights and the Politics of Literary Representation*. New York: Palgrave.

Spindel, Carol. 2000. *Dancing at Halftime: Sports and the Controversy over American Indian Mascots*. New York: New York University Press.

Staurowsky, Ellen. 2007. "'You Know, We Are All Indian': Exploring White Power and Privilege in Reactions to the NCAA Native American Mascot Policy." *Journal of Sport and Social Issues* 31(1): 61–76.

Strong, Pauline. 2004. "The Mascot Slot: Cultural Citizenship, Political Correctness, and Pseudo-Indian Sports Symbols." *Journal of Sport and Social Issues* 28(1): 79–87.

Young, Kevin. 2014. "Toward a Less Speciesist Sociology of Sport." *Sociology of Sport Journal* 31(4): 387–401.

Wyshynski, Greg. 2010. "Inside Story of How Shark with Octopus Hit the Ice in San Jose." *Yahoo Sports Canada,* May 4. https://ca.sports.yahoo.com/nhl/blog/puck_daddy/post/Inside-story-of-how-shark-with-octopus-hit-the-i?urn=nhl,238543.

Chapter 13

On Empathy, Anthropocentrism, and Rhetorical Tropes: An Analysis of Online "Save the Bees!" Campaign Images

Christina Victoria Cedillo

Activist organizations defend vulnerable species by using images that rally support. These visual appeals create emotional connections between the human audience and non/human subjects by featuring evocative and shocking imagery. For example, Animal Liberation Front (ALF) publications depict the horrors of vivisection on living non/humans, while PETA anti-fur ads employ naked human models and celebrities in a variety of suggestive or violent poses. Such shocking imagery relies on pathos, or an "emotional influence [exerted] on the audience, potentially affecting attitude or choice" (Cockcroft and Cockcroft 2014, 87). Visual appeals that employ pathos to arouse human sympathy for suffering non/humans work to influence the emotions and connect those stirred emotions to social and cultural frameworks. According to philosopher Jacques Derrida, these "pathetic" images "open the immense question of pathos and the pathological, precisely, that is, of suffering, pity, and compassion," and ask audiences to consider "the place that has to be accorded to the interpretation of this compassion, to the sharing of this suffering among the living, to the law, ethics, and politics that must be brought to bear upon this experience of compassion" (2002, 395). Drawing out these connections, critics have found that shock-based campaigns can advance racist, sexist, or ableist assumptions while attempting to promote non/human rights (Kim 2011; Deckha 2008; Richter 2014). In so doing, they attempt to elevate the status of one subjugated group at the expense of another.

Likewise, non/human rights campaigns can promote the very speciesism that they are created to counter. Campaign images build pathos by using rhetorical tropes that influence their reception, often automatically. Typically, a trope is the use of figurative language. However, a rhetorical trope is primarily characterized by its capacity to serve as a lens that translates one idea in terms of another, whether verbally or visually. Tropes transcend their status as figures of speech to become "figures of ideology" that influence perception and perpetuate social inequalities (Villanueva 2006). The four master tropes through which Western audiences interpret words and images are metaphor, metonymy, synecdoche, and irony (Burke 1941). General unfamiliarity with these tropes allows humans to construct an impression of "animality" that bolsters human subjectivity and superiority while remaining unquestioned. As a result, even mundane campaign images can reinforce the anthropocentric perspective that threatens and endangers non/human species. While it is impossible to trace here the origins and maintenance of the human-non/human divide, extensive research supports that this dichotomy is primarily enacted rhetorically (Elder et al. 1998; Steel 2008; Cohen 1999; Lewiecki-Wilson 2011; Armstrong 2002; Salvador and Clarke 2011). A rhetorical analysis focused on Internet campaigns concerning the plight of honeybees demonstrates how tropes reinforce the divide and the bias it accommodates.

A comprehensive survey of Internet campaign images turns up four prevalent patterns of bee representation which are here designated "Bee as Tragic Figure," "Bee as Social Creature," "Bee as Worker," and "Bee as Activist." These image types emerge vis-à-vis the four rhetorical master tropes through which people create connections between unique ideas and objects: metaphor, metonymy, synecdoche, and irony. Rhetorician and literary critic Kenneth Burke outlines these terms in "Four Master Tropes," and he theorizes how, through these tropes, human beings construe the world (1941). *Metaphor* means speaking of A in terms of B; *metonymy* is the assumption of an underlying association between A and B; *synecdoche* is the acceptance of a piece as representative of the whole; and *irony* is the reflection of the similarities and differences between A and B. However, beyond stylistic figures of speech, tropes are also lenses that permit humans to interpret information and affect how that information is processed. He explains,

> For *metaphor* we could substitute *perspective*;
> For *metonymy* we could substitute *reduction*;
> For *synecdoche* we could substitute *representation*;
> For *irony* we could substitute *dialectic*. (Burke 1941, 421)

Tropes encourage specific kinds of semantic relationships. As delineated by Burke, these four tropes together provide a useful framework for analyzing

Internet images. Their use as analytical tools clarifies how human beings posit relationships between things that differ in both meaning and significance, and how conventional ideologies inform the construction of these relationships (Rice and Schofer 1983, 19).

The trope of metaphor illuminates a popular kind of "save the bees" campaign image through its use of bees to clarify its properties through comparison. This pattern of depiction is "Bee as Tragic Figure" because, instead of using text to explain meaning, the viewer must interpret the image as metaphor via the bee's palpable mortality. Bee-centered campaigns have become more widespread in recent years due to an upsurge in colony collapse disorder, which has been linked to the use of neonicotinoid pesticides (EFSA 2013). Researchers assert that "one mouthful in three in [the human] diet directly or indirectly benefits from honey bee pollination" and that "[b]ee pollination is responsible for more than $15 billion in increased crop value each year" (USDA 2013). Consequently, images designed to inform the public about the plight of bees have become common sights across the Internet. The Scottish Wildlife Trust's website features an example of the "Bee as Tragic Figure." It is designed to establish a direct connection between humans and bees. A dead bee rests with its body turned away from the viewer. The image features no text; only the deceased bee's wings and fuzzy striped body are visible. The careful framing and positioning of the dead bee creates pathos intended to inspire human action by inciting an emotional reaction.

Metaphor hinges on a change in perspective and what that change says about something when viewed in a new light. The "Bee as Tragic Figure" image type alters human perceptions regarding bees, seeking to elevate their cultural status due to the major role they play in human culture. Bees are not just insects, but fellow contributors to national economies and food production. If this realization does not exactly place bees on a par with humans, it aligns the interests of both parties in a co-mission to ensure human existence. Burke terms this alignment *identification*, a joining of unique parties based on "some principle they have in common" (1969, 21). The "Bee as Tragic Figure" image type encourages identification by creating the impression that one gazes upon a human casualty. The key attribute of the image located on the Scottish Wildlife Trust website is how the bee's body is deliberately turned away. The compound eyes and many legs that distinguish bees from humans remain hidden. This absence matters because humans are generally trained to engage in identification as a "visual process," with distinct parties attempting oneness primarily through the eyes (Kaufman 1996, 31).

Derrida expounds on this point of human-non/human identification. Discussing "animal encounters," Derrida notes that perception of one's humanity depends on the recognition of its bounds, signified by the non/human that looks back and therefore proves a subject.

> As with every bottomless gaze, as with the eyes of the other, the gaze called
> animal offers to my sight the abyssal limit of the human: the inhuman or the
> ahuman, the ends of man, that is to say the bordercrossing from which vantage
> man dares to announce himself to himself, thereby calling himself by the name
> that he believes he gives himself (Derrida 2002, 381).

In the Scottish Wildlife Trust website image, the bee's eyes do not return the gaze so human viewers do not identify the casualty. Instead, the bee remains an Other that allows viewers to more easily impose human attitudes and sentiments onto the bee's image. The bee's image promotes cross-species empathy through identification. However, this empathy is based on the viewer's recognition of a human construct and the notion of "beeness." Hence, the question of "what or who is and is not grievable according to what or who is or is not humanized" highlights the ambivalence accommodated by metaphor (Weil 2012, 113). Bees are near enough to humans to make their demise a matter of human interest, but only if we ignore the "absolute otherness" of bees' bodies (Derrida 2002, 280). The primacy of human embodiment remains the unquestioned assumption underlying this ostensible alignment, both in terms of basic survival and acceptable representation.

It is important to understand how the trope of metaphor works because metaphor provides the relational base for the incongruous relationships created by the other tropes. Burke states that "perspective" can be substituted for "metaphor" because metaphors allow readers to glean new information based on perceived connections between the "thisness of a that, or the thatness of a this" (1941, 422). Metaphor involves a "carrying-over" of meaning in "a process that necessarily involves varying degrees of incongruity in that the two realms are never identical" (Burke 1941, 422). A metaphor states that one thing *is* another, but that comparison is only possible because the two things are overtly dissimilar. Burke claims that the "nature" of any distinct thing, or "character," can be demystified by considering it from the perspective of another and that through diverse comparisons "we establish a character's reality" (422). The metaphor trope requires difference to determine points of possible sameness since, were the things compared identified as equal, there would be no significant semantic gap to bridge. This sameness-difference matters because this correspondence sustains the kinds of symbolic violence that lead to material violence. Metaphor—and subsequently, every other trope—can encourage the view that any posited similarity or difference is "real" rather than a calculated comparison. Metaphor permits what Julie Matthews describes as an elision of "internal distinctions between animals," meaning that humans and non/humans are similar enough to be compared even as their differences can be exploited (Matthews 2012, 128).

The image of "Bee as Social Creature" relies on metonymy to create a rhetorical connection. In these kinds of images, bees are portrayed at home in groups, either in colonies or the comb. Burke associates metonymy with reduction because this trope reifies intangible states or concepts; metonymy renders forms of consciousness like emotions and ideas in concrete terms (1941, 425). For instance, buildings, emblems, and rituals embody notions of social order, but they cannot capture the richness and breadth of the concept itself. Metonymy presumes a fundamental relationship between two things and the material object must share some essence of the idea. This is why the former can represent the latter. Typically, that association is accepted as a natural fact rather than a commonly accepted assumption, which has obtained its power through frequent repetition in cultural texts. An image on the EcoWatch website illustrates how this process works. The image shows two bees with their heads together, their front legs touching as though one bee is assisting the other in unloading pollen. The picture accompanied a news story on President Obama's campaign to "act now to save the bees" (Iberle-kamp 2013). Several environmental groups joined forces to petition the U.S. President to follow the European Union's example by enacting protective measures to safeguard bees. These activists asked Obama to order the Environmental Protection Agency (EPA) to recognize the dangers posed by neonicotinoids and ban their use as the European Food Safety Authority (EFSA) has done. The juxtaposition of visual and verbal appeals exemplifies how metonymy reifies an idea and creates associations between unique entities based on an underlying, often unspoken, similarity rooted in that idea.

In this example, an ideal organized society, along with its attendant structures and relationships, is the concept hypostatized. It is personified by the bees, the President of the United States, its citizens, the environmental advocates petitioning him, the EPA, the EFSA, and the citizens of the European Union, and manifested through the constellated interactions of these diverse parties as they are ideally envisioned. The bees pollinate the crops that foster human survival, and humans, in turn, champion the bees. Environmental groups solicit Obama as an elected leader to exercise his authority over a governmental agency that citizens grant the ability to make decisions, which affect the health of millions. The Office of the President and the EPA have authority over particular aspects of social life but are also indebted to each citizen in having the power to execute their authority. In asking Obama to follow the lead of the European Union, which has already allowed the EFSA to ban neonicotinoids to protect its own citizens, the activists presume that sovereign nations are obligated to defer to one another in service to the greater good. Ultimately, the greater good is the ruling principle that ties the image-petition dyad to the notion of an ideal society that is "reduced" to a variety of lifeforms and a series of acts.

Over millennia, Western philosophers from Aristotle to Martin Heidegger have deployed an ideologically laden image of the bee in their attempts to categorize nature and theorize about the social order. In *Generation of Ani-*

mals, Aristotle describes the hierarchy of bees, deeming them insects whose colonies resemble the human *polis*, though the misogyny of his own culture leads him to believe that bees have kings rather than queens (1943, 335; Mayhew 2004, 20; Pomeroy 1994, 279). An ethical ambivalence concerning bees characterizes Pliny's encyclopedia, *The Natural History*. There bees display the "natural habits of industry" (1856, 125). Unlike humans, who go to war for morally ambiguous reasons, bees fight only for survival, a trait that frames the bee as a "*munificum animal*" from whose example humanity might learn something of ethics (Ash 2011, 16). Francis Bacon describes different approaches to philosophy in terms of insect behavior in *The New Organon*, comparing bees' pollen collection from garden and wild flowers as a middle ground between Empiricism and Rationalism (2000, 79). Bernard Mandeville's controversial *The Fable of the Bees* transforms apian community into a complex, potent metonym useful for examining human economic structures and the formation of human nations (1714). More recently, Martin Heidegger's contemplation of consciousness as the difference between humans and non/humans in *The Fundamental Concepts of Metaphysics* sees bees "trapped" by instinct, as are the other non/humans with whom they form a general animality (Aho 2009, 77). Unlike that of humans who are capable of "world-forming," "[t]he bee's world is limited to a specific domain and is strictly circumscribed" (Heidegger 1995, 193).

Social theories advanced by these authors render the bee a highly tractable signifier, one that becomes a commonplace yardstick for thinking about human behavior. On a fundamental level, humans can identify with the bees' embodied proximity to and interaction with one another, to those recognized as peers and who share functional space. This amity is based solely on human knowledge of closeness. Like humans, bees are communal beings. Their social hierarchy may or may not necessarily embody a human ideal of community, but their existence reflects for humans something of a social contract that governs human life. Differences in associations between human parties, and associations between humans and bees evident in the above example of "Bee as Social Creature," reveal the limits of that resemblance.

The complex network of actors involved in campaigning against nicotinoids seems to cohere under Lockean social arrangements where representative leaders and agencies must answer to those who embody the higher authority in whose name the agent acts (Locke 2012; Fieser 2001). Inversely, associations between humans and bees rest on the idea that bees are "poor in the world" and have less Being than humans (Heidegger 1995, 196). This notion has endured through repetition. For example, Pliny ascribes some degree of rationality to bees and connects human and non/human forms of culture. However, like Aristotle and Heidegger, he distinguishes between human and non/human nature and claims for the latter a greater teleology (Ash 2011, 118, n.39; Laehn 2013, 17). In addition, as anthropologist and philosopher Barbara Noske explains, an unquestioned assumption that only humans have culture engenders a tautological view that non/humans cannot have their own cultures because they do not maintain the same material practices as humans (2008, 24). Thus, bees embody an ideal society from a human vantage point. This happens even as bees are viewed primarily as objects and their deaths are "losses to farmers, consumers and the economy" (Iberlekamp 2013). Bees participate in the production of societies and yet they are not participants. Despite the similarities between humans and non/ humans that the metonymic trope permits, it still bolsters the assumption of human supremacy.

The third pattern of representation, the "Bee as Worker," depends on the synecdochal trope. Synecdoche is a figure of speech or thought wherein a part stands in for the whole, as when a car is a "nice set of wheels." Burke defines synecdoche conventionally to mean both that a part may represent the whole and that the whole may represent a part. According to Burke, "The 'noblest synecdoche,' the perfect paradigm or prototype for all lesser usages, is found in metaphysical doctrines proclaiming the identity of 'microcosm' and 'macrocosm'" (1941, 427). Synecdoche informs most political societies vis-à-vis the tendency to treat individuals as representative of the group. Images associated with this trope show bees simply doing what they do in the everyday, which people perceive as typical "bee-activities." However, the bees in these images tend to be situated in natural settings filled with plants, flowers, or trees. They occupy the majority of the frame while the remainder of the scene falls out of focus, providing the perspectival background against which the bee emerges as the central figure.

The Scottish Wildlife Trust website features a picture by Rachel Scopes of a male red-tailed bumblebee that is in midair, about to land on some flowers. The bee's legs are clearly displayed and its large red tail contrasts with the soft lilac of the blooms. Only a sprig laden with flowers and buds is in focus. The rest of the flowers are only perceptible as blotches of blurred purple at what seems like a distance. The image accompanies a blog entry by Laura Whitfield, a ranger based at the Falls of Clyde reserve in Scotland, explaining the dangers posed by neonicotinoids and asking blog visitors to write the Scottish government to ban these pesticides (Fallsofclyde 2012). The image of bee and flowers reinforces the information shared in the blog: neonicotinoid pesticides prove a solemn threat to both flora and fauna. The material existence of the bee and flowers is intertwined beyond their natural interdependence in that humans rely on both for their survival. A focus on their interaction ties directly to a larger picture. Here emphasis lies beyond the frame to connote the global human sphere that will be disastrously affected if change does not occur. This transference of meaning occurs via the reverse telescopic perspective of the picture. The juxtaposition of the blurred background with the subject in focus points attention outward of the image.

The "scene" becomes distinct, more complex, and more real as perception shifts from the mono-dimensional background, to the two-dimensional figure of the bee, to the three-dimensional world of the viewer that encompasses the other two visual fields.

Perspective is key given synecdoche's connection to representation because during observation a substitution occurs. The target object is replaced by a new one that typifies those attributes that the viewer selectively emphasizes.

> Sensory representation is, of course, synecdochic in that the senses abstract certain qualities from some bundle of electro-chemical activities we call, say, a tree, and these qualities (such as size, shape, color, texture, weight, etc.) can be said "truly to represent" a tree. Similarly, artistic representation is synecdochic, in that certain relations within the medium "stand for" corresponding relations outside it. (Burke 1941, 427)

In direct contrast to the previous trope, the bee and flowers form a symbolic pairing that signifies a space distinct from that of human culture. Presented here is a more pristine and organic realm, given that the threat comes from outside in the form of human-made compounds. Nature is framed as separate from the human sphere, existing as an idealized Other against which human civilization may be posited as hyper-constructed and dangerous. Through such ideologically laden framing, bee and flower alike are interchangeable things. Both are synecdochic representations of a collective notion of Nature that bolsters the impression of a humanity-non/humanity dichotomy.

Last, the pattern "Bee as Activist" underscores the significant cultural impact exerted by the trope of irony. Burke links irony to dialectic since irony reveals semantic relationships between terms that are neither "precisely right or precisely wrong" and therefore must be negotiated according to all the possible meanings available within given contexts (1941, 432). Irony uses humor, satire, or surprise to accentuate the differences between audience expectations and what is presented. Consequently, such representation abandons the presumed verisimilitude of the patterns examined above in favor of a dramatic display. These images depict bees as active participants in the very campaigns aimed at securing their survival. Even when the image does not satirize its subject by featuring a bee in a battle helmet or breathing through a gas mask it casts the bee as warrior. In a picture originating from the Organic Consumers Association, reposted on the This One Wild Life website, a bee faces the viewer. Its compound eyes, wings, and legs are clearly displayed, its hindquarters laden with pollen. Against a background that replicates the bright yellow of the pollen, black and white text above the image states, "Swarm the EPA: Tell Congress to Ban Neonicotinoid Pesticides before They Devastate the U.S. Bee Population." Below the image, the message reads, "Then, Join the Earth Day Swarm to Ban Bee-Killing Pesticides" (2013). Captured in midflight, with its wings outspread and legs upheld, the bee appears to turn its gaze directly on the audience. Indeed, based on its bearing and central position within the frame the bee appears defiant and proud, even as its head remains dusted with pollen.

The human viewer may or may not be able to demarcate the feelings and attitudes of the bee. However, the figure appears bold because, unlike the dead bees that turn away in the "Bee as Tragic Figure" image type, this bee is a viewer as the eyes look into the eyes of the humans looking at the image. The ironic trope that informs the image works based on the ignorance of bees' emotional states even as humans know that the recognition of bee bravado is not unfounded. Anyone who has ever suffered a bee sting knows all too well that bees are willing and able to defend themselves and their communities. Nonetheless, images such as the one described above play with irony in ways that affirm anthropomorphism. Rather than simply being asked to see themselves in the bees, audiences are encouraged to see some of the bees in themselves, too. By imposing human intent on non/human beings and imbuing humans with seemingly non/human qualities, these images universalize struggles for survival and obscure important species-specific distinctions. They make it appear as though identification is a two-way street. They also frame humans and bees as possible allies in the fight against bee death and pesticide use rather than stressing that this relationship is one between an aggressor who uses poisons and the injured party. Human consciences are assuaged because it is "those other humans" who are harming bees, not the audience viewing the image, even if their reliance on bee exploitation makes them complicit through ignorance.

In rhetorical studies, divergent opinions that question whether non/humans can be subjects rely on communication-based definitions. Burke distinguishes human beings, more precisely "man," as the "symbol-using (symbol-making, symbol-misusing) animal / inventor of the negative (or moralized by the negative) / separated from his natural condition by instruments of his own making / goaded by the spirit of hierarchy (or moved by the sense of order) / and rotten with perfection" (1966, 14). For Burke, what differentiates humans from non/humans is their ability to use language to create and organize reality and bring into being even that which is not. It is interesting that he positions humans as squarely within the bounds of animality, albeit a special variety. In contrast, George Kennedy argues that non/humans use "a combination of vocal sounds and body language to express their feelings, influence others, and get what they want from human masters" (Kennedy 1998, 12). Of significance is that he does not limit rhetoric to words but asserts embodied rhetorics as a potent way of communicating. He argues that non/humans employ rhetoric among their peers and others in many of the same ways that humans do, using deliberative and epideictic forms, deploying purposely arranged postures and calls to convince or memorialize peers. In either case, however, communication as a marker of subjectivity is defined according to how human beings use rhetoric. Under this logic non/humans speak as humans speak and for the same reasons, even if their "language" takes on different forms.

Despite Burke's ambivalence toward non/human communication, his delineation of tropes proves practical and crucial because tropes can create connection while obscuring harm. In each image type examined above, the tropes used are based on privileging humans. Human embodiment remains the presupposed measure by which bees' value is determined even when humans try to create positive, empathetic connections to "save the bees." Tropes privilege the perspectives of those who are making the comparisons and frame those viewed as mere facts. In doing so, they obscure the anthropocentrism inherent in human observations of the non/human world. As this examination of select bee images shows, tropes may also provide a lexicon for the way humans identify with bees (or other non/humans) critically. The classification permitted by their use does not denote "beeness" or form the basis for imposing value on their lives, but instead signifies a very human desire to identify with the "animal Other." This is not to say that there is no essential similarity or distinction between humans and non/humans. It is to say, however, that these connections are difficult to contemplate in an unprejudiced manner when human definitions are being used. As Kennedy explains, "Our own experience and metaphors from human life are often the terms we have to describe what we observe among animals" (1998, 12). If human audiences are to be conscientious consumers of such images, they must be cognizant that these images depict anthropocentric fantasies. Human audiences should also be aware that these images reinforce the tautological process through which the power to define others is constructed to affirm the definers' authority to do so. Escape from a perspective based in human experience may prove difficult, if not impossible. Fortunately, by recognizing this conundrum, humans may at least begin to recognize that the subjectivity of bees remains distinct from the images of bees constructed from a human viewpoint.

Philosopher Lorraine Code seeks to articulate a model of empathy that attempts to avoid the oppression that comes along with imposing one's definition of subjectivity on those with whom one seeks to identify. She states, "A human subject may never be wholly—or permanently—transparent, never fully knowable either to herself or to others, as the person that she is. Nor is 'the person that one is' a fixed or static entity" (1995, 95). Code speaks of human interactions. Yet her words seem fitting when applied to non/humans whose essences humans may never know, and whom humans must regard as complex and worthy of respect. Realizing the biased quality of identification demands questioning one's motives and full recognition that impressions of others are always even if partially fabricated.

Until humans find a means to escape anthropocentric perspectives alto-gether, anthropocentrism can be problematized in a constructive manner that does not equate human interpretation with a non/human essence. Kennedy notes, on the one hand, a tendency for "animal lovers" to anthropomorphize companion animals and, on the other hand, the tendency for "radical human-ism" to deny non/humans a soul or sentience (1998, 12–13). The attitude that non/humans are more complex than commonly assumed because humans share something essential with them, whether rhetoric, culture, or corporeal-ity, is a judgment based on human notions of what matters. The point is not to erase diverse non/humans's natures by attributing or denying them what's been asserted as "human" characteristics. However, as Kennedy argues, a "modest degree of anthropomorphism is not a negative factor in studying animals" if humans can forge useful ways of empathizing with non/humans, especially those whose existence is threatened (1998, 12). Cary Wolfe states in *Animal Rites*,

> Practically speaking, we must use what we have, in the same way that one might very well want to invoke the discourse of universal human rights to prohibit the torture of human beings, even though in theoretical terms the model of universal human rights has been thoroughly dismantled as a very historically specific relic of Enlightenment modernity—and for many of the same reasons as in the foregoing critique of *animal* rights. (2003, 192)

Hence, cross-species identification must be promoted if it saves non/human life, but so must conscientious awareness that such identification is a biased process. This bias should be purposefully negotiated each time humans at-tempt to communicate with or understand non/humans.

A collective, assumed notion of animality can no longer form the disre-garded background against which humanity emerges. Likewise, animality can no longer be the absent presence that bolsters the oppression of human and non/human subaltern groups alike (Elder et al. 1998). Cynthia Lewiecki-Wilson asks,

> Rather than extending humanist arguments of liberal rationalism to the dis-abled and animals . . . and to poor nations . . . how might the centering of the perspective and paradigm of a complex ecology of situated, interconnected embodiment help us invent a new rhetoric of interdependency that could influ-ence public, civic debates and decisions? (2011, 94)

Where bees and other non/humans are concerned, what if, rather than seek to view them as being on the same level with humans, humans came to recog-nize those levels as rhetorical constructs?

Perhaps the issue of non/humans and humans' obligatory ethics should remain problematic so that their unresolved status compels interrogation of the presumption of human authority. That process of negotiation can help reveal that any supposed understanding of "the animal Other" is a reflexive statement about the human condition. Rhetoric is always contextual and interpretive. Rhetoric always calls attention to the relationship between individuals and constructed groups as contingent and variable. This uncertainty demands an ongoing negotiation of relationships between humans and diverse non/humans. As Wolfe states, "Precisely *because* the rules of the game are ungrounded, unchecked, and uninsured by anything else, it is all the more critical that we not abandon them when the judgments they require bump up against our most deep-seated prejudices—in this case, prejudices based on species" (2003, 191). Identification proves crucial in the promotion of non/human rights, but so does understanding that the vector of identification works one way from the human side. Humans see themselves in other non/humans. Still, ethical relativism cannot dictate that those more closely related to humans biologically, and therefore more likely to demonstrate "human" behaviors, are more worthy of respect. Knowledge of rhetorical tropes should draw attention to these behaviors as part of a constructed lexicon created to sustain the illusion of humanity as an entirely distinct category.

One of the most commonly shared images of bees appears on a trendy blog titled *This Blog Will Blow Your Mind* (2013). The image accompanies various links to information about the dangers of genetically modified foods and a call to boycott corporations like Monsanto that create GMOs. In this picture, a dead bee faces away from the viewer. Beside the body, large block text reads, "Genetically modified crops have killed millions of bees. Save our pollinators. Boycott GMOs" (*This Blog* 2013). Such images establish human dominance as a given—they are "our" bees and their existence proves crucial to that of humans. Yet even images that forgo openly proprietary language by rejecting references to human interests, or by avoiding text altogether, can cast bees in a hierarchical relationship where humanity is always dominant. This assumption must be questioned because it is the same one used to justify human consumption of non/humans, as well as non/human experimentation, abuse, and trafficking (Peggs 2009; Sollund 2011). Indeed, images that do not make such overt claims may demand closer examination since their reception relies on preconceived notions of what or who matters disguised as plain reality.

Ultimately, identification and dissociation between parties is contingent on the imposition of cultural discourses on embodied Being. Acknowledging this does not provide a straightforward methodology for dealing with the question of Others. Instead, it demands consideration of ethical stances toward others that a set approach might render dangerously uncomplicated. Humanity has long sought to establish the basis of its connection to non/human Others as a means to determine the quality of interspecies ethical relationships. Comprehending human identification and dissociation with non/humans as rhetorical processes means humans must acknowledge that they have deliberately constructed categories of life in their favor. Rhetorician Victor Villanueva cautions, "We are affected, often not consciously, by the language we receive and use, by trope. And that means that we are ideologically affected. What I mean is that our assumptions about how the world works are influenced by—might even be created by—the language we receive and use" (2006). Although Villanueva speaks to current issues of race relations rather than human views of non/humans, his words remain relevant. All forms of observation are informed by interpretive schema. Consequently, humans cannot presume a natural fact of dominion over non/human lives, either physically or philosophically.

Becoming familiar with humanity's reliance on tropes is a small but critical step in understanding the effects rhetorical processes have on human and non/human lives. Then it becomes possible to analyze even seemingly objective images that subconsciously promote anthropocentric cultural assumptions and organize the human world. Images such as those used in ad campaigns highlighting the plight of honeybees prove indispensable in the creation of effective appeals. When this kind of visual process is employed to create empathy to persuade individuals to act on behalf of others, it is said this helps to "humanize" the problem. This kind of emotional engagement becomes problematized when humans seek to identify with non/humans. This expression highlights not only the ethical obligations borne by humans toward each other as social creatures, but also a tendency to posit that responsibility as a strictly human transaction based on the presumption of the inferiority of other species. Even eschewing such tropes linguistically, humans still participate inadvertently in identification predicated on predispositions epitomized by the erasure of non/human subjectivity. Therefore, it proves crucial that audiences interrogate how online images that accompany petitions, and informational resources, engage in furthering an anthropocentric perspective. Not only does such a perspective lead to threatened and endangered species, but the unconscious influence of campaign images themselves contributes to the problems they seek to combat.

REFERENCES

Aristotle. 1943. *Generation of Animals*. Translated by A. L. Peck. Cambridge: Harvard University Press.

Armstrong, Philip. 2002. "The Postcolonial Animal." *Society and Animals* 10(4): 413–419.

Ash, Rhiannon. 2011. "Pliny the Elder's Attitude to Warfare." In *Pliny the Elder: Themes and Contexts*, edited by Roy Gibson and Ruth Morello, 1–19. Leiden: Brill.

Bacon, Francis. 2000. *The New Organon*, edited by Lisa Jardine and Michael Silverthorne. Cambridge: Cambridge University Press.

"Boycott GMO's—We Need Healthy Food." n.d. *This Blog Will Blow Your Mind*. http://wewillblowyourmind.blogspot.co.uk/2013/02/boycott-gmos-we-need-healthy-food.html.

Burke, Kenneth. 1941. "Four Master Tropes." *Kenyon Review* 3(4): 421–438.

Cockcroft, Robert, and Susan Cockcroft. 2014. *Persuading People: An Introduction to Rhetoric*. New York: Palgrave Macmillan.

Clune, Kim. n.d. "Save the Bees to Save Our Food." *This One Wild Life*. http://thisonewildlife.com/protect-honey-bees.

Code, Lorraine. 1995. *Rhetorical Spaces: Essays on Gendered Locations*. New York: Routledge.

Cohen, Jeffrey J. 1999. *Of Giants: Sex, Monsters, and the Middle Ages*. Minneapolis: University of Minnesota Press.

Deckha, Maneesha. 2008. "Disturbing Images: PETA and the Feminist Ethics of Animal Advocacy." *Ethics and the Environment* 13(2): 35–76.

Derrida, Jacques. 1969a. *A Rhetoric of Motives*. Berkeley: University of California Press.

———. 2002. "The Animal That Therefore I Am." *Critical Inquiry* 28(2): 369–418.

Elder, Glen, Jennifer Wolch, and Jody Emel. 1998. "Race, Place, and the Bounds of Humanity." *Society and Animals* 6(2): 183–202.

"EFSA Identifies Risks to Bees from Neonicotinoids." n.d. European Food Safety Authority. http://www.efsa.europa.eu/en/press/news/130116.htm.

Fieser, James. 2001. *Moral Philosophy through the Ages*. Mountain View, CA: Mayfield.

"Honey Bee Health and Colony Collapse Disorder." n.d. USDA Agricultural Research Service. http://www.ars.usda.gov/News/docs.htm?docid=15572.

Iberlekamp. n.d. "President Obama, Act Now to Save the Bees." *EcoWatch: Transforming Green*. http://ecowatch.com/2013/07/03/obama-save-the-bees.

Kaufman, Gershen. 1996. *The Psychology of Shame: Theory and Treatment of Shame-Based Syndromes*. New York: Springer.

Kennedy, George A. 1998. *Comparative Rhetoric: An Historical and Cross-Cultural Introduction*. New York: Oxford University Press.

Kim, Claire Jean. 2011. "Moral Extensionism or Racist Exploitation? The Use of Holocaust and Slavery Analogies in the Animal Liberation Movement." *New Political Science* 33(3): 311–333.

Laehn, Thomas R. 2013. *Pliny's Defense of Empire*. New York: Routledge.

Lewiecki-Wilson, Cynthia. 2011. "Ableist Rhetorics, Nevertheless: Disability and Animal Rights in the Work of Peter Singer and Martha Nussbaum." *jac* 31(1–2): 71–101.

Locke, John. 2012. *The Second Treatise of Government and A Letter Concerning Toleration*. N.p.: Dover Thrift Editions.

Mandeville, Bernard. (1714) 1989. *The Fable of the Bees*. London: Penguin.

Matthews, Julie. 2012. "Compassion, Geography and the Question of the Animal." *Environmental Values* 21:125–142.

Mayhew, Robert. 2004. *The Female in Aristotle's Biology: Reason or Rationalization*. Chicago: University of Chicago Press.

Noske, Barbara. 2008. "The Animal Question in Anthropology." In *Social Creatures: A Human and Animal Studies Reader*, edited by Clifton P. Flynn, 22–28. Brooklyn, NY: Lantern.

Peggs, Kay. 2009. "A Hostile World for Nonhuman Animals: Human Identification and the Oppression of Nonhuman Animals for Human Good." *Sociology* 43(1): 85–102.

Pliny the Elder. 1856. *The Natural History of Pliny*, Vol. IV. Translated by John Bostock and H. T. Riley. London: Henry G. Bohn.

Poisoned Bees. n.d. Digital image. Greenpeace USA. http://www.greenpeace.org/usa/en/campaigns/genetic-engineering/Bees-in-Crisis/.

Pomeroy, Sarah. 1994. *Xenophon: Oeconomicus: A Social and Historical Commentary*. Oxford: Oxford University Press.

Rice, Donald, and Peter Schofer. 1983. *Rhetorical Poetics: Theory and Practice of Figural and Symbolic Reading in Modern French Literature*. Madison: University of Wisconsin Press.

Richter, Zack. 2014. "Intersectionality and the Nonhuman Disabled Body: Challenging the Neocapitalist Technoscientific Reproduction of Ableism and Speciesism." *Journal for Critical Animal Studies* 12(2): 84–94. http://www.criticalanimalstudies.org/wp-content/uploads/2014/04/JCAS-Vol-12-Issue-2-May-20145.pdf#page=21.

Salvador, Michael, and Tracylee Clarke. 2011. "The Weyekin Principle: Toward an Embodied Critical Rhetoric." *Environmental Communication* 5(3): 243–260.

Scottish Wildlife Trust. n.d. *Scottish Wildlife Trust*. http://scottishwildlifetrust.org.uk/.

Sollund, Ragnhild. 2011. "Expressions of Speciesism: The Effects of Keeping Companion Animals on Animal Abuse, Animal Trafficking and Species Decline." *Crime Law and Social Change* 55:437–451. doi: 10.1007/s10611-011-9296-3.

Steel, Karl. 2008. "How to Make a Human." *Exemplaria* 20(1): 3–27.

Villanueva, Victor. 2006. "The Rhetorics of the New Racism or the Master's Four Tropes." FYHC: First-Year Honors Composition 1. http://fyhc.info/ArticleOneVillanuevaPDF.pdf.

Weil, Kari. 2012. *Thinking Animals: Why Animal Studies Now?* New York: Columbia University Press.

Whitfield, Laura. n.d. "Save Our Bees—A Scottish Wildlife Trust Campaign." Falls of Clyde Blog. *Scottish Wildlife Trust*. http://blogs.scottishwildlifetrust.org.uk/fallsofclyde/2012/11/28/save-our-bees-a-scottish-wildlife-trust-campaign.

Wolfe, Cary. 2003. *Animal Rites: American Culture, the Discourse of Species, and Posthumanist Theory*. Chicago: University of Chicago Press.

Index

About the Contributors

Joseph Anderton is assistant professor in Drama and Performance at the University of Nottingham, where he teaches Animals and Humans in Twentieth-Century Literature and Drama, among other modules. His monograph *Beckett's Creatures: Art of Failure after the Holocaust* (Bloomsbury Methuen Drama 2016) examines the historical and biopolitical relevance of the "creature" and "creaturely life" as it appears in the literary works of Samuel Beckett. Recent publications on nonhuman animals include "Hooves! The Equine Presence in Beckett" in "Beckett and Animals" and work on creaturely poetics in stage adaptations of Franz Kafka's stories in the "On Anthropomorphism" special issue of *Performance Research*. He also has an article on canines and otherness in Kafka, Beckett, and Auster appearing in *Twentieth-Century Literature*. Joseph has reviewed and peer reviewed for journals such as the *Journal of Beckett Studies*, *Literary Geographies*, and the *Journal of European Humour Research*, and acted as article editor for Sage Publications.

Michael Atkinson is a professor in the Faculty of Kinesiology Physical Education at the University of Toronto, where he teaches physical cultural studies, policy, bioethics, and research methods. He earned a PhD in Sociology from the University of Calgary in 2001. Atkinson's central areas of teaching and research interests pertain to the experiences of human and nonhuman animal suffering in/as physical cultures, the cross-national study of bio-pedagogical practices, radical embodiment, issues in bioethics within global and local physical cultures, and ethnographic research methods. His ethnographic research efforts have included the study of ticket scalpers, tattoo enthusiasts, fell runners, cosmetic surgery patients, greyhound and fox hunting cultures, Ashtanga yoga practitioners, Straightedge and Parkour youth cultures, and triathletes. He is the author or editor of nine books, and his research has appeared in diverse academic journals around the world. In October 2004, he was honored to receive the Aurora Prize from the Social Sciences and Humanities Research Council of Canada, as the outstanding young scholar in Canadian social sciences. Atkinson is editor of the *Sociology of Sport Journal* and has served on editorial boards of journals including *Deviant Behavior*, *Sport in Society*, *Qualitative Research in Sport*, *Exercise and Health*, and *Qualitative Sociology Review*.

Fernando Gabriel Pagnoni Berns currently works at the University of Buenos Aires (UBA) in the department of Arts as a graduate teaching assistant. He teaches seminars on American Horror Cinema and Euro Horror. He is director of the research group on horror cinema called "Grite" (shout) and has published articles on Argentinian and international cinema and drama in the following publications: *Imagofagia*, *Stichomythia*, *Anagnórisis*, *Lindes*, and *UpStage Journal*, among others. He is a PhD student and has published chapters in the books entitled *Undead in the West*, edited by Cynthia Miller, *To See the Saw Movies: Essays on Torture Porn and Post 9/11 Horror*, edited by John Wallis, *Reading Richard Matheson: A Critical Survey*, edited by Cheyenne Mathews, *Dreamscapes in Italian Cinema*, edited by Francesco Pascuzzi, *Time-Travel Television*, edited by Sherry Ginn, and *For His Eyes Only: The Women of James Bond*, edited by Lisa Funnell, among others.

Christina Victoria Cedillo is currently assistant professor of Writing and Rhetoric at University of Houston Clear Lake in Houston, Texas. Her primary area of interest is the interplay between rhetorics of embodiment and embodied rhetorics, particularly how the embodied experiences of denigrated groups can counter and contest dominant ontological discourses. In addition to focusing on intersections of race and gender and how they affect the deployment and reception of embodied rhetorics, she has also started to examine how transhistorical cultural assumptions regarding a human-non/human divide undergird oppressive regimes of power. Her work has appeared in several edited collections, including *Argumentation and Advocacy* and the *Journal of Feminist Studies in Religion*. Her chapter in this volume is based on research presented at the 2014 North American Conference for Critical Animal Studies.

Amber E. George is the program coordinator for the Intergroup Dialogue Project at Cornell University, an initiative that advances social justice education. Dr. George is a member of the Eco-ability Collective, the Conference Awards Chair of the Central New York Peace Studies Consortium, and the Director of Finance for the Institute for Critical Animal Studies (ICAS). She has taught courses in ethics and social philosophy at Le Moyne College,

Misericordia University, and the State University of New York at Cortland. Dr. George has presented her work at several Eco-Ability and Critical Animal Studies conferences. She published a book chapter, "Disney's Little 'Freak' Show of Animals in the Environment: A Dis-Ability Pedagogical Perspective on the Disney Industrial Complex," in *Earth, Animal, and Disability Liberation: The Rise of Eco-Ability*. She has also served as an editor on several projects for the *Journal of Critical Animal Studies* and *Social Advocacy and Systems Change Journal*, and is on the review board of *Green Theory and Praxis Journal* and the *Transformative Justice* book series.

Stella Hockenhull is a reader in Film and Television Studies at the University of Wolverhampton, where she is also co-director of the Research Centre for Film, Media, Discourse and Culture. She has an undergraduate degree in Film and the Visual Arts and a Master's degree in Screen Studies. She gained a PhD in the correlation between film and painting in the films of Powell and Pressburger in 2006 and has published widely in the subject area, including two monographs entitled *Aesthetics and Neo-Romanticism in Film: Landscapes in Contemporary British Cinema* and *Neo-Romantic Landscapes: An Aesthetic Approach to the Films of Powell and Pressburger*. Her more recent research focuses on nonhuman animal representation in film and television, which she has presented at a number of national and international conferences. Recent publications in this field include "Creaturely Stars: Animals and Performance in Cinema" in *Bhatter College Journal of Multidisciplinary Studies: Special Issue on Animal Studies*, "Horse Power: Equine Alliances in the Western" in Sue Matheson (ed.), *Love in Western Film and Television: Lonely Hearts and Happy Trails*, "Celebrity Creatures: The Starification of the Cinematic Animal" in *Revisiting Star Studies*, and "Mythical Mounts and Sturdy Steeds: Equine Reverence in Iceland" in *Urban-Rural-Wilderness: the Co-Living of Humans and Animals in the North since the Nineteenth Century*. She is a member of a number of organizations, including the British Animal Studies Network, H-Network on Animal Studies, British Sociological Association, Animal/Human Studies Group, and Institute for Critical Animal Studies.

Anja Höing studied English and Biology at the University of Osnabrück, Germany. She obtained her B.A. in 2009, followed by a Master of Education (MEd) in 2011, and is now employed as a research assistant at the Institute of English and American Studies at the University of Osnabrück, where she is working on her PhD on religion and culture in English animal stories. Her main research interests lie in the fields of animals in literature, especially talking animal stories, representations of nature, ecosystems and environmentalism in literature, children's literature, and interfaces between literature and the natural sciences. She presented first findings at the Cosmopolitan

Animals conference organized by the University of Kent in 2012. In 2013, she contributed to the postgraduate workshop Environment, Literature, Culture in Frankfurt, Germany. In 2014, she read a paper on the topic of "Snit's a Good Dog – Dogs' Innate Duty in Richard Adams's *The Plague Dogs*" at the first Global Conference: The Animal and Human Bond, hosted by Inter-Disciplinary and held in Mansfield College, Oxford. She also presented her research at the University of Sheffield's 2014 Reading Animals conference, where she read a paper on "Writing Animals: Culture Transmission in Talking Animal Stories."

Prof. Dr. Harald Husemann is professor of English Literary and Cultural Studies at the Institute of English and American Studies, Osnabrück University, Germany. After studying at Hull University (GB) and Kiel University (Germany), he obtained his "Staatsexamen" from Kiel University in 1966 (majors English, History). In 1971 he obtained his PhD in History. After two years as lecturer in English Literature at Kiel he became Professor of English Literature and British Cultural Studies at Osnabrück University in 1974. During his time at Osnabrück University he has been visiting professor to many universities, among others the Catholic University of the West in France, the University of Southern Indiana, Southwestern University (Texas), Janus Pannonius University in Hungary, University of Izmir in Turkey, Islamia University in Pakistan, and Doon University in India. He has published widely on contemporary British politics and Anglo-German relations in media, fiction, and cartoons. Among his publications are "Cartooning the Krauts," The Foreign Language Edition - English, "The Colditz Industry" in C. C. Barfoot (ed.), *Beyond Pug's Tour*, "Laughing all the Way to the Euro Bank. Euro-Cartoons, Euro-Myths and British Apprehensions of German Domination" in Hard Times, "Dr. Strangelove: Or How I Came to Love the Stereotype" in Gerhard Bergmann (ed.), USA Studies, Contributions to Cultural Studies, and "Skeletons in Their Cupboards: The Image of Germany in Post-War English Novels," in Claus Uhlig and Rüdiger Zimmermann (eds.), Anglistentag 1990 Proceedings. He also edited several publications, among them *Anglo-German Attitudes*, *Coping with the Relations: Anglo-German Cartoons from the Fifties to the Nineties*, and *As Others See Us: Anglo-German Perceptions*. He also is co-editor of the series "European Education in Dialogue." His teaching and research interests include, among others, media in fact and fiction, fiction into film, and intercultural communication.

Fiona Yuk-wa Law, PhD (HKU), is a lecturer in Comparative Literature at the University of Hong Kong. Her research interests include Asian cinemas, visual cultures, animal studies (animal rights, posthumanism, zoo poetics), healing and death, and nostalgia and affect. She teaches courses on Sinophone cinemas and cultural studies in the context of globalization, Hong

Kong culture, modern poetry, and visual studies, and was a guest curator at the Hong Kong Film Archive in 2011 and 2012. Her writings are primarily about Hong Kong cinema, such as an article on Chinese New Year films (1950s–1960s) in the *Journal of Chinese Cinemas*, a book chapter on Stanley Kwan's films in *Critical Proximity: The Visual Memories of Stanley Kwan* (in Chinese), and a book chapter on Hong Kong middle-class comedy published by the Hong Kong Film Critics Society (forthcoming, in Chinese), among others. In recent years, she has extended her research interests to animal studies in the Asian context, with particular focus on cinematic representations, photography, animal welfare, and urban culture. She has presented several papers about different representations of animal-human relationships on Asian screens. Her recent article on animal/human deaths and healing narratives in East Asian cinemas can be found in *Animal Studies Journal*.

Matthew Lerberg received his PhD from the University of Texas at Arlington. He is interested in the relationships between humans and nonhumans in literature, film, and art. In his dissertation he advocates what he calls "a(e)s(th)et(ics)," or the importance of the convergence of aesthetics and ethics when considering human and nonhuman relationships. He has published on the film *Winged Migration* in ASLE UK's *Green Letters* and has a forthcoming article with the University of Wales Press that analyzes the cultural legacy of werewolves in the popular television series *Grimm* and the comic book series *Fables*. When not researching and writing he enjoys rock climbing, cycling, hiking, and camping.

César Alfonso Marino is professor of Literature. He graduated from the University of Buenos Aires (UBA) in the department of Arts. He is a lecturer on popular culture in literature, film, and videogames. He has taught workshops on images as texts in mass culture and has published chapters in the books entitled *The Comics of Joss Whedon*, edited by Valerie Estelle Frankel, *Dick Grayson, Boy Wonder: Scholars and Creators on 75 Years of Robin, Nightwing and Batman*, edited by Kristen Geaman, and *The Ages of Hulk*, edited by Joseph Darowski.

Guilherme Nothen is a doctoral candidate in the department of Kinesiology and Physical Education at the University of Toronto, where he is currently focusing on historic gymnasiums. He is interested in exploring the ethnographic and historical methods of inquiry concerning the gradual transformation of sport spaces over the course of the twentieth century, soccer-related violence in Brazil, and the use/abuse of nonhuman animals in sports. He obtained his Master's degree from the University of Brazil in 2010. He has produced a number of articles and book chapters in both Portuguese and English, including a conversation with Michael Burawoy—president of the

International Sociological Association at the time. He also serves as executive editor of *Movimento Journal*, a Brazilian scholarly publication devoted to the dissemination of sociocultural perspectives on sport and physical culture.

Dr. Sean Parson is an assistant professor in the Departments of Politics and International Affairs and Sustainable Communities at Northern Arizona University. He is finishing a book manuscript titled *Cooking up Revolution: Food not Bombs, Anarchist Homeless Activism and The Politics of Space* and is currently working on a project that explores what superhero comics and movies tell us about our relationship with the more-than-human world. His musings on comics and culture can be read at https://readingsuperheroespolitically.wordpress.com/. He has been involved in a range of social movements: from animal liberation and forest defense to immigrant rights and climate justice. When not working or grading he spends his days hiking the mountains of Northern Arizona with his best four-legged friend, Diego.

Jennifer Polish teaches writing at CUNY Queens College and is a PhD student in English at the CUNY Graduate Center, from which she received her Master's degree in Liberal Studies. Her research interests include the intersections of dis/ability, race, and animality in children's literature and media. She has published an article on queerness and dis/ability in group homes for people with intellectual disabilities in *Zeteo: The Journal of Interdisciplinary Writing*, and is currently pursuing the relationship between affective whiteness and dis/ability in composition classrooms. She has taught and written extensively about trauma and dis/ability in *The Hunger Games* and other young adult media, and is currently working on her first novel, a queer young adult fantasy.

J.L. Schatz is an instructor of English and Feminist Evolutionary Theory at Binghamton University, where he also serves as the director of Speech and Debate. He has served as the Institute for Critical Animal Studies (ICAS) North American Representative from 2013 to 2015 and has been a member of ICAS' Executive Board since 2014. As the Director of Speech and Debate, he has coached his team to a decade's worth of consecutive top ten finishes and was ranked first in the nation in 2008 by the Cross-Examination Debate Association. He has published articles on disability studies in popular media, environmental managerialism, apocalypse and technology, critical pedagogy, veganism, and critical animal studies. He has helped organize several conferences, including two ICAS annual North American conferences and the Central New York Peace Consortium's annual conference. He has also headed several protests directed against animals used in circuses for entertainment as well as restaurants serving factory-farmed animals.

Carter Soles, PhD, is assistant professor of Film Studies in the English Department at the College at Brockport (SUNY). His research interests include ecomedia studies, gender and identity studies, geek studies, and film genre studies. He has published articles on queer theory and the rise of geek culture for *Jump Cut* and on the sexism of geek-centered romantic comedy for *Bright Lights Film Journal*. Carter is particularly interested in the ecocritical dimension of the horror genre, and has published essays on the figure of the cannibalistic hillbilly in 1970s slasher cinema for *Ecocinema: Theory and Practice* (2013), and on post–Silent Spring 1960s ecohorror in *Interdisciplinary Studies in Literature and the Environment*. He teaches film theory, film history, and ecocinema courses at the College at Brockport, and is the director of the college's Interdisciplinary Film Studies Minor. He is working on a book-length project on apocalyptic ecohorror cinema.